War or Common Cause?

A Critical Ethnography of Language Education Policy, Race, and Cultural Citizenship

A volume in
Education Policy in Practice: Critical Cultural Studies

Series Editors:
Bradley A. U. Levinson and Margaret Sutton, *Indiana University*

Education Policy in Practice:
Critical Cultural Studies

Bradley A. U. Levinson and Margaret Sutton, Series Editors

War or Common Cause?

A Critical Ethnography of Language Education Policy, Race, and Cultural Citizenship

by

Kimberly S. Anderson
University of North Carolina at Greensboro

Information Age Publishing, Inc.
Charlotte, North Carolina • www.infoagepub.com

Library of Congress Cataloging-in-Publication Data

Anderson, Kimberly S.
  War or common cause? : a critical ethnography of language education policy, race, and cultural citizenship / by Kimberly S. Anderson.
      p. cm. -- (Education policy in practice: critical cultural studies)
  Includes bibliographical references and index.
  ISBN 978-1-59311-985-0 (pbk.) -- ISBN 978-1-59311-986-7 (hardcover) 1. Linguistic minorities--Education--United States. 2. Language and education--United States. 3. Language and culture--United States. 4. Educational anthropology--United States. 5. Language policy--United States. I. Title.
  LC3731.A746 2008
  371.826'912--dc22

                                                                                    2008032862

CONTENTS

EDITOR'S INTRODUCTION

Bradley A. U. Levinson

It is a singular pleasure to introduce the work of Kim Anderson, an educational anthropologist whose deep knowledge of immigrant and bilingual education, both as practitioner and scholar, informs this illuminating book.

The book is based partly on Dr. Anderson's 2003 dissertation, which earned the Outstanding Dissertation Award of the Council on Anthropology of Education (American Anthropological Association). That dissertation provided a compelling empirical and theoretical account of debates about bilingual education, and about "implementation" of new language education policy, at a diverse Southern California elementary school. Yet Anderson was not content to work that dissertation alone into a book. Rather, she felt drawn to include an account of similar debates that she discovered to be occurring in the "new Latino Diaspora" of the Southeastern United States, especially the state of Georgia, where she began working in 2005. The result is a powerful, wide-ranging portrait of language education policy debates as they played out in different locales over a period of more than 10 years.

Several important features of Anderson's book bear mentioning here. A key term in Anderson's scholarship is "policy process," and she uses this concept to illuminate the multifaceted, often unanticipated dimensions of policy appropriation in different venues—but especially schools and classrooms. The book represents a multidimensional and longitudinal study of "policy processes" as they play out on the ground (a single school in Los

Angeles), and over time (both within the same school, and also within the state of Georgia). In order to reconstruct this complex policy process, Anderson impressively marshals a great variety of forms of "discourse." Most of this discourse, of course, comes from overheard discussions and spontaneous interviews conducted at a particular school—the voices of teachers and administrators. Such discourse forms the heart of her ethnographic findings. Yet Anderson also brings an ethnographer's eye to national and regional debates as they are conducted and represented in different forms of media, especially newspapers and magazines. She then uses the key theoretical concept of "articulation" to conceptually link these media representations with local school discourse. The result is an illuminating account of how everyday debates at a particular school and media debates occurring more broadly mutually inform one another.

Another key concept is that of cultural citizenship, through which Anderson contributes an important new way to conceptualize the appropriation of policies in practice. Anderson takes the concept of cultural citizenship from Latino studies scholarship to insist on the dimensions of citizenship that go beyond political rights and juridical status, to the ways that people collectively construct their sense of identity and belonging at the local level. What she discovers in her research at the elementary school is that local constructions of cultural citizenship clearly inform the way people react to and contextualize language education policies, such as California's English-Only Proposition 227. In this particular case, cultural citizenship is tragically rendered in dichotomous Black-Latino terms, thereby oversimplifying the actual complexity of local identities and practices.

Finally, Dr. Anderson has provided us with a "critical ethnography," a multisited ethnography, and perhaps most importantly, a kind of "insider-outsider ethnography," born of Anderson's dual role as teacher and ethnographer at the same school. While many scholars founder on the perilous shoals of such a task, Anderson has managed to navigate it astutely and gracefully. Although she has a clear and unabashed stance on bilingual education and cultural inclusion, Anderson's account of the political and ideological conflicts within the field of bilingual and immigrant education is remarkably judicious.

This is a book passionately written, aimed at a broad audience, with telling anecdotes and trenchant theory skillfully interwoven. War or common cause? Dr. Anderson poses this question in her title because she believes that the ethnography of policy can serve as the basis for critical reflection and, possibly, reconciliation. She holds out the hope for common cause, the transcendence of conflict born of misunderstanding, for the larger purpose of an equitable and culturally empowering education for all children. We should applaud her efforts and urge her to succeed.

FOREWORD

Douglas Foley

For over 50 years, anthropologists have been trying to make policymakers and teachers aware of how their social and linguistic practices create racial and social inequalities in public schools. The hope has been that critical ethnographic portraits of schools will challenge well-meaning educators to create policies, curricula, and teaching for ALL students. Kim Anderson's study of one Los Angeles school is an imaginative, useful addition to the field. She conceptualizes the teachers' talk as a "war over bilingual education," thus a "struggle over cultural citizenship." Amidst this Brown-Black war of words over who is the real American citizen, each ethnic group creates "collective fictions" of the other that echo White racial attitudes towards Latino immigrants and African Americans in the media. Meanwhile, too many of the local White teachers imagine themselves as neutral and "above" the Black-Brown racial battle over citizenship identity. Such a posture turns liberal White teachers and administrators into rather ineffectual actors in this racial drama. Dr. Anderson, herself a White bilingual teacher, tries to break with that posture through a consciousness-raising discussion group for teachers, following the dictates of "activist anthropology" and "participatory action research." Unfortunately the effort did little to create a more unified environment on campus.

Although her attempt to mediate between local teachers was unsuccessful, Dr. Anderson's ethnography demonstrates many important lessons for educational policymakers. She makes the point that too many educational policies like California's Proposition 227 are seen as top-down edicts, which set off a chain of unintended events. She argues that policymakers must understand their policies as "a socio-cultural process" that require local level evaluations. Only a complex, in-depth ethno-graphic portrait will capture how local people enact and accept, or resist and undermine a particular educational policy. Perhaps few educational policymakers anticipated the local implementation barrier of a cultural citizenship battle that the author uncovers. Nor did they foresee that kill-ing bilingual education through Proposition 227 would do little to end the local historical residue of xenophobia and racism. Like all good criti-cal ethnographers, Dr. Anderson is providing educational policymakers with a snapshot of what their policies inadvertently produce. This act of unveiling or "witnessing" local policy consequences is the power and beauty of her ethnographic study. One can only hope that reading her lively story will became standard practice among educational policy-mak-ers, who, like high flying aviators, are prone to drop policies on schools and communities and fly away from local evaluation.

Finally, I would also like to underscore what Dr. Anderson's innovative ethnography can teach her fellow educational anthropologists. She deploys the idea of a multisited ethnography to greatly expand our notion of "school ethnography." This leads her to focus on the "articula-tion" between public discourses on immigrants, race, and citizenship and the local discourses of teachers. Because she takes the notion of critical discourse analysis seriously, she provides detailed empirical samples of the way local teachers reason, conceptualize, and talk. She shows us how their rhetorical flourishes, key terms, and metaphoric references are often appropriated from media circulated discourses. Although critical dis-course analysis is not an entirely new methodological approach, Dr. Anderson deploys it in a particularly interesting manner that redefines the school-community connection. She shows us how the wider discursive contexts of California and of Georgia partially shape community-school relations. The media circulated immigration debates in Georgia repro-duce that same national culture of xenophobia and racism that she found in California. With more in-depth studies in local Georgia schools, we will surely find Georgia teachers embroiled in cultural citizenship battles simi-lar to those in California.

Another innovative aspect of Dr. Anderson's study is her efforts to create an engaged, activist type of educational ethnography. By returning to her school as a teacher-researcher, she utilizes a more "auto-ethnographic" approach. Being a teacher/educator first, and an anthropologist second, Dr. Anderson avoids bashing and essentializing teachers. In some ways, she is the consummate insider, but her critical ideas on race and White privi-lege also distance her from fellow teachers. Consequently, she is able to produce an unflinching, yet sympathetic portrait of her colleagues. She shows them to be more unwitting products of larger racial discourses than hateful individuals. Moreover, she searches for teacher agency and diversity and concludes that not all teachers are trapped in these larger racist discourses. Educational ethnographers of all ideological stripes would do well to study Dr. Anderson's subtle use of theory and autobiography to produce an intimate, politically engaged style of ethnographic interpretation. Her work represents the best of what some anthropologists (Foley, Levinson, & Hurtig, 2000) have dubbed the "new educational ethnography."

I should close by revealing my own "positionality" as the advisor of Dr. Anderson's original dissertation project. I have had the pleasure of watching her develop the worldview and voice that inhabits this fine book. I have no doubt that she will produce other excellent ethnographies, but I suspect this one will always remain particularly close to her heart. It represents the best of her youthful idealism, passion, and creativity. And like all good activist scholars, she will continue to search for ways to promote and produce a better world.

REFERENCE

Foley, D., Levinson, B. A. U., & Hurtig, J. (2000). Anthropology goes inside: The new ethnography of ethnicity and gender. In W. Secada (Ed.), *Review of Research in Education* (pp. 37–98). Washington DC: American Educational Research Association.

ACKNOWLEDGMENTS

First and foremost I give thanks to my family and my friends for their love and support that literally keeps me going! Thank you to everyone at "California Elementary School" for all that I was able to experience and learn as a teacher and researcher in the community. Thank you to Richard Handler, Doug Foley, Pauline Strong, Joe Johnson, Jr., Marta Menchaca, and Charles Hale for guiding me and this project from its inception, and to fellowships from the University of Texas at Austin that provided support at critical junctures. Thank you to Henry Robles for editing and moral support. Thank you to Bradley Levinson for shepherding this project into this book. Thank you to Zi (and Mr. Baker and Oso and Nisha and Shakti's) for the knowledge, skills, and community that made the completion of this book possible.

CHAPTER 1

INTRODUCTION

The Anthropology of Language Education Policy, Race, and Cultural Citizenship

---

Debates about what language/s to utilize in the instruction of students in American public schools have always been connected to debates about immigration and national identity, with underlying disputes about race politics and civil rights. Within debates about language education policies have been questions about, Who are we as a community, as a nation? What will America look like and be like in the future? And, what can we do now to create the kind of community and nation that we want (Gómez-Peña, 1987)?[1]

These debates came home to me when I embarked upon my journey in the field of education in 1991, as a bilingual teacher. In an effort to gain a more sophisticated understanding of debates about bilingual education and their educational and political implications, I began research in 1996 at an elementary school in Los Angeles. I will call it "California Elementary." This school was an ideal place to conduct this research for several reasons: California has been characterized in the media as a prime example of "the changing face of America," the destination point for the largest numbers of immigrants nationwide (Morganthau, 1997). By the year 2025 Latinos are expected to be nearly 43% of the state population

---

(p. 60). California has political clout, commanding a large number of seats in Congress and a large number of electoral votes ("As goes California, so goes the nation," it is often said). California was host to groundbreaking legislation mandating bilingual education (*Lau v. Nichols*, 1974). The Los Angeles Unified School District (LAUSD) alone educates one fourth of the nation's English Language Learner (ELL) students (Los Angeles Unified School District, 1996c, p. 3). And, *this* Los Angeles elementary school is the school that I taught in, where my research questions arose.

In my research I sought to understand language education policies as more than just instrumental, administrative directives to be implemented (the traditionally acknowledged function of "policy"). I asked, how can policies be more thoroughly understood as themselves complex, culturally situated resources in daily life—as contested cultural *processes* through which people understand and create ways of living, relationships, and political agendas? This is what Levinson and Sutton (2001) call a sociocultural approach to the study of education policy. Further, how can such a nuanced conceptualization of language education policies impart an understanding of people's struggles for cultural citizenship? "*Cultural* citizenship," departing from the legal concept of citizenship, is defined as a person or a group having voice, belonging, institutional access, and the power to participate fully in the various facets of community life (Flores & Benmayor, 1997; Ong, 1996; Rosaldo, 1994, 1997). I wanted to examine how struggles for cultural citizenship shape the social contexts of schooling, and inform relationships to, and outcomes of, language education policies.

To get at these questions I first explored how my elementary school community in South Los Angeles negotiated controversial language policies that shifted dramatically in the late 1980s through 2000, from establishing a bilingual program for Latino newcomers in the school that had previously been predominantly African American and monolingual, to abruptly implementing English immersion in 1998 as per the state's English for the Children Proposition 227 ballot initiative. I looked at how Latino, African American, and White school community members defined the community and its parameters for cultural citizenship through debates about these shifting language education policies. I examined how school community members' discourses about language, immigration, race, and education policies articulated to national media and political discourses on these topics, and how these discourses gave shape to people's experiences of and relationships to our changing instructional mandates. And I interrogated how all of this shaped the academic and professional environments on campus.

A few years later and all the way across the country I asked, How does the social terrain and public dialogue about immigration, language, race, and education in the Southeast, and particularly in Georgia, compare to the California case? Are there common dynamics in these two contexts—one a long-time destination area for immigrants (California) and one a relatively new hypergrowth region for immigration (the Southeast)? What could this tell us about issues that more and more communities nationwide are experiencing, with increasing diversity and growing pressure to improve the academic achievement of all students? And, what are the implications of this for improving education policy processes so that they are more responsive to diverse school communities? Ultimately I hope that this work contributes to struggles for cultural citizenship and educational equity in all school communities.

I outline my personal journey here to provide the reader with a sense of the evolution of these research questions, and to expose the perspectives and biases that I am conscious of bringing to the project. As Behar (1996) would say, I want to unveil the biography within the ethnography.

BIOGRAPHY WITHIN ETHNOGRAPHY

I began teaching in 1991, fresh out of college, as part of the Teach For America (TFA) program. True to the TFA national motto ("One day, all children in this nation will have the opportunity to attain an excellent education"), I wanted to contribute to improving education for all kids, and I believed I could make a difference. I taught a fourth grade bilingual class for one year in a school district neighboring downtown Los Angeles, and in 1992 I transferred to an elementary school located in South Los Angeles, in the LAUSD. I will call it "California Elementary."

I worked at California Elementary for 2 years (1992–1994), teaching third and fourth grade. Of the roughly 1,200 students at the school, the vast majority were Latino, many immigrants, and a small percentage were African American. My students were all Latino. I taught in the bilingual program. The LAUSD had a "transitional" model of bilingual education: Instruction in core content areas (language arts, math, social studies, and science) was conducted in students' native language (Spanish at our school, but bilingual programs were offered in many languages in the district), while intensive English as a Second Language (ESL, also called English Language Development, ELD) lessons were given daily and subjects such as physical education, music, and art utilized English. Also important was an emphasis on the histories and cultures of Latinos and on multicultural pedagogy. More English was added in content area instruction as was appropriate to students' growth until they mastered enough to flourish in a monolingual English environment. At that point they "transitioned" (or were "redesignated fluent English proficient") and were placed in the English Only program, or the "EO" program as we called it on campus.

The program at California Elementary was large and growing in 1992. Administrators and Latino parents were generally enthusiastic about it. They expressed high expectations for us and the program was seen as fostering academic achievement. But after a short time on campus I began to feel this sense of value around bilingual instruction as a point of contention. Questions about resources for the bilingual program *versus* for the EO program often arose. For example, when we voted on who would fill a new instructional coordinator position on staff: Did the candidate need to be bilingual or not? When we voted on purchasing new curricular materials: Just how much of the materials should be in Spanish as opposed to in English? What the questions implied was, What is our "policy" about the importance of each language vis-à-vis the other? And since the bilingual and EO programs mapped fairly directly on to race, What is our "policy" about the relative value of African Americans and Latinos on campus?

Questions about bilingual education constantly arose in my life off campus as well. When I mentioned to people what I did for a living, they became either very impressed or very agitated. The latter asked questions like, "Why teach in Spanish when we want them to learn English?" and, "What kind of message are you sending to the students—don't they want to be American?" I became frustrated with what I felt were my simple answers to these questions. I wondered about my own positioning as a White, middle-class teacher in this urban, high poverty school, where I did not look like my students and where I taught in a language of which I was not even a native speaker. And I became uncomfortable with my sense of sliding through the debates without critically engaging in them.

In 1994, upon earning my California Clear Professional teaching credential and my Bilingual Cross-Cultural Language and Academic Development Specialist credential, I was invited by the LAUSD's District Intern Program (at the time the second largest alternative credentialing program in the nation, of which I was a recent graduate) to become an instructor. At that point I really began to wonder, did I see things critically enough to facilitate the professional education of *other* new teachers all over the city? I didn't think so. I took a break from teaching and began graduate study in anthropology.

In 1995 I heard from friends at California Elementary that since I had left the earlier tensions over resources had erupted into full-blown debates about the future of our bilingual program. Right away I called the principal and asked if she would approve my return to campus that summer to study the controversy. Research in the summer of 1996 became the first phase—and chapter 3—of this book.

By 1997 and 1998, as school community members at California Elementary continued to debate the future of their own bilingual program, statewide a massive anti-bilingual education campaign was launched by the conservative Republican millionaire, Ron Unz. The goals of the campaign were outlined in its legislative form, the Proposition 227 English for the Children ballot initiative. Proposition 227 sought to dismantle bilingual education statewide and to require that all ELLs be taught using the untried, unresearched, controversial, structured English immersion approach. Proposition 227 garnered national media attention, and I knew that passions about it would be running high at California Elementary. My friends there told me that teaching positions were opening up for the 1998–1999 school year, so I got on the phone again to the principal.

I returned once more to California Elementary in August of 1998, just 2 months after Proposition 227 passed, to continue my study of the politics of language education policy. But this time I did not want to just collect data and leave. I wanted the process of conducting research to contribute to the school community in palpable ways—this was "my school," after all, where I had been a teacher, where I had had the privilege of working with students and their families, and where I had made many friends. I had been a part of the school community before and still felt connected to it, so I wanted to be more involved than an ethnographer typically is. Thus for 2 school years, from 1998 through 2000, in addition to inhabiting the identity of "anthropologist" I also took a teaching position. I was again "Ms. Anderson, third grade, room 212." I relished the opportunity to work with students and to be part of the staff again as we implemented the changes mandated by Proposition 227. After 2 years of teaching and research I left California Elementary in 2000.

In 2001 my career in education took a new turn. From 2001 through 2004 I worked for a nonprofit, policy advocacy and technical assistance organization in Los Angeles. I served as a school improvement coach in local schools (some of them, just down the road from California Elementary), I contributed to the organization's policy advocacy work at the state and district level, and I conducted evaluation projects for the organization. In 2005 I left Los Angeles for Atlanta, to take a position at a regional education research and policy center. In my position there, which I am still in as of the submission of this manuscript, I work on research studies, program evaluations, and policy analysis projects, with a specific focus on the state of Georgia.[2]

As soon as I arrived in Atlanta I realized that I had not left my language education policy research topics behind in California. The Southeast had become a hypergrowth region for immigration, with Georgia in particular ranking amongst the top new immigrant destinations in the nation. I constantly read in the newspaper and saw on television and heard on the radio about immigration. For example, it was not uncommon at this time to read newspaper editorials expressing the fear that Georgians would soon be living in "Georgiafornia" (Campos, 2006a)—fear that the wars over immigration, culture clashes, and education policy that erupted in California were now imminent in the Peach State. In the region's schools, I began to read and to see that educators "struggle[d] to integrate Latino immigrants successfully into southern educational institutions" (Tomás Rivera Policy Institute, 2004, p. 2). Research "on inter-ethnic relations in emerging immigrant communities" was sorely needed (p. 12) in order to address the strengths and challenges of schools serving increasingly diverse student populations, if indeed such lofty goals as the Georgia Department of Education's motto that the state would "lead the nation in improving student achievement" (Cox, 2005) was to be realized.

The anthropologist in me got to work tracking media discourses, education news, and legislative politics. On any given day I could find a lot going on—for example an *Atlanta Journal-Constitution* front-page article about national immigration politics, a Metro section article on immigration in Atlanta, and a few editorial/opinion pieces; as well I would find a local TV news segment on immigration and a *CNN* special report on the issue. What started out in my mind as gathering information for a brief epilogue chapter in a book about my California research became an intense 2-year phase of research and a full chapter (chapter 7) in this book about the politics of language education policy on *both* coasts.

I hope this book provides a rich, reflective, teacher-anthropologist's account of changes in language education policy and politics over the last several years, as lived in one school community that experienced them relatively early on (vis-à-vis the rest of the nation), and in another place where these shifts are newly taking shape. I aim to illuminate relationships between policy as traditionally conceived (as official, imposed, administrative mandate) and policy *processes*—between the various meanings that a policy can take on, and the varied interpretations, appropriations, and effects of it as it is actually lived (Levinson & Sutton, 2001). I wish to contribute to understandings of the sociocultural contexts of schooling, and of the local and national structures of exclusion and participation that shape relationships and outcomes in schools. Being (or having been) a member of the communities researched, I have a stake in creating a "polyphonic" text that places the voices of the researcher and the researched "in dialogue with each other and with historical material," in order to tease out the common ground between people supposedly diametrically opposed on an issue (Ginsburg, 1993, p. 175). As such I hope to contribute to dialogue about how the politics of language education policies can be seen as less as "language wars" or "culture wars" or "racial discord," and more as opportunities for coalition building to address the complex needs of today's school communities (Flores & Benmayor, 1997; Haraway, 1988; Rosaldo, 1994).

EXAMINING CULTURAL CITIZENSHIP

The concept of *cultural citizenship* has become a powerful heuristic device for me to think about the politics of language education policy. The concept has been championed by Latino scholars as a framework for understanding the dynamism of the highly complex communities in which people live today. Flores and Benmayor (1997, p. 5) explain that the usual theoretical concepts used in the social sciences to understand diverse social settings, such as multiculturalism, assimilation, and acculturation, "somehow [miss] the point of the dynamic processes taking place with Latino and other 'minoritized' communities" (p. 9). Assimilation focuses too much on absorption and disappearance, while pluralism and multiculturalism assume a stable and unchanging country where immigrants simply add color and spice to the salad bowl but do not challenge traditional hegemonic views of "America" (p. 10). They argue that conventional legal definitions of "citizenship" are also insufficient for deep understandings of current-day sociopolitical dynamics. Flores and Benmayor argue that the notion of "citizen as political subject" is a more comprehensive concept for describing the current realities of diverse communities. As such, they maintain,

> immigrants who might not be citizens in a legal sense or might not even be in this country legally, but who labor and contribute to the economic and cultural wealth of the country, would be recognized as legitimate political subjects claiming rights for themselves and their children, and in that sense as citizens. (p. 11)

This idea also allows scholars to examine how a community defines its "cultural citizenship": its interests and purposes, its binding solidarities, its boundaries, its criteria for membership, and its voice (Flores & Benmayor, 1997, p. 13). It enables interrogation of the ways in which people understand and construct the world in which they live, how they interact with each other and how they negotiate their roles to define "the distribution and allocation of rights, privileges, and institutional access" (Rocco, 1997, p. 98). These dynamics in turn can shape the educational environment in which teaching and learning occur, affecting opportunities and academic outcomes for children and communities. By examining issues and events through the conceptual lens of cultural citizenship, we can understand today's ever-more diverse communities as complex, fluid "sites not only of contestation, but also of affirmation and cultural production" (Flores & Benmayor 1997, p. 9).

A key analytical process in explorations of cultural citizenship is to unwrap the "collective fictions" that communities construct about themselves and how they employ them to create a sense of belonging, entitlement, agency, and dignity for members, as well as to manage dynamics of negotiation, dispute, and conflict (Flores & Benmayor, 1997, p. 13; Rosaldo, 1994, pp. 243–244). One also asks how "cultural artifacts" look and feel from subject positions both dominant and subordinate in the community, to understand the "multiplicity of socio-material concerns" that people negotiate, and the differential political and material outcomes that they experience (Rosaldo, 1994, pp. 244–245). This can entail a nuanced look at the fluidity of identity and political categories, how they are deployed strategically in struggle (Ong, 1996), and to what effects.

Examining dynamics of cultural citizenship, then, requires more than just the traditional ethnographic focus on the "micro." Scholars must examine both the local *and* national (even global) arenas that people negotiate (Rosaldo, 1994, pp. 244–245). Scholars must interrogate the distinct and overlapping vernacular and mainstream "fictions" of belonging and legitimacy, and how actors construct experience within structures of local and national participation (Flores & Benmayor, 1997, p. 15; Rosaldo, 1997, p. 38).[3]

Research on struggles for cultural citizenship is timely because debates about the identity and future of America have been raging as of late (I explore this in-depth in chapters 2, 4, and 7). Notions of what is "American" have been hotly debated in, for example, campaigns for laws to eliminate affirmative action, to limit immigration and to restrict the rights of immigrants, and to outlaw bilingual education. Such debates expose our feelings, our "collective fictions," about nation, race, the ideals of equality and fairness. They expose our expectations for interaction with each other, and ultimately our goals for what type of society we want to build. Indeed, the debates about what language/s we should use in American schools are less a single topic of contention than a complex constellation of sites across which "groups with distinct political, economic, and cultural visions" attempt to define what the socially legitimate means and ends of a community and a society are to be, and whose knowledge is of most worth" (Apple, 1993; McCarthy & Crichlow, 1993).

This kind of research is not only timely but also necessary to understand the myriad issues at play in school communities implementing improvement efforts. For example, in her study of school restructuring in a southern city, Lipman (1998) found that because school community members failed to confront the underlying issues of race and class that shaped the beliefs and practices of teaching and learning in their school, the reform effort implemented with the hopes of improving the achievement of African American and working class students produced the same inequitable results that the reform was put in place to ameliorate. With Lipman (and critical multiculturalists and critical race theorists, more generally), I believe that we must address the fundamental struggles for cultural citizenship that flow through educational reform and policy processes. What we believe about who belongs, who can learn, who should have a voice, how we are interconnected, and what goals we have as communities must be openly discussed for the technical requirements of any policy mandate to be able to meaningfully improve schooling for *all* children. We must ask, "Who are *WE*, what does this mean, and with what effects for all of us—and for each of us?"

The theoretical concepts of hegemony and cultural production are helpful in understanding the ways in which actors experience and shape dynamics of cultural citizenship. Stuart Hall (1988) argues that in contestations over power and ideological dominance, a certain discursive framework comes to gain popularity. People on all sides of the conflict accord this framework the "symbolic power to map or classify the world" (p. 44). Hence, when an issue is debated and a struggle waged, it is that circle of dominant, or "hegemonic," ideas that poses the questions around which the conflict rages (p. 54). This is evident in debates about language education policy in the United States, as I point out in the media chapters.

But Gilroy (1987) points out that it is not so simple: positions vis-à-vis this circle of dominant ideas are often more complex than a dichotomy between the powerful and the powerless, between the "hegemonic" and the "counterhegemonic." The underlying assumptions of both are variously employed in the discourses of actors across both "sides" (pp. 40, 64). Why? Hall (1988) reminds us that individuals and social collectivities often have multiple agendas: They "have both the interest of advancing and improving their position" within a certain arena, "and of not losing their place" within another (p. 45). Actors often assume a number of specific subject positions in relation to the issues at hand (p. 49). And these positions can even be contradictory.

Gilroy (1987) argues that in struggle, while battle lines may be drawn discursively in very definitive ways, people are not simple or essential but are part of loosely assembled "interpretive communities" (p. 235) that constantly form and reform around shared sets of experiences, perceptions, forms of expression, and goals. Membership in interpretive communities is indicated by the shared use of a "multi-accented symbolic repertoire" (p. 235). To understand an interpretive community's "symbolic repertoire" we can ask, What are the salient, charged discourses and symbols used, what are their stable and enduring elements? What are their contradictory and shifting logics? How do these discourses and symbols manifest in particular argumentative structures, and how do they change with context? What determines their solidity as well as their inner fractures (p. 56)? And, what implications does this have for differently-placed actors in the political terrain?

The concept of interpretive community is similar to Bourdieu's concept of class: In *Language and Symbolic Power* (1991), Bourdieu defines "classes" not in terms of relationships to the means of production in Marxist terms, but as "sets of agents who occupy similar positions in the social space, and hence possess similar kinds and similar quantities of capital, similar life chances, similar dispositions, etc." (cited in Thompson 1991, p. 30). Classes come together under a shared vision of the social world and of themselves as having a particular place within that world. As feminist standpoint epistemology would argue, it depends on "where you stand" at any one time in relation to each other and to structures of domination, how much power you have to leverage (or think you have, or think another has), or the extent to which you ally with the dominant (hooks, 2000). I utilize this idea of class and Gilroy's (1987) concept of interpretive community, because I see California Elementary school community members' struggles for cultural citizenship as constituting attempts to secure better "places to stand" in the moral, professional, economic, and institutional spaces on campus, in the neighborhood, in America, and even in the world.

ENGAGING IN THE ANTHROPOLOGY OF POLICY

When I began to see contention over bilingual instruction at California Elementary I knew that what I wanted to understand was the politics of policy. Cris Shore and Susan Wright's work on the anthropology of policy (1997) was my starting point. They point out that, "Policy has become an increasingly central concept in the organization of contemporary societies" (p. 4). Through policy, individuals and communities are "categorized" and given particular statuses and roles in different social, political, and power contexts. "The study of policy, therefore, leads straight into issues at the heart of anthropology: norms and institutions; ideology and consciousness; knowledge and power; rhetoric and discourse; meaning and interpretations; the global and the local—to mention but a few" (p. 4). Indeed, they argue, "to use Mauss's concept [1954], policies can be studied as a 'total social phenomenon' as they have important economic, legal, cultural and moral implications, and can create whole [sets] of relationships between individuals, groups and objects" (p. 7).

Levinson and Sutton (2001) and Stein (2004) carry this idea forward, arguing that studies of policy must move beyond the traditional instrumentalist paradigm. The traditional instrumentalist paradigm defines policies as "systems of thought and action used to regulate and organize behavior. Policies are seen as mandates set forth by a governing body that are carried out by a separate entity, the identified policy implementers or beneficiaries" (Stein, 2004, p. 5). Levinson and Sutton champion the need to account more thoroughly for the "cultural, contextual, and political dimensions of educational policy" (p. 2). Through the fine-grained methodology of ethnography, anthropologists can examine policies as not only forms of governance but also as discursive or symbolic expressions of normative expectations that are appropriated, created, and contested across diverse social and institutional contexts (p. 1). Tracking moments in the lives of policies—moments in policy *processes*—then, can illuminate "the place and role of values, beliefs, and identities" when individuals and groups engage in decision making (p. 3).

Levinson and Sutton (2001) argue that a sociocultural perspective on policy studies can not only enrich understandings of policymaking and implementation, but also contribute to efforts to democratize policy processes (p. 15). When the multiple meanings and effects of policies are illuminated decision-makers can craft policies that better engage and serve diverse constituencies. School community members can become more savvy implementers and creators of policy in their daily lives. I believe this then benefits the ultimate goal of education—high achievement and success in life for all students.

SPEAKING OF LANGUAGE

Bourdieu and Passeron (1977) state that one cannot talk about a language without also talking about a set of relations to that language (p. 116; see also Fishman, 1976). Working from this assumption, I explore how issues of language are hardly ever "about language as such but about what kind of political community we are and wish to be" (Schmidt, 2000, p. 183). Looking at the "political economy of language" (Urciuoli, 1996, p. 4), I track how people construct the meaning of languages as a kind of index of power relations (see also Gal, 1987, 1989; Irvine 1989).

I draw on works from critical linguistic anthropology to ask how discourses about language and language policy inform school community members' experiences and their relations to dynamics of cultural citizenship.[4] I ask how rhetorical "place markers" (McCarthy & Crichlow, 1993; see also Gal, 1994; Roediger, 1991) and "key symbols" (Woolard, 1989) like "America," "immigrant," "illegal," "English Only," "Spanish," and "bilingual" function: Locally, I examine how talk about these key symbols becomes what Bourdieu (1991, p. 128) calls "performative utterances": speakers' attempts "to produce and impose representations of the social world" "to transform "in accordance with their interests" (p. 128). How do these performative utterances become "metacommunicative" (Urciuoli, 1996), signaling a whole set of assumptions and agendas in struggle?

One example of such research in a neighboring community to California Elementary is Horton's (1995) study of the politics of immigration in Monterey Park, California in the 1990s. He found that a key metacommunicative discourse, that of "newcomers vs. established residents," was enduring yet fluid over time (p. 8). Who was "newcomer" and "established resident"—and the very definition of these—changed according to demographic shifts, coalition building, electoral outcomes, and dynamics of assimilation. Horton concluded that if we leave unexplored the complex nature of such discourses we are left with partial, fragmented views of the dynamics that impact lives in diverse communities, and hence we are left much less able to effect positive change.

In this spirit I seek to challenge assumptions about the essential nature of linguistic, racial, and political categories (Black, Latino, White, Spanish, English, illegal, American, etc.) (Yon, 2000). It is within specific social contexts that these categories gain meaning and value (Urciuoli, 1996, p. 51). In my research I show how language often indexes race (English standing in for African American and Spanish for Latino). The categories become co-constitutive, with language becoming "an important dimension of racial 'subject-ification' " (Ong, 1996, cited in Harrison, 1998, p. 620). I take particular heed of Roediger's (1991) assertion that a change in signifiers over time can signal "a new set of social realities and racial [and material] meanings" (p. 15). Acknowledging that the content of social categories are negotiated in struggle, we can trace how semantic shifts leave "fingerprints" of transformations in human relations (Shore & Wright, 1997, p. 19).

This addresses what is sometimes a shortcoming in anthropological research about language politics. As Duranti (1994) notes, scholars have produced innumerable fine-grained analyses of speech acts (e.g., Searle, 1972) and ethnographies of speaking (e.g., Gumperz & Hymes, 1972; Heath, 1983; Hymes, 1972), examining the ways in which the intricacies of speech shape and are shaped by daily life, genre conventions, and belief systems. However, much more critique is needed of the wider-scale systems of domination and power that these local language practices exist within. Ethnographies of education have also tended to focus on the micro level (Luykx, 1999, p. xxxiv), looking at language issues only in the classroom or school community. In all this study of language, there is still a need for more exploration beyond the local—and beyond simple dichotomies (national/local, mainstream/subaltern, Black/White).

Attinasi (1997) argues that investigating through dichotomies and critiquing systems of domination helps take scholars from studying language to contributing to the politics of language—to countering what he calls "the linguistics of racism" (p. 281). He points out that a "communicative apartheid" (p. 286) exists in the United States, with dichotomous views of correct and incorrect language use, shutting out not just one group or another from structures of power but "all groups who do not share" the "language of power" (p. 294, pp. 279–280). An important example, he states, is the English Only movement, which can be seen to target people in America who speak nonstandard varieties of English as much it targets speakers of other languages (p. 292; see also Smitherman, 1992, 2002). Delpit and Kilgour Dowdy (2002) also examine ways in which language maps on to race and how struggles for cultural citizenship are impacted dually by our tongue and our phenotype.

This is a long-needed departure from common constructions of the issue of bilingual education in the United States. In mainstream research and political/media treatment of the issue, bilingual education is overwhelmingly characterized as a "Latino issue." While the existence of bilingual programs utilizing languages other than Spanish is sometimes acknowledged (many large urban districts in the United States have had bilingual programs utilizing multiple languages), most attention is paid to programs for Latino, Spanish-speaking students.[5] This trend is so extreme that August and Hakuta (1997) report a need for research on even "the most basic" aspects of how bilingual education affects communities and students "with native languages other than Spanish" (p. 7). By looking at how issues of language at California Elementary affect Latino, Black, and White school community members, native Spanish and native English speakers, this book takes a step towards providing some of that basic information.

TAKING A CRITICAL STANCE TOWARD RACE

The conflict at California Elementary made it obvious to me that dynamics of race are deeply interwoven into the politics of immigration and language policy in the United States. My understanding of race is based on Omi and Winant's (1994) definition: "A concept which signifies and symbolizes social conflicts and interests by referring to different types of human bodies" (p. 55). Like Du Bois (1940) and Visweswaran (1998), I believe that these "types of human bodies" are not biological entities but social constructions shaped by shared sets of historical experiences and shared dynamics of struggle (not unlike Gilroy's concept of interpretive community and Bourdieu's concept of class). I draw on the fundamental assertion of critical race theory, that racial difference and White supremacy are organizing principles of American society, underlying such basic concepts as citizenship, property rights, and equality[6]; and shaping the politics of culture, class, identity, education, and immigration, to name a few.[7]

McCarthy and Crichlow (1993) point to a persisting "crisis" in the theorization of race in education (p. xiv). Questions of race, they argue, threaten traditionally unchallenged methodological and ethical assumptions about the privilege of established agendas (p. xvii). Indeed I was surprised when I went to the literature looking for a body of work to help me understand Black-Latino-White interrelationships. Much of the literature on race and education in the United States shows a tendency to focus on African Americans in a bipolar Black/White framework (Flores & Benmayor, 1997). Given this dichotomy, Latinos and other groups are often left out, leaving unexamined the "different ways policy and actions affect different groups and sub-groups" (Attinasi, 1997; see also Seller & Weis, 1997). When Latinos are discussed,[8] it is usually an exploration of dichotomous Latino/White relations. Weis (1996) confirms that in the educational literature "there has been excellent research on various groups as they struggle for emotional, intellectual, cultural and economic space," but "we have not spent enough time focusing on the ways in which these groups struggle in relation to each other" (p. x). I hope that this book will contribute to the growing body of education research that takes into account multifaceted, not dichotomous, dynamics of race.

In the burgeoning body of race literature on Whiteness, much has been written to expose and critique White people's spaces of privilege.[9] This work is of paramount importance. At the same time, in this literature I find a tendency that can, in certain ways, limit understandings of the complex nature of race as it functions in everyday life: Whiteness tends to be essentialized, placed simply in opposition to a "racialized other" and conceptualized as only applying to phenotypically White people (e.g., Fine, 1997; Frankenberg, 1993; Hartigan, 1997). I believe this overlooks how sometimes, racial categories can be produced and experienced in multifaceted ways. Domínguez (1997), for example, discusses the ways in which terms like "Black," "Mulatto," "Indian," and "White" have historically been variously inhabited and defined in social struggles in Louisiana. Ellsworth (1997) has looked at how the racial category of "White" manifests not only as a signifier of a certain set of phenotypic characteristics ("White" people) but also as a shifting set of practices, forms of property, performances, locations of privilege, and political symbols available to be strategically employed by people in a variety of subject positions ("Whiteness").[10]

The inescapable question after asking *how* race manifests in these complex ways is asking *with what effects, and for whom.* I explore how racial and language categories and discourses function both in and between each other, and how they co-construct one another along with other political categories such as "immigrant" and "American." Thus I ask, for example, how the term "African American" is used interchangeably with "English Only," and then tied to particular constructions of "America" in moves to legitimize a policy agenda or to stake a claim to cultural citizenship. I take Pollock's (2004) challenge to "wrestle" with race: One must analyze both the production of "simple," historic and straightforward orders of racial inequality, *and* the complexity of racial dynamics as lived (p. 56, 57).

DOING MY "HOMEWORK"

I have never been a very traditional anthropologist. Anthropologists traditionally have gone to do "fieldwork" in places that are far away, exotic and "wild" (Gupta & Ferguson, 1998, p. 8). It has been assumed that only by going to some "Other" place can an anthropologist find the difference and distance necessary for analytical clarity and neutrality. The goal I brought to my research, however, was to understand something that I was smack in the middle of: a topic that I was close to personally, activities that I myself was doing, and a place that I was *in.*

The traditionally-assumed remove and neutral omnipotence of the ethnographer started bending to scholarly critique as early as the late 1940s and 1950s, when anthropologists began exploring the "field" as a place for research and a place for social activism (Foley, 1999). Work in feminist, post-colonial, native, and auto-ethnography has also asserted that the *insider's* perspective on data and political involvement in the field, can generate powerful analytical insights.[11]

Inspired by this work, I investigate a community from which I "come." California Elementary is a place where I have worked and played a role in campus life; it is the place that shaped my very identity as a professional and as a researcher. Of course, talking about being a member of the California Elementary school community is complex—the neighborhood and the student body were all Latino and African American. In this sense I was indeed an outsider. The "school community" as a whole, however, included a staff that was quite diverse, comprising Latino, African American, White, and Asian teachers, administrators, and other staff. In this sense, because my research focuses on the dynamics between the adults on campus, I was an insider. Being a teacher there both before and during the research afforded me the position of someone who "was a part of" the very questions that I asked people. While certainly there were things that people *wouldn't* tell me for the very reason that I *was* a teacher there (and I was a *White* teacher there, and I was a *bilingual* teacher there), there were also many times that I had access to events, information, insights, and histories that someone who was not a teacher there would not have had.

So, I found that I asked and answered questions from shifting positions (Haraway, 1988), sometimes as anthropologist, sometimes as teacher, sometimes as White person, sometimes as "Latino/Bilingual" advocate, sometimes as "African American/EO" advocate. This evokes Haraway's idea of the anthropologist's split and contradictory self, and Abu-Lughod's (1991) idea of a "halfie" anthropologist. Somewhere between anthropologist and "informant," I negotiated less the traditional anthropological idea of rapport and more that of complicity (Marcus, 1998). This project was "homework" for me as much as it was "fieldwork" (Gordon, 1998, p. viii [citing Visweswaran, 1994]).

Atweh, Kemmis, and Wilkinson's (1998) idea of participatory action research (PAR) takes this idea of "homework" even further. They define PAR as investigating reality in order to change it and changing reality in order to investigate it (p. 21 [drawing on Fals-Borda, 1979; Fals-Borda & Rahman, 1991]). Similar to Freire's (1973) idea of *conscientização*, PAR requires that people do research on themselves. Participants explore and critique their knowledge, interpretive categories, communication, and experiences. They strive to understand the ways in which these are shaped by social structures, discourses, and power relations. When these connections are understood dynamically, people are poised to improve their realities.

This is the approach with which I undertook my research—I wanted to become a better-informed educator, able to do research and to use research to improve my own practice, and to contribute to knowledge in the field as a whole. One particular aspect of this I describe in chapter eight: My efforts to establish, in collaboration with colleagues at California Elementary, a professional discussion group (PDG) at California Elementary. We sought to create in the PDG a forum where teachers could address concerns about conflict on campus and about our classroom practice. We hoped to use this forum as a springboard for projects that would better our school community and our sense of agency. Such a form of teacher professional development is a powerful way for educators to collaboratively investigate, critique, and reenvision their habits, assumptions, and beliefs—in order to affect real, positive change together (e.g., Duncan-Andrade, 2005; Johnson, 2002; Killion & Bellamy, 2000). In this spirit, it is my hope that the things I have learned throughout this research project strengthen my own ongoing work in the field of education; and I hope that this book can in turn be used as a tool by others to spark critical reflection on the work they do.

MULTISITED AND CRITICAL ETHNOGRAPHY

As my questions about the politics of bilingual education at California Elementary began to formulate in my early years of teaching, they did so against a backdrop of swirling debates in the media and national politics about the virtues and sins of immigration, bilingual education, and changing American demographics. When I decided to conduct research on language education policy, then, I knew I had to look at more than just the goings-on at our one campus. Drawing on the work of George Marcus (1998), I formulated a plan to undertake multisited ethnographic research. Marcus states that a multisited ethnography rejects anthropology's traditional local/place-focused approach and instead adopts a *places*-focused strategy (p. 50). These places are sites or levels of analysis (such as "global/national/local") that are often seen as only loosely related, or perhaps even incommensurate. The ethnographer "follows the conflict" (p. 94), tracing and mapping its manifestations, and examining the ways in which each locale makes a "critical commentary upon the other" (p. 52). This can enrich knowledge of how social categories, discursive practices, and relations of power function and change in society.

This is similar to Stein's (2004) idea of the cultural analysis of education policy. In her analysis of congressional debates about the federal Elementary and Secondary Education Act and qualitative observations in urban elementary schools receiving Title I funds, she furthers an approach that does not look at policy unidirectionally but rather explores the "recursive relationship" of influence between local practice and national policymaking (p. xii). She looks at both of these sites of policy process because, "Although all locations of the policy process influence one another ... there is no necessary stability or convergence in the meanings of policy constructed by the individuals engaged.... Meanings, unlike other elements of policy, cannot be mandated" (p. 6). Interpretive analysis of education policy processes, then, contributes to the understanding of how the varied contexts of the policy processes interact, shape, and constrain one another.

A multisited approach for me involves engaging the often-thought distinct arenas of national media discourse, and everyday experience and talk in schools. In the first two phases of research, in the local context I explored how actors in a Los Angeles school community imagined, employed, and challenged widely-circulating discourses of race, language, immigration, and Americanness through their negotiations of shifting language education policies. In the national context, I conducted research at the "site" of media discourses about these issues, analyzing newspaper, television and radio texts. I sought out articulations and divergences between local narratives and these "mediascapes" (Appadurai, 1991, p. 6), and asked how each set of discourses related to the other in shaping subject positions, agendas, and outcomes.

In 2005, I "followed the conflict" into a third phase of research. The topic of immigration was still hot nationwide but it was relatively new in the Southeast. Georgia and North Carolina were suddenly and consistently on the list of the most popular destinations for immigrants to the U.S. Southern cities like Atlanta and Raleigh were now receiving extra support from immigration and customs enforcement task forces; and senators from Georgia (as opposed to longtime immigration-heavy states like California) were now making headlines as key players in the fate of federal immigration legislation.

And so, I added another research "site": the politics of immigration, language, race and education policy going on in Georgia (and comparatively, nationally at the time), as viewed through media coverage of events, debates, and legislation. I wanted to see how similar or different the themes and sticking points were in the Southeast compared to the earlier ones I examined in California. I wanted to see what could be learned from a comparison of politics in a new immigrant destination to those in a more mature immigrant destination—a comparison of dynamics across decades, as well.

At California Elementary I used the ethnographic research techniques of participant observation, interviews, and document collection. In 1996, my participant observation involved the traditional sitting in on meetings, interviewing, chatting at lunch and in the hallways, and just being around to experience things. In 1998–2000 participant observation was much more intense, as I was truly a "participant"—I was a teacher there, too. I kept tape recorders and note pads in various locations to record observations and reflections on the run. I conducted interviews with teachers, staff members, administrators, and parents (at lunch time and after school, being careful not to interfere with any of our professional duties). Over these two research periods I did over 100 interviews in all. I also sought out casual conversations with people in hallways, during breaks, on the playground, and at social gatherings. These conversations were countless. I maintained a personal journal where I recorded reflections, experiences, and questions. As for documents, I collected many types, all publicly available: regular faculty meeting agendas, weekly staff bulletins, select school-home communication documents, school employee and classroom rosters, district-wide pamphlets and notices, and certain documentation about classroom organization and our student population.

At the national level I looked at newspapers, TV, radio, and magazines. The print media I most closely followed were *The Los Angeles Times*, *La Opinión* (Los Angeles Spanish language newspaper), *The New York Times*, and (from 2005 through 2007) the *Atlanta Journal-Constitution*; and less frequently, *Time* magazine, *USA Today*, *Newsweek*, and *Education Week*, and also professional publications from the National Education Association and National Association for Bilingual Education.

To analyze my local data I utilized the frameworks of content analysis and discourse analysis (Agar, 1996; Carspecken & Apple, 1992; Glaser & Strauss, 1967), looking at the ways people organized their accounts of events, their explanations of opinions, and their answers to questions, and searching for emerging themes. I searched for the ways in which ideologies were expressed (Bourdieu, 1991; Foucault, 1972) and the ways in which speakers "contextualized" themselves vis-à-vis local and national discourses (Alvarez-Cáccamo, 1996; Gumperz, 1982; Hill & Irvine, 1992). To analyze my media data I conducted textual content analysis. I searched here, too, for recurring themes. To make sense of what I was finding across the local and national sites, I used the constant comparative method to trace co-occurrences, articulations, and divergences (Merriam, 1998).

I used all these methodological tools less to ensure that I got "the right" depiction of things and more to help me get as close to how school community members themselves characterized things as possible, while still being able to comment critically on that--including the clarification of my own positioned objectivity (Haraway, 1988, p. 196). I strove for what Marcus (1998, p. 97) calls "reflexivity as method."

LOOKING FORWARD

I offer this book to policymakers, scholars, educators, and people in school communities alike. We all share the work of making policy, practice, and research more effective in, and responsive to, our diverse communities. I strive to present the following chapters in an engaging, grounded style (less traditionally "academic"). In doing so I follow bell hooks' (1989) reminder that "to speak in a language accessible to all of us is a political choice about whom we are speaking to, whom we want to hear us, and whom we want to motivate with our words" (cited in Lipman, 1998, p. 21). I hope this book provides food for thought, for all of us.

NOTES

1. For an in-depth discussion of the history and politics of bilingual education I refer the reader to Keller and VanHooft (1982), Wrigley (1982), Estrada (1979), Higham (1994), Almaguer (1994), Takaki (1990), Trujillo (1996), Applewhite (1979), McDonnell (1996), Tollefson and Tsui (2004).

2. My professional work for the center is separate from this research project, which I completed independently. Though certainly working on the center's projects informs my perspective on issues in the region in a general sense, all of the inquiries that I made for this book were separate from my professional work, and the sources that I cite in this book were all publicly available.

3. See also Anderson (1983), Smith and Heckman (1995), Ginsburg (1989), Handler (1988), Williams (1991), Urciuoli (1996), and Fordham (1996).

4. Gal (1994, 1989), Woolard (1989), Urciuoli (1996), Hill and Irvine (1992). Some have called this type of approach a study of "folk linguistics" (Beck & Allexsaht-Snider 2002). For similar work on the multifaceted, fluid political content that social symbols carry in schools and societies, see Heller (1995), Smith and Heckman (1995), Woolard (1989), and Zentella (1990).

5. Corson (1999), August and Hakuta (1997), Attinasi (1997), Crawford (1997), Smitherman (1992), Crenshaw, Gotanda, Peller, and Thomas (1995), Porter (1990), Fillmore (1992), Trujillo (1996), Fishman and Keller (1982).

6. For example, Bell (1997a, 1997b), Crenshaw et al. (1995), Delgado and Stefanic (1995), Harris (1995), López (1995), Peller (1995), Flagg (1997a, 1997b), Goldberg (1996).

7. For example, West (1994), Gregory and Sanjek (1994), Hall (1996, 1988), Williams (1989), Almaguer (1994), Giroux (1993), Roediger (1991).

8. E.g., Barrera (1997), Foley (1990), Menchaca (1993, 1995), Trujillo (1996), Valenzuela (2005).

9. For example, Harris (1995), Peller (1995), Morrison (1992), MacCannell (1992), Foley (1990), Hartigan (1997, 1999), Frankenberg (1993), Fine (1997), McIntosh (1989).

10. See also MacCannell (1992), Fanon (1967), Winddance Twine (1997), Fine Weis, Addelston, & Marusza (1997), Frankenberg (1993), Segal (1993), Strong (1992).

11. For example, Reed-Danahay (1997), Abu-Lughod (1991), Behar (1993), Kondo (1990).

CHAPTER 2

DEBATES ABOUT IMMIGRATION, LANGUAGE, RACE, AND EDUCATION POLICY IN THE NATIONAL MEDIA IN THE MID-1990s

Debates about immigration and bilingual education in the national media leading up to and in the mid-1990s were vigorous. The "pro-" and "anti-" camps, though they presented opposing agendas, tended to anchor their arguments in common terms: First, whether the idea of languages other than English in school was a threat or a benefit to things "American," and second that bilingual education was strictly a "Latino issue" (A. Valdés, 1979, p. 180). The opposing sides also utilized the similar discursive strategies of talk about equal opportunity, leveling the playing field, and essentialized characterizations of "America." "Both sides often conflated concepts of language and national identity in their arguments, and typified race relations in similar ways. In the rest of this chapter I lay out the major themes in the debates as they manifested in the "anti-bilingual education" arguments and the "pro-bilingual education" arguments.[1]

War or Common Cause? A Critical Ethnography of
Language Education Policy, Race, and Cultural Citizenship , pp. 21–26
Copyright © 2008 by Information Age Publishing
All rights of reproduction in any form reserved.

THE "ANTI-BILINGUAL EDUCATION" ARGUMENTS

Most arguments against bilingual education leading up to and in the mid-1990s constructed the English language as the defining essence of American identity and culture. These arguments can be seen as what Bourdieu (1991) calls the struggle for a "normalized language" with which to fashion an ideal national "community of consciousness" (p. 48). Handler (1988) argues that in such nationalist discourses, a certain language is painted as defining the nation both sociologically and territorially. Given this static conception of the nation and its culture, "the notion that people exposed to two cultures or two languages lose their identity and become confused and unable to function is commonplace" (p. 166). Bilingualism comes to symbolize a threat of cultural pollution and the impending "death of the nation" (p. 169).

For example, the *Los Angeles Times* reported that a local government official exclaimed, "We as a nation need to have a central functional identity in the English language" (Phinney & Reza,1996). And in a 1996 TV news report on issues of language and schools, the opinion of a New York school board member was as follows:

> Well, here we are in the multicultural heartland and everything is in Spanish here. I don't even feel like I'm in the United States. I feel like I'm in the middle of Latin America.... In the old days, when they used to refer to an ethnic neighborhood, an Italian neighborhood ... everything was still in English.... You knew you were Americans. (*20/20*, 1996)

Meanwhile, in the *Washington Post* it was said that while Chinese, Haitian, Russian, Korean, Vietnamese, French, Greek, Arabic, and Bengali speaking students received bilingual instruction in the United States, the "real threat" was posed only by Spanish-English programs: "Hispanic cultures" were "less interested in assimilating" than other groups, particularly when compared to earlier immigrants from Europe who assimilated to become productive contributors to society (Astroff, 1988; Glazer & Moynihan, 1974). Latino immigrants, the *National Review* pronounced, preferred to stay in "linguistic welfare" bilingual programs that "did not really teach English" and that drained the national coffers. By "rejecting" monolingual English instruction, then, Spanish-speaking immigrants "doomed themselves" to an uneven social and economic playing field, and shunned the "American Dream" (McQuillan & Tse, 1996; Porter, 1990).

This "problem" was presented in even graver terms when major news magazine stories began to report that the "face" of America was changing (Morganthau, 1997, p. 58), becoming more Latino and Asian, more Brown. Latinos were then the second-largest and fastest-growing minority group in the United States, and "whites could become a minority as early as the 2050s" (p. 59). The alleged lack of linguistic and cultural assimilation, coupled with characterizations of Latinos as harboring "traditions of corruption," "political apathy," and "soaring birth rates," constructed Latinos as threatening the nation's peace and prosperity (Cooper, 1994, p. 28). Bilingual education was portrayed as just one of the many problems—but the signature one—that this growing population brought to the United States.

In 1994 the issue came to a head in California. Proposition 187, the "Save Our State" ballot initiative, was proposed by conservative anti-immigration groups. The measure passed by a 59% vote in that year's statewide election. The initiative sought to amend state law so that anyone who could not prove their legal status in the United States would be denied the benefits of any public services such as health care (except for emergency medical care as required by federal law), social services, and public education. School districts were mandated to verify the legal status of all students and their parents, and to report any illegal students and their parents to the federal immigration authorities. All illegal immigrants would be deported. Upon its passage, Proposition 187 was immediately challenged in court and a judge imposed a temporary restraining order barring its implementation until its constitutionality could be determined. In 1996 the restraining order was still in effect, and so while its mandates were not yet enforceable the cloud of 187 hung over the state.

Balibar (1991) calls these types of discourses and agendas examples of an "immigration complex": a myriad of social concerns condensed into one overwhelming malady and posited as caused by the singular "fact of the presence of immigrants" (p. 220). The term "immigrant" becomes racialized in its connection to "Latino," and becomes "a gloss for national Other" (p. 222). It then functions as a powerful political category in public debate, accommodating various meanings in shifting contexts of struggle (Gilroy, 1987, pp. 24, 38; see also Darder, 1997).

THE "PRO-BILINGUAL EDUCATION" ARGUMENTS

In surveying national debates about immigration and bilingual education leading up to and in the mid-1990s, I found much more coverage given to the "anti-" arguments. Though passionate, outspoken, and often experienced in the field, bilingual education advocates were given less attention and bestowed less legitimacy by pundits and reporters. There are volumes of research showing the benefits of bilingual instruction, but this literature did not generally reach the public and was not referenced much in media coverage (McQuillan & Tse, 1996).

Pushing for the recognition of languages other than English as legitimate vehicles for academic instruction, bilingual education advocates challenged the increasingly powerful movement to make the public space of education monolingual. They rejected the hegemonic stereotype of a homogeneous "American" identity in favor of a pluralist, multicultural one (Crowley, 1989, p. 223; Lee, 1996). This provided, at least potentially, for a space of difference, a stance from which to nurture a diverse yet "united utterance" (Crowley, 1989, p. 223) against the monolingual status quo.

Pro-bilingual education arguments often focused on the necessity of a plurality of languages in a global economy. Contrary to the other side's opinion that speaking diverse languages sapped patriotism and left speakers of other languages in a linguistic and economic ghetto, advocates argued that being bilingual could advance one's own career and benefit the nation's economy (Colvin, 1996).

While running directly counter to the anti-bilingual education discourses, however, many bilingual education advocates constructed their position similarly to their opponents. First, they discussed bilingual education vis-à-vis an ideal American national community, the identity of which was assumed to manifest through language. Though they extolled the benefits of a linguistically and culturally plural nation, they often did so while reinforcing the primacy of English in America, and while framing the advantages of bilingualism in a nationalistic manner. In other words, they argued, one can champion diversity but must base it in uniformity. While bilingual people can have "two worlds" in private or in classrooms or during a business deal, in the end the national community must be a "social unit" within which assimilation to English prevails. For example, in a *Los Angeles Times* editorial an advocate stated that, "It is dehumanizing to steal a person's language, their culture, their identity" by abolishing bilingual education. But while Spanish could be a kind of personal or family "treasure" that should be honored, English *must* be spoken by all. And a *New York Times* editorial opined that while "multilingualism improves communication" in our global economy and society, and helps immigrant communities share in the "reality" of American economic betterment, this betterment must still be grounded in English (Velásquez, 1995).

Second, bilingual education defenders portrayed the programs as tools to boost English Language Learners (ELLs) on to a linguistically, culturally and economically level playing field with "mainstream" English speakers. In the *Los Angeles Times* a Chilean immigrant pleaded, "Of course everyone should learn English ... but there needs to be a system to assist in the transition. That's what bilingual [tax and voting] forms and bilingual education are all about." Like the anti-bilingual education arguments, many bilingual education advocates constructed English as the ultimate goal, portraying the use of other languages as a stepping stone.

Third, as in much anti-bilingual education literature, bilingual education advocates often characterized non-English speaking communities as inherently inferior to English-speaking ones. For example, a teacher argued in the *Los Angeles Times* that,

> The higher my students' skills are in their own dominant language, the more successful they're going to be in all subject areas in English.... [As a result,] if you have students who feel confident and positive about who they are, they won't need to reach out to gangs or to other negative situations in the community. (Loar, 1995, p. B3)

It seemed that by simply learning English—through bilingual instruction—children could steer clear of the destructive influences of their own non-English-speaking community.

Additionally, most "pro" arguments also racialized bilingual education narrowly as a "Latino issue," establishing a Latino versus mainstream and Spanish versus English dichotomy. Though people insisted that multilingualism in general was desirable, the bilingual programs discussed were usually only Spanish-English. Hardly any mention was ever made of the many other languages utilized in bilingual programs across the nation. The personal success stories of bilingual program graduates were about Latinos, and the ELLs mentioned or quoted were Latino (Loar, 1995; Pyle, 1996; Velásquez, 1995).

STATE-LEVEL POLICY BACKTRACKING

It was not just on the national scene that debates about bilingual education raged in the mid-1990s. The institution of bilingual education was coming under attack by the mid-1990s at the state level. At the very time that conflict at California Elementary erupted over the value of its bilingual program, anti-bilingual education factions were raising questions with California's State Board of Education about the efficacy and future of the program--and they were finding an audience. By 1995 the California State Board of Education began easing the terms of its strict bilingual instruction mandate. They began allowing districts to implement alternative programs utilizing methods other than native language instruction with ELLs, as long as districts could prove that student progress would not be slowed down. Exactly how they would prove this was left vague (Pyle, 1996, p. A1). This state-level policy backtracking would provide fuel for the massive anti-bilingual education campaign, Proposition 227, in 1998.

THE TYPIFICATION OF
LATINO/AFRICAN AMERICAN/WHITE RELATIONS

Also leading up to the conflict at California Elementary was increasing media coverage of polarizing racial tension in Black and Latino neighborhoods. In *Racial Ideology in U.S. Mainstream News Magazine Coverage of Black-Latino Interaction*, Shah and Thornton (1991) contend that "Rapidly changing demographics over the past decade have brought blacks and Latinos into political and social conflict over scarce resources" (p. 119). However, "Despite the importance and implications of these conflicts for American social relations—and especially for the 52.3 million blacks and Latinos in the United States—there has been little news coverage" that goes beyond the surface, and almost no in-depth research on these dynamics (p. 119).

Shah and Thornton (1991) found that the "typification" of African American/Latino/White relations in media coverage was extreme (p. 133). These portrayals were usually "incomplete because they block[ed] alternative ways of understanding issues" (p. 133). Propagated by the mostly White press rooms, this then served "to organize public debate about race by establishing parameters within which inter-minority interaction is understood" (p. 199). African American/Latino interaction got presented in an "ahistorical manner," portrayed shallowly as savagely conflict-ridden and constructed in stark opposition to a White mainstream. Thus it became commonplace to present Latinos and African Americans as in opposing camps, battling out an issue of their own making—and to present Whites as naturally "above" such "racial" battles. As we will see, this typification permeated assumptions about the boundaries within struggle at California Elementary.

NOTE

1. For other discussions of this see for example Crawford (1995, 1992a, 1992b), Gallegos (1994), Estrada (1979), Crowley (1989), and Casanova (1991).

CHAPTER 3

CONFLICT OVER IMMIGRATION, LANGUAGE EDUCATION POLICY, AND RACE AT CALIFORNIA ELEMENTARY IN THE MID-1990s

As outlined in chapter 1, I take a sociocultural approach to the study of language education policies (Levinson & Sutton, 2001), examining how they function as complex, culturally situated practices of power, and how they are created by technical mandates and by daily praxis. I analyze the language education policies at issue at California Elementary as resources through which people understood and constructed experience, relationships, and agendas. I explore how they became frames for, and tools within, struggles for cultural citizenship. After Rosaldo (1994), Ong (1996), and Flores and Benmayor (1997), I define cultural citizenship as an individual or group having access to institutional structures and opportunities; feeling a sense of belonging, participation, and voice; and being recognized for contributions made to the social collective. More

War or Common Cause? A Critical Ethnography of
Language Education Policy, Race, and Cultural Citizenship , pp. 27–62
Copyright © 2008 by Information Age Publishing
All rights of reproduction in any form reserved.

than just in the legal sense, *cultural* citizens are recognized as, and feel they are, full members of their community.

In 1996 I conducted a summer of research in the school in South Los Angeles that I had taught in from 1992 through 1994, where my curiosity about the politics of language education policy first arose. I investigated how in the late 1980s and through 1996 the school community negotiated dramatic shifts in local demographics and attendant changes in language education policies. I asked, how did Latino, African American and White school community members experience and construct these dynamics, and how did they struggle to define the community's parameters for cultural citizenship through debates about them? How did school community members' intertwined discourses about language, immigration, nation, and race reflect national media and political discourses on these topics, and how did these discourses shape people's experiences of and relationships to the shifting instructional policies? And, how did all of this impact the educational environment on campus, and with what effects?

When I first returned to campus in 1996, I was flooded with memories of my time there as a teacher. I was happy to be back, but I was surprised to feel hesitant at first. I wondered, can I hold my "insider" personal perspectives together with—and in tension with—my "outsider" anthropologist's gaze (Fordham, 1996)? As a particularly situated ethnographer, can I conduct the kind of research that will critically engage the multiple perspectives there are on the issues? Can I write the kind of text that will spark dialogue and action among practitioners, researchers, and policymakers?

A SCHOOL COMMUNITY IN TRANSITION

The neighborhood surrounding this school not too far south of downtown Los Angeles is bordered on one side by a set of train tracks and on another by a major freeway through the city. The area was very economically depressed in the mid-1990s. Residentially, there were mostly small houses with front porches and small yards, and some two- and three-story apartment buildings. There were also large factories, produce distribution centers, strip malls, and many empty lots. Some buildings had painted murals of African American historical figures, Mexican countryside scenes, and the Virgin of Guadalupe. The school's campus was comprised of two, two-story buildings and several trailer classrooms, a large blacktop yard, and an outdoor lunch pavilion. All was enclosed by a high chain-link that was locked from 7:30 A.M. until 2:30 P.M. every day.

The community had seen drastic demographic changes over the previous several years. This area of South Los Angeles had been predominantly

African American, middle and working class. Explained one African American parent,

> My parents bought a house here in 1955. I went to California Elementary. It was a nice area. From '56 to '82 you still had older Black parents living here. Then they got better jobs and moved on to suburbs such as Rancho Cucamonga, Upland, Rialto, San Bernardino, and Fontana. But the grandparents stayed until they died, and now things are being sold to Latinos.

Los Angeles Unified School District (LAUSD) statistics reflected this change. The enrollment of English Language Learners (ELLs) in the district in 1981 was 117,388; by 1996 it was 300,980 (LAUSD, 1996a). At California Elementary, the student body went from being overwhelmingly African American to being 53% African American and 47% Latino by 1980 (LAUSD, 1996a). Of the Latino students in my bilingual classes in 1992–1993 and 1993–1994, some were first or second generation U.S. citizens, some were legal immigrants, and some were undocumented immigrants (they would tell me stories of coming to the United States, running over the hills in San Diego by night, or riding across a border checkpoint in the empty gas tank of a truck). By the 1995–96 school year the K–5 student body was just over 10% African American and just under 90% Latino, and that year only a small handful of Black youngsters matriculated to kindergarten.

Though the community population was changing from mostly African American to mostly Latino in the years leading up to 1987, until that year a large majority of the school's staff remained monolingual English speakers, many African American. The demographic shifts that were occurring were basically absorbed into that organizational and cultural structure: As ELLs entered the school they were placed in the existing English Only (EO) classes. Over time as more ELLs matriculated, bilingual teacher's assistants (TAs) were hired so that students could be placed in classrooms where teachers delivered instruction in English but a TA was there to offer small group native language support for a few hours each day (to clarify instructions, review the academic concepts in Spanish, help students with the English vocabulary needed for the lesson, etc.). These were called "modified bilingual classes." While this arrangement did modify instruction to varying degrees to meet ELLs' needs, it was overall the ELLs who had to adapt to the English speaking environment. Several staff members described the school's pedagogical focus prior to 1987 as "getting the new kids into English, fast."

In 1987, things changed. The LAUSD implemented the Master Plan for Bilingual Education, a comprehensive policy mandating bilingual instruction and bilingual teachers for ELLs (LAUSD, 1996c). New administrators were brought to California Elementary to implement the Master

Plan, and this brought about lots of changes, quickly. The administration began to group the ELLs into full bilingual classes taught by newly-hired, district- and state-certified bilingual teachers. Those monolingual teachers who had been teaching the ELLs up until that point were now being told that they "did not qualify" to teach them. Each year more bilingual staff was hired, and more EO staff was displaced from the "modified" classes into the dwindling number of full EO classes. Across campus, classrooms became more and more segregated by language and race. The majority of new bilingual teachers were Latino, some of whom were immigrants themselves; a few were White (me for example), and still fewer were African American (a fellow Teach For America corps member of mine, for example). The overwhelming majority of us were also in the LAUSD's District Intern alternative credentialing program. Many of African American TAs found their positions dropped from 6 hours a day to 3 so that 3 more hours could be filled with a new bilingual TA. As well, cafeteria, campus security, and office staff positions began to be filled by bilingual personnel. By the 1996–1997 school year, 17% of the school's personnel were African American, 63% were Latino, 1% were Asian, and 19% were White. There were 4 EO classes and 39 bilingual classes.

Not only were bilingual jobs proliferating, but the LAUSD was also paying a bilingual stipend to teachers who passed district fluency exams and state Bilingual Cross-Cultural Language and Academic Development specialist exams. So, new bilingual teachers in positions once occupied by veteran EO teachers were getting paid up to $5,000 more a year. Monolingual teachers could take a state exam in English as a Second Language (ESL) methods to earn a Language Development Specialist stipend half the size—$2,500. Moreover, when it came time each year for teachers to choose which class they would teach the next year,[1] bilingual certification trumped years experience (seniority) and bilingual teachers were accorded first pick.

These differences in compensation and professional opportunity became major points of contention, as did student achievement statistics. Bilingual program Latino students were consistently outscoring English speaking African American students in *both* languages: Latino students transitioning from the bilingual program into EO classes were scoring higher on state standardized tests in *English*. Upper-grade EO teachers who received the transitioned students reported that, in the words of one, "The bilingual transitioned kids, nine times out of ten they are your top kids." And students in the bilingual program were scoring higher, comparatively, on their exams in *Spanish* than were African American students in English (LAUSD, 1994–95).

These developments, and the tensions that began to build around them, were exacerbated by another major change in the school community in 1994: the reorganization of campus decision-making structures according to the new Los Angeles Educational Alliance for Restructuring Now (LEARN) school reform model. Briefly, LEARN was an organizational model based on the principle of site-based management: "Virtually all decision making is moved to the school level, and central administration shifts from the traditional role of command and control to one of advice and support" (LAUSD, 1994–95). No longer did the principal have concentrated authority. Parents, staff, administrators and other community members were now all "stakeholders" invested with decision making powers.

Decision making was now based on the concept of "consensus" in various committees. Consensus was considered the point at which all stake holders agreed that a decision was satisfactory. Though this was one of the foundations of the LEARN philosophy, I found it to be a problematic concept at this school. People did not seem to know how important decisions were actually made if there was contention among stakeholders (Did the principal have the power to break a tie, for example?). Hence, when changes were made that were not unanimously popular, people sometimes seemed unsure just how that decision was finalized (a vote they missed? the handiwork of a persuasive somebody on a certain committee?). Consequently, they did not always know to whom they should address a formal objection.

Some people I spoke with attributed the growing conflict over bilingual education in part to this confusion. Said one TA, "Before, the principal was in charge. Now no one is willing to give up their opinion and compromise. And since no one has the final say, nothing gets done. LEARN has divided this school." On the other hand, many agreed with the parent who said that, "LEARN really helped us because now everyone is heard and we're learning to communicate." Overall, it was difficult to say just how much of an effect this organizational change had on politics at California Elementary. Certainly it complicated the question of who had control over issues important to dynamics of cultural citizenship—just who held the keys to access to decision-making power, to the ability to include or exclude, to the ability to be heard?

A financial "zero-sum game" was another major factor in the conflict that raged on campus in 1996: The EO and bilingual programs were in competition for limited resources. The school received funds for basic costs, federal Title VII bilingual education funds, and Title I funds for socioeconomically disadvantaged students. With the adoption of the LEARN model, the school site had significant freedom in deciding how to spend these funds. The trouble was, as many people told me, given the set allotment to work with, "One more dollar for bilingual is one less for EO and vice versa." Decisions about expenditures came to be interpreted as moral valuations, as how the school community prioritized the two programs and the programs' student and staff needs.

OUTLINES OF A CONFLICT

All of the teachers, TAs, other staff members, parents, and administrators I spoke to that summer portrayed these dynamics of change, competition, and struggle as overwhelming and conflict ridden. In the words of many, it was literally "a war." One "side" of this "war" was described to me as those supportive of the bilingual program. They were "the bilingual people," "the Latinos," the "Spanish people." That there were a few White and African American people in bilingual positions, or who were supportive of bilingual education, was glossed over, generally not mentioned. I refer to the people on this "side" of the conflict as "Latino/bilingual." I use this combination of terms because they were so often used together and interchangeably (even by the same person in the same sentence), and because they together contain the constructed lines of division of the conflict—the racial and the linguistic/pedagogical.

The other "side" was described to me interchangeably as "the African Americans," or "the EOs." The fact that there were a few White EO teachers and a few bilingual teachers who actually believed it was better to teach ELLs all in English was also hardly ever mentioned. I call this "side" "African American/EO." Again, I aim to remain true to the characterizations that school community members used to describe school community dynamics, and to maintain the terms in tension, in quotes throughout the text, to emphasize the constructed, strategic nature of this articulation of racial, linguistic, and pedagogical categories.

As the "Latino/bilingual," "African American/EO" constructions highlight, I found that it was the racial categorizations *as connected to* the linguistic and pedagogical ones that became, in Urciuoli's (1996) terms, "metacommunicative" (p. 8), serving as rhetorical "place markers" for a whole set of assumptions about beliefs, group membership, and political agendas. It was these place markers that gave shape to the lines of division on campus.

KEY VOICES IN THE CONFLICT

I was not long into my summer of research before I perceived that a few key voices were emerging in people's stories. It was these individuals who were mentioned and quoted most often when people told me what had been happening since I left in 1994. These individuals appeared to symbolize for many school community members the oppositions at hand. There were those on the "African American/EO" "side" and those on the "Latino/bilingual" "side." I perceived greater heterogeneity, however. I found that on both "sides" there was a group of voices that I call "border crossers" (following Foley, 1995; Giroux, 1992). Border crossers were school community members who did not neatly fit the ascribed profile of "their" "side"; they showed that these interpretive communities were heterogeneous within. The people considered "African American/EO" were African American and EO, and a few were White and Latino, *and* a few spoke some Spanish or even taught in the bilingual program. Those considered "Latino/bilingual" were Latino and bilingual, *and* a few were White and a few African American, and some spoke little Spanish. And regarding policy agendas, there were times when people on either "side" would agree with aspects of the other "side's" agenda. (Further, though I focus in this research on the adults in the community, it should be noted that as for students, there were a small number of Latino students who began enrolling in kindergarten as EO in those years. Those students were mentioned in only two discussions all summer. Most people completely glossed over their existence in conflations of EO with African American and bilingual with Latino.)

In conversations, any diversity within and across the dichotomy of this "war" was not generally acknowledged. I came to see, though, that this had simultaneously a confounding and a necessary effect: In one sense I saw the simple dichotomy as confounding understandings of people's multifaceted subject positions and agendas (people's membership on one "side" or the other was often not as simple as it was portrayed). In another sense, I came to see that constructing the tightly-drawn "Latino/bilingual," "African American/EO" dichotomy gave necessary shape and momentum to each "side's" arguments and agendas, flowing from their experiences as interpretive communities (see Gutiérrez, 2002, & Pollock, 2004 for discussion of this issue).

The personal profiles below are intended to give a basic feel for these "key voices" on the California Elementary School campus in 1996. Of course, the names of these people have been changed.

"African American/EO" Key Voices

Michael attended California Elementary as a student and became involved at the school again as a family member of then current students in 1994. He volunteered on campus in a variety of capacities for awhile, and then became TA. He became active on the school's LEARN council and as such became involved in many important decision making processes. Also an employee union representative, Michael was well known and active in many areas of campus life. He was often characterized as a vocal advocate for Black students and staff.

Eleanor was TA and had been at the school for many years. She was very active, often volunteering to help with holiday celebrations, Career Days, and other activities. She was popular and people were always talking with her about goings on. For me, she seemed to be a gauge of community feelings.

"African American/EO" Border Crossers

Janice was probably the most often quoted voice for this "side." She had been a teacher for almost 20 years, and at this school site since 1982. She held a lifetime credential and a master's degree in education. Janice had taught full EO classes a majority of the time but had also taught modified bilingual classes. She had served as a teachers' union representative and was on several committees at the school. Some people in the school community told me they were intimidated by her because, they said, "she's so outspoken." She said it was because, "I'm a strong Black woman, and that's scary to some people." While not everyone I spoke with on the "African American/EO" "side" agreed with everything Janice said, she was often the one from this "side" to stand up in meetings and voice opinions.

Frank had been a teacher at the school for several years. African American, he often argued forcefully in meetings for the "African American/ EO" position. However, Frank taught full bilingual classes. This seemed to make some people uncomfortable and suspicious of his loyalty. One African American teacher explained, "I applaud Frank for being *that way*," meaning, bilingual, "but I told him, 'You're still a Black man. Your mom and dad and you, are Black. Don't you forget that!'" In this teacher's opinion, Frank seemed to be poised to commit racial treason through bilingualism.

Roslyn had been at the school since 1992. A young African American teacher, she taught both EO and modified bilingual classes. In 1996 Roslyn took the administrative position of Title I program coordinator. She was known to many as an advocate for the African American students at the school. As she explained, while she had Latino and Black children in her classes, all of whom she loved, "of course Black children are going to be closer to my heart, I share their experience. I'm going to fight for them." Roslyn was a graduate of the District Intern Program, and several people on the "African American/EO" "side" told me they were concerned about this because, "all the DI's" were "only taught to care about the LEPs [ELLs]."

A final border crosser on the "African American/EO" "side" was Elizabeth. Elizabeth was a border crosser for the simple fact that she broke the mold by being White. Elizabeth had been at California Elementary for several years. She was not a particularly vocal participant in public conflict, but she was well recognized as an exemplary EO teacher and she would argue a very forceful "pro-EO" position in lunchtime and parking lot conversations, expressing many opinions I found to be representative of others on this "side."

"Latino/bilingual" Key Voices

Enrique was cited by most people as, to put it in the words of one, the "bilingual ringleader." Enrique came to the United States from Mexico as a young child. A graduate of the District Intern Program, from 1993 through 1996 he taught full bilingual classes. In 1996 he took the administrative position of bilingual program coordinator. As bilingual coordinator Enrique was in charge of program placement and transition/redesignation for all ELLs. He oversaw the large bilingual program budget and managed professional support of bilingual staff. Consequently, many on the "African American/EO" "side" charged that Enrique was responsible for what they saw as the neglect of African American students and for "the ELLs not transitioning into English fast enough."

Crystal had been a TA in the bilingual program since 1990. In 1996 her sister and brother also worked at the school, as TAs and campus security aides. Crystal's family had come to the United States from Mexico when she was a young child. She took pride in being bilingual and in working to help other immigrants achieve success in school. Crystal was well liked among bilingual program teachers, parents, administrators, and TAs, and I found her opinions about school politics to be reflective of many of the TAs'.

"Latino/bilingual" Border Crossers

Like Elizabeth, simply by being White Scott etched a fissure into the discursively constructed "Black-Brown" dichotomy of the conflict. In 1996 he had been at the school only a few years. Scott was the perpetrator of "the blackface incident" (a defining moment in this conflict that I discuss in the next section). In fact, he often did and said things offensive to "African American/EO" school community members. However, his Whiteness seemed to be overshadowed by his bilingualism, because his actions and statements were always described to me as examples of the offenses of "the bilinguals."

Linda was a White teacher who had taught in the bilingual program since 1990. She was a controversial figure at California Elementary because she was very vocal in defending the bilingual program during faculty meetings, in the lunch room, and in personal interactions. She was also a teacher's union representative in the mid-1990s. Her pro-bilingual stance was noted by many "African American/EO" school community members as an example of how the campus environment was becoming increasingly hostile to Black and monolingual English speaking people.

Andrea had been the bilingual program coordinator for several years when, in 1996, she ran for the newly vacated assistant principal position. School community members on the "Latino/bilingual" "side" expressed unreserved support for her candidacy. "She really has the kids' needs at heart," they told me, citing her work as a coordinator. Many on the "African American/EO" "side" expressed disapproval of her candidacy. If she were elected, one parent said, "Our kids wouldn't have a chance against the bilingual agenda." When Andrea was elected to the position she was either portrayed as yet another threatening "bilingual" force or as another needed "bilingual" advocate. She was not usually characterized as a "white person" in a position of authority.

Throughout this text I quote these key voices and many other school community members. I will sometimes indicate who a speaker is, when it will help to enrich the reader's understanding of that person's position or motivations. I also follow certain key voices through time in 1998 in, chapter 5, in order to trace experiences across the years and shifting language policies. At other times I will refer to a speaker in general terms like, "a teacher," or, "one staff member," and so forth.

"IT'S A BLACK-BROWN THING"

Imagine this scene (excerpted from my field notes, 1996):

It's mid-February, 1996 in this South Los Angeles community. At the school today the auditorium is the center of activity. The long-anticipated Black History Month Program is about to begin. People file in and sit on long wooden benches facing the stage, whispering in anticipation. The room is packed with students, staff, and parents. As they wait, they gaze up at the large banners on the walls that proclaim, "Believe and Achieve! ¡Piensa y Realiza!" Backstage, Scott prepares his students to perform a song about African American activists in the Civil Rights era; he is applying theater makeup to their faces. The stage manager, also a white teacher in the bilingual program, sees this but says nothing and ushers them onto the stage. Out in the audience a hush falls as the lights dim and curtains rise. People watch as a group of fourth grade students, all Latino, walk out onto the stage painted in blackface. As soon as the song ends, several African American faculty and staff members rush to the offending teacher and to the administrators. The arguments, anger, disbelief, and apologies that ensued in the following weeks became known collectively on campus as, "the blackface incident."

The "blackface incident" was the story most frequently told to me when people explained the "war" on campus. But while there was a certain level of common interpretation (it was unfortunate that it happened), the import ascribed to it varied. In fact, I heard tell of the incident so many times that in its retelling it seemed to become a lens through which other moments of the conflict were interpreted, constructed, and conveyed. In Woolard's (1989) words, the incident became a "key symbol" for school community members as they experienced and debated issues of language and immigration, race relations, professional status and opportunity, teaching and learning, and community belonging. It became a key symbol as they negotiated dynamics of cultural citizenship. Stories about this emotionally loaded event also seemed to me to be what Bourdieu (1991) calls performative utterances (p. 128): discursive attempts to legitimate the speaker's position in a struggle, and to delegitimize the position of others. I saw school community members attempting "to produce and impose representations of the social world" that would shape understandings of what should be done to end the "war." Indeed, how people discussed the "blackface incident" gave me insight not only into "what happened" on stage that day but into how people understood all manner of points of contention, how they constructed their own and others' positionalities and cultural citizenship status, and how they saw all this relating to politics on a national scale.

"WE'RE NOT EVEN WORTH A REWRITE": "AFRICAN AMERICAN/ EO" CONSTRUCTIONS OF SCHOOL COMMUNITY DYNAMICS

For many "African American/EO" school community members, the "blackface incident" brought up questions that had already been brewing: Who are "we" as a school community, anymore? Just who belongs? Are African Americans and monolingual English speakers valued? In addition to the affront of "the blackface incident" itself, most people I spoke with on this "side" of the school community felt that the way it was dealt with was appalling: A few days after the incident the school sent a letter of apology from Scott to all parents. Like most official documents that were sent home, the letter was in a bilingual format and was prepared by the office staff (which was majority Latino). But unlike with most official documents, there were glaring discrepancies between the English and Spanish copies of this letter. The English version was just a xerox of

Scott's apology scribbled on a piece of notebook paper. It appeared hastily written and utterly unedited. The Spanish version, however, was neatly typed in business letter format, placed on letterhead, and translated into the properly formal language. An African American parent said to me, "See? This whole 'blackface' thing is just another example of how bilingual people treat Blacks in the community. We're not even worth a rewrite."

The lack of worth of African Americans in the school community was further described to me as evidenced and caused by the following issues: unequal representation in positions of power; unfair hiring practices; disrespectful treatment of staff, parents, and students; an inferior academic program for EO students; racism; and "Latino/bilingual" greed for power and money. The Black-Brown "war" was also sometimes attributed to a culture clash between African Americans and Latinos, and between Latinos and "America." These issues could be seen to form what Gilroy (1987) called a "multi-accentuated symbolic repertoire" of discourses through which people understood dynamics on campus, and which people utilized to argue their case.

Regarding unequal representation in positions of power, numerous people argued that a higher "Latino/bilingual" student population did not justify what they saw as disproportionate representation of "Latino/bilingual" people in leadership posts. The principal was very "pro-bilingual" (hardly mentioned was the fact that she was White). She had just replaced a Black principal who had held the position between 1994 and 1996, and who had been perceived by most on campus as very "pro-EO." The vice principal, Andrea, used to be the bilingual program coordinator and was outspokenly "pro-bilingual" (also hardly mentioned was that she was White). Moreover, folks argued, one of the few "African American/EO" school community members in a position of power was not receiving proper support. The school's official parent representative on various committees, an African American man, was having difficulty getting concerns heard and was rumored to be the target of a plot to replace him with a Latina. And so I heard repeatedly some variant of this teacher's sentiments:

> We're treated as if we're outsiders. They say, "We're a bilingual school ... oh, yea, and there's a few African Americans." It's as if, "Soon there won't be any EOs so let's not bother with them." But the way I see it, even if there's only one EO student he deserves attention! If there were more Black people here things like this wouldn't happen.

Hiring practices and treatment of staff members were also unfair, many argued. People who were bilingual but otherwise inexperienced were hired to fill open teacher and TA positions. Eleanor explained,

I missed a job once because they *claimed* they needed a bilingual person. The woman who got the job spoke Spanish but she failed the basic skills test and I passed. And in the end there weren't even any LEP [ELL] kids in the class! I don't have anything against Spanish speakers. In certain areas they need a [bilingual] TA, but here Black people could at least work on the yard [supervising recess and lunch]. I got nieces and things coming up who need jobs but they won't be able to get one. It's not fair!

Worse yet, several people explained, was the district's refusal to offer monolingual English speaking professionals opportunities to become bilingual and hence marketable. The district offered free language courses, but this was not enough, said one teacher. "I don't know how the district expects us to become bilingual if they don't give us bilingual classes to teach. How can you learn it without speaking it every day?"

Stories of unequal treatment of students were also ubiquitous. "African American/EO" students were unfairly stereotyped as troublemakers, many reported, and they got harsher punishment for misbehavior than "Latino/bilingual" students. Explained one teacher, "There are always three or four Black boys, Black boys only, sitting on the bench in the office [i.e., punished]. I find it hard to believe that they are so bad inherently." And recently, "there was an African American child and a Latino child who both did bad things. The Hispanic one, who was worse, got nothing, got sent home. But the African American child got hand-cuffed by the police and taken away!"

Of paramount concern to those on this "side" of the community was the perceived inferior academic program for "African American/EO" students. The large discrepancy in test scores between students in the EO program and students in the bilingual program was cited as the ultimate proof. Said one parent, "Black students are being allowed to fall behind. They're not given a fair chance. People here, their major concern is bilingual education. We are overflowing with Spanish books. Our kids don't have access to the same kinds of resources." One educational aide commented, "Spanish students get all kinds of homework and hard work but African American kids don't get any, or they get worksheets accidentally sent home in Spanish! Who's monitoring the EOs to make sure they get the right homework, or that they can read by second grade?" Not the administration, one parent told me. She recounted the story of her last visit to campus, one that she said typified the experiences of other parents as well:

I was never told anything until I was called for a meeting about my son's progress by the principal and the psychologist. When I got there they left to go look at something in the hall and they never came back! They just left me sitting there and never even told me what the meeting was for!

One respite in these dynamics, I was told, had been provided by the previous principal (who held the position 1994–1996). He was Black and a vocal proponent of the EO program. "African American/EO" school community members portrayed him positively: He was "fair, he paid attention to the needs of *all* kids, not just the bilinguals." They cited for example his purchase of the Proficiency in English Program (PEP). PEP was a supplementary program designed to provide instruction in standard English (it involved vocabulary practice, oral recitations practice, and included a monthly assembly to introduce new skills and build motivation). It was seen as a resource for improving all students' command of standard English, but it was culturally associated with African American students in the EO program.

Many people maintained that racism was behind what "Latino/bilingual" school community members believed, said, and did. "Latino/bilingual" teachers, I was told, avoided Black students due to racist sentiments and assumptions. Said one TA,

> None of the so-called bilingual teachers want to bother with Black kids, especially the boys. I've heard a few say so. It's a race thing. Some of the Latino teachers are scared of the Black kids! Many Black students do have hard lives, don't have two parents at home like the Latino kids. But that doesn't make them inherently bad kids! We need to work with *all kids*, not a color. We need to get away from pro-color and be pro-*education*.

People reported frequent racist public remarks. For example, Scott was quoted by many to have said in a staff meeting about school discipline, "I don't have any behavior problems in my class because my kids are all Hispanic." That statement, said a parent, "was an accusation that African Americans *are* the problem."

People also argued that this racist behavior took the form of using "African American/EO" students' native English language skills in order to help teach ELLs English. Federal antisegregation laws mandated that where the division of students along language lines amounted to de facto racial separation (as was the case at our school), at least 20% of every school day had to be spent in joint activities—for example during art, music, and physical education. These "mixing" activities were supposed to be language-rich, in English, and carefully geared to the linguistic strengths and needs of both the native English speaking and ELL participants. At California Elementary, we implemented "mixing" time in the afternoons. We divided our classes (on grade levels) into groups, and combined and traded groups so that at any one time I, for example, would have a class full of small groups of students from all my colleagues' classes. Students rotated like this to different teachers a week at a time for music, art, or physical education lessons. "Mixing" was supported by many on the "Latino/bilingual" "side" because it offered ELLs the opportunity to interact with native English speakers. To the contrary, many on the "African American/EO" "side" agreed with Janice that,

> It's racist. Bilingual teachers are supposed to bring Hispanic kids to my room, and my African American kids are supposed to talk to them and prepare them for life? No. Black people, we think mixing is like going back to slavery, that you're treating our kids like quote unquote niggers.

Amidst all these points of contention money was also a key factor, as seen in the pay differentials that bilingual teachers received and in unequal program funding. The bilingual teacher stipends of up to $5,000 (depending on how many of the required tests teachers had passed) were seen as blatantly unfair. Argued one teacher, "People get to come here and take a test in their native language and get the $5,000. I can't come here and take a test in my native language and get $5,000!" Not only was the differential unfair but it contributed to bilingual teachers not wanting to teach Black children *and* not wanting to teach English to ELLs, many people told me. A parent explained to me that teachers purposefully kept their students' level of English proficiency low: "There's a lot of money in bilingual education and they don't want to give it up." And analyzing the issue on a larger, programmatic scale she added,

> As a whole program there's more money in bilingual ed. Think about it, they have to keep bilingual ed going because if all the kids transition to English, there goes their money. It's not fair and it doesn't make any sense. What about spending our money on English stuff?

Articulating to National Media Discourses

People often explained the conflict at California Elementary in terms prevalent in the national media at the time, articulating discourses of culture, language, and nation. They attributed a certain amount of the problems in the community to what they characterized as Latinos' unruly, dirty, or otherwise disreputable living habits and culture. English was posited as synonymous with the American nation, and Spanish characterized as an illegitimate threat, a place marker for the "borders" of appropriate national belonging (Williams, 1989). Constructions of Spanish-speaking Latino immigrants as unassimilating, noncitizen "invaders" positioned them as troublemakers.

On the contrary, as American-born citizens and as English speakers, African Americans were constructed as having a superior, more

American culture. This was portrayed in ways similar to the ways that in the media White middle class culture is unproblematically described as quintessentially American: African Americans were described as the prototypical Americans, suffering the burdens of welfare and other social problems at the hands of culturally deficient Others. For example, when I asked the parent representative to explain why he had said that the neighborhood's demographic shift had lead to this conflict, he said:

> These new Hispanic folks, they do things that African Americans just don't do, it's not their [African Americans'] culture. One African American family moves out and five Hispanic families move in—to one house! I don't wanna sound prejudiced or racist, but the value of the property goes down, the attraction to the area diminishes when you see vendors on the street, when you see clothes hanging on fences, or when you see a yard with five or six dogs, and I'm not talking well kept animals, I'm talking hounds! I went recently to a parent workshop here and they had a Spanish presenter and no English translation. I don't think I should have to go to a meeting in my own country and wear translation devices. Is this America or what? I have nothing against Hispanics, but I believe they are the sole reasoning behind welfare reform, year-round schools, a lot of our problems.

And Eleanor stated,

> Programs get jeopardized because some bilingual teachers here don't speak English well and they aren't American citizens, they're Mexican or Spanish citizens [the school employed a few teachers from Spain and Mexico as part of the district's international exchange program]. ESL has gone ka-boom. Kids aren't learning English. We get fifth graders who've been here since kindergarten and they still can't transition. How can that be? It doesn't make sense. Do we want our kids to be good, successful citizens and know American language and culture? What's the goal?

What it came down to, numerous people argued, was that "Hispanics are trying to take over." According to some, they already had. One teacher chalked up all the school's ills to the fact that, "This district went crazy when it went 100% Hispanic."

These quotes echoed not only the hegemonic anti-bilingual education and anti-immigration media discourses of the time that linked "Americanness" to English, but also drew upon assumptions about culture and belonging made popular in the American consciousness decades earlier. In Oscar Lewis's (1964, 1966) theory of "the culture of poverty," Lewis argued that poor people adapted to poverty by developing a way of life utterly outside the mainstream. Typical were disorganized and female-centered families and a refusal to assimilate to dominant values of upward mobility and thrift. These characteristics were passed from mother to child, Lewis maintained. This process of quasi-biological cultural transmission was so thorough, he argued, that by the age of 5 or 6 children's mental and social growth were forever stunted. Hence, even improved economic or other opportunities became useless. Poor people, he argued, would just naturally remain poor and pass these debilitating, alienating cultural characteristics on to the next generation.

Since the culture of poverty theory was published, in the public arena it has almost exclusively been applied to explanations of the chronic poverty and academic underachievement of racialized groups (e.g., Puerto Ricans [Bourgois, 1995], Mexicans [O. Lewis, 1964]), constructing them as inherently inferior to "mainstream Americans" (as gloss for the White middle class). These constructions have served to rationalize and provide stability to systems of White dominance and privilege. In particular, debates about *African American* language and culture (and their implications for learning and success in mainstream arenas) have been lively for decades.[2] Hence this move to align Black Americans with these hegemonic ideals of superior American culture and English monolingualism (that were usually deployed *against* them) can be seen as very strategic performative utterances (Bourdieu, 1991)—discursive efforts to secure a better place to "stand" (hooks, 2000) in relation to "Latinos/bilinguals" in the local community, and in the American racial and socioeconomic hierarchy.

This move to champion the ideal that English (only) was appropriate in American schools can be considered even more strategic when we note that it completely contradicted the policy agenda espoused by most "African American/EO" school community members I talked to during this time. This agenda, as we will see, proposed a dual immersion bilingual program so that Latino *and* African American students could attain Spanish-English biliteracy—so that all of the students at California Elementary could have access to ever-more diverse economic and social opportunities.

Where Should We Go From Here? "African American/EO" Policy Agendas

"African American/EO" school community members' answers to the question, "Where should we go from here?" were almost uniformly two-sided. When discussing the bilingual program in its current form, available to only Latino ELLs, I heard vehement accusations similar to those in anti-bilingual education media discourses: that bilingual education was un-American, unfair, and ineffective in providing students with the dominant cultural capital that they lacked, English. In this case,

English was the valued competency and Spanish the devalued competency. However, these condemnations of the current situation often dissolved when it came to creating future agendas for the school. When discussing what direction the school should take, people reminded me that monolingual African American students were falling behind their biliterate Latino counterparts academically, and that biliterate adults had more job opportunities, job security, and professional advantages. Though many charged that "Latino/bilingual" students were not learning English fast enough, in daily experience at California Elementary English no longer appeared to be the status quo competency that ELLs had to acquire in order to have an equitable chance in a monolingual English "mainstream."

Now Spanish seemed to be the "legitimate competence" (Bourdieu, 1991) that students needed *in addition to* English to be appropriately educated for an *increasingly bilingual mainstream*. Many "African American/EO" school community members now argued that without Spanish students would grow to be "de facto excluded" from the required bilingualism (p. 55), such as the jobs that people competed for on campus. They argued that without biliteracy "African American/EO" students would be "condemned [to] silence" (p. 55) as their "Latino/bilingual" counterparts passed them by.

In this sense, people stated that American public education had to live up to its commitment to equal access and opportunity for all by providing a program that would allow all students to achieve biliteracy. The words of Frank were echoed by several others:

> We've been talking about bilingualism forever. But "bilingualism" here means Spanish speakers get to learn Spanish and get pushed into English. I always thought that "bilingual" meant everyone learns two languages. Black kids are getting a second-rate education. Why can't they learn Spanish? Why can't they be bilingual and get ahead, too? Huh, "bilingual," what a misnomer.

One day during recess Janice and I were talking and she added this perspective on bilingual education policy at California Elementary—a perspective others shared:

> I know there's a need for bilingual education. People don't know this but I have studied bilingual education, I know the theory. I see it work at this school and I agree with it in principle. But I don't support it here because of how it was pushed on us. When they started the bilingual program we got no input and suddenly EOs became disrespected, second class citizens in our own school. Bilingual ed has to go!

Just a few moments later, when I asked her what we could do to improve the education of Black students on campus, she reflected, "I see all the jobs here going to bilinguals. Things are changing, Spanish is an important skill.... So why leave EOs behind? Why can't African American students have bilingual education, too?"

This brings to mind Urciuoli's (1996) discussion of language. Urciuoli studied the politics of English and Spanish in a New York Puerto Rican community. She explains that for the people she worked with, Spanish and English as codes were not themselves imbued with socially meaningful qualities. It was the "structures," or "specific relations and contexts" (p. 76) within which these codes were spoken that lent them their social significance (p. 50). I see similar dynamics expressed in the contradictory stances taken towards Spanish and English by actors in this Los Angeles school. Spanish was not always considered un-American or devalued; it was only considered so when it was positioned vis-à-vis currently dominant, pro-EO national media rhetoric—and when it was seen as unattainable by "African American/EO" school community members. When Spanish was placed in relation to actual local experiences, where bilinguals held advantageous positions and where there seemed to be a possibility to empower all students through a dual language program on campus, Spanish became desirable, and bilingualism became a goal.

This proposal for a dual language bilingual program amounted to a firm rejection of national media typifications of bilingual education. It was now clearly not just a "Latino issue." Nor was it simply about a group of students catching up to an established status quo. It was now about connecting to an emergent reality in a changing American ethnoscape. This redefinition of the stakes of bilingual education was situated, however, squarely within the enduring hegemonic discourse of American public institutions' responsibility to provide equal opportunity for all. The same logic that went into legislating bilingual education in the first place (e.g., in *Lau v. Nichols,* 1974) was now used to reenvision its scope.

Whose Knowledge is of Most Worth?

Among all these debates about what was going on and what changes should be made, a big question became what educators should know and what experience should be valued. "African American/EO" faculty and staff saw the number of positions open to them dwindling. Their two-pronged, anti- and pro-bilingual education agenda found many school community members in the dilemma of demanding for the children something they themselves did not possess. Though Spanish now seemed crucial for "African American/EO" students, it was often still presented as unnecessary for educators. Janice shared with me her response to people on the hiring committee who argued that teachers applying to teach bilingual classes, which were the only open positions at the time, had to pass the district fluency test (a Master Plan requirement):

> I have a lifetime professional multi-subject kindergarten through adult credential, a master's degree, a Language Development Specialist credential, and three times as many years' teaching as them [new bilingual teachers]. Don't come at me with that Spanish! People think that's all they need, but just because they have shoes on doesn't mean they can walk. Someone said I couldn't teach a bilingual class because I don't speak Spanish. I told them I can teach any kids, I'm a professional! We'll make up our own language!

In these reflections, we see a tension inherent in this kind of transformative vision for universal biliteracy: How to forge the future with the tools of the present? How to validate something for the next generation that invalidates or "dates" important aspects of our own current knowledge and experience?

As we will see in the following section, the experiences, discourses and agendas of "African American/EO" school community members, while constructed as opposing those of "Latino/bilingual" school community members, were actually analogous in many ways. To this "other side" of the "war" I now turn.

"I USED TO HEAR 'WET BACKS' A LOT": "LATINO/BILINGUAL" CONSTRUCTIONS OF SCHOOL COMMUNITY DYNAMICS

One Latino teacher told me,

> I couldn't believe it, the "blackface thing." I couldn't believe that teacher was so insensitive. But he said it was an accident, that he didn't know what blackface meant. So we just have to get over it and move on.

Many others concurred. Some did not even understand the excitement over "the blackface incident" to begin with. Explained one parent,

> Afterwards some of the Latino people didn't understand what was so offensive. They didn't grow up in this country and didn't know the history of it. Their indifference made people even madder. I might be one of them who didn't understand what the big deal was. But I still feel some things need to be put behind us.

Indeed, most on the "Latino/bilingual" "side" whom I spoke with saw the incident less as an affront to Black school community members and more as evidence that conflict had to be "put behind us" because, *everything's going crazy around here.*" And to a few, the after-event dynamics even became proof of an anti- "Latino/bilingual" environment in the community. A few teachers recounted the faculty meeting just after the incident like this one:

> When the Black teachers were expressing their feelings about the prejudice they felt towards them, they were expressing prejudice about Latinos! So I said—near tears—that I'd just been insulted. Some of them didn't understand that and some didn't care, and some thought it was good. They felt satisfied that I was offended, and this was allowed to go on at the meeting!

For most on this "side," then, "the blackface incident" became something that needed to be dealt with so that the "main issues" plaguing the school could be addressed: a perceived campaign to keep "Latino/bilingual" people out of positions of power; racism; unequal treatment of Latino staff members; the uphill battle to provide Latino students with robust bilingual instruction; and Latinos not being accepted in the community. I saw this as a set of issues analogous to those articulated by "African American/EO" school community members, a similar "multi-accentuated symbolic repertoire" of discourses through which people understood the goings-on at California Elementary, and through which people forwarded their agendas. Asserted a teacher,

> We're a majority Latino school and we have to serve the community. Bilingual education here suffers because of resentment and misunderstanding. The EO program is doing its job. The kids are learning at their level. EOs ask, "Why are Spanish kids pushed on reading and writing and not Blacks?" We should address why second grade EOs aren't reading. But you can't help it. We're a predominantly Latino school and we have so far to go with the bilingual program. LEPs [ELLs] have to be given a fair shot and they don't have that yet. When I first came here they said lots of insulting things about bilingual education, about District Interns and about Hispanics in general. I used to hear "wetbacks" a lot.

Hearing such slurs were not the only instances of discrimination that people related to me. Many maintained that certain Black school community members had been plotting the "unfair" election of more Black people to positions of power. For example, at that time the reelection of the school's parent representative to the LEARN leadership council (a Black man, mentioned earlier) was vehemently opposed by some on the "Latino/bilingual" "side." They told me they opposed his reelection because he was "illegally elected" in the first place: the previous principal had held "a secret meeting," they told me, on a day when Andrea (the vice principal) was absent. "He only invited African Americans. That's how [the representative] got elected." So it was obvious, many contended, that "African American/EO" school community members had been systematically attempting to exclude those on the "Latino/bilingual" side from fair participation in decision-making processes. Other people cited the previous principal's perceived efforts to help only African American candidates for the vice principal position, which had opened up a few months before my research began. They said that the principal was a member of a professional organization for Black administrators that wrongly held "secret" study groups for African Americans who wanted to sit for the district's administrative exams (exams which had to be passed in order to qualify for open vice principal or principal positions). "It's always a racial thing," a few people argued. "To me," said one, "any group shouldn't preclude the success of other groups. Racism always comes from those who say they don't have it. It has really hurt the school community."

Explaining their opinion that "African American/EO" school community members were receiving unfair special treatment as of late, many on this "side" of the conflict accused the previous principal of having "favored the EOs." Shared one teacher, "We asked him for substitute release days so we could work on preparing for the Cinco de Mayo celebration and he said, 'No.' Then for celebration days important to EOs, like Career Day, they did get substitutes." Worse still, another commented, he

> tried to destroy bilingual education. He said we couldn't have a bilingual advisory council any more [a parent-administrator-teacher group to guide program decision making]. We did the best we could anyway, but he made it hard. And he said he was going to modify all the classes! That's taboo!

Modifying the bilingual classes would have involved reorganization of the entire school. As I described earlier, "modified bilingual" meant that a class had EO students and ELLs, and the teacher delivered the instruction mainly in English, with a bilingual TA to provide limited first language support to ELLs (like it had been prior to the Master Plan implementation in 1987). If the principal modified all the bilingual classes, it was also therefore possible that "Latino/bilingual" teachers' Spanish fluency would be less of a factor in determining who could teach which classes, thereby lessening their advantage in choice of grade and track assignments. Because of this principal, several people agreed, "The bilingual program began to fall apart. He just about ruined the school."

Additionally, many felt that "Latino/bilingual" school community members were underrepresented in school politics. One teacher pointed out that,

> I'd show up at meetings and I'd be the only Latino. African Americans had learned the game: If you want to change things, go to meetings. If I was the only Latino and there were six African Americans, concerns at the meeting were only about EOs. If African American kids are only ten percent [of the student body], how can they say EO kids are not represented, when the bilingual program isn't even fully implemented yet? I told the bilingual teachers, "You all have to start showing up!"

Finally, monetary and material concerns often arose: As discussed in the preceding chapter on the national media, the mid-1990s were a time of growing anti-bilingual education and anti-immigrant sentiments in the United States. When I asked one TA about any news she had heard recently that might affect the school, she replied, "Proposition 187. Governor Wilson doesn't want to give education to immigrants." She then looked at me nervously and exclaimed, "If 187 goes into effect where would our [bilingual program] jobs go?!" When teachers mentioned Proposition 187, corresponding concerns often arose about the potential loss of lucrative bilingual stipends (that would result from the drop in the need for bilingual teachers if "illegal immigrants" were banned from California schools). Linda told me, "I need that money! They're never going to get the teachers they need if they take away those stipends."

A perceived greed for money and political power on the part of "African American/EO" school community members was frequently mentioned, and cast in terms of a "turf war." Enrique's assessment was shared by several others I spoke with:

> Any time you have a Brown wave enter an African American area there's a turf war. Blacks in this country saw the beginning and the end of Affirmative Action in their own lifetimes. Here in South Central LA, Blacks still dominate politics and so they feel the threat of Latino business power. They're fighting to keep control. Latino gangs are also starting to control the drug trade in the illegal realm. In order for Latinos to move up, others have to move out, and so this thing is Black versus Brown.

This monetary and political greed surfaced, several people opined, when "African American/EO" staff members objected to certain things that "Latino/bilingual" school community members saw as fair and logical. A prime example noted was the objection to the bilingual teacher stipend. Another was the disapproval of the first pick that bilingual teachers were given over EO teachers when choosing their class (grade level and track) for the next year. The reason for bilingual teachers having these advantages, they reminded me, was because of the needs of the growing ELL population. "African American/EO" staff members were "just complaining," TAs and teachers would say. In the words of one: "They're not taking into account what's good for the *kids*. They're only worried about themselves. They just want the money and positions we can get because of our expertise."

I saw these sentiments reflecting concerns analogous to those on the "African American/EO" "side." Not only were unequal treatment and discrimination, unequal representation in decision making, and the equitable education of all children important issues. Economic opportunity was clearly at stake.

Articulating to National Media Discourses

In constructing their cases about the "war" at California Elementary, a few people explained it to me in terms common in national media discourses. Recalled a TA at lunch one day,

> When I came here [to the US] I was mystified about English. There was so much hostility towards Latinos! If you spoke Spanish people would say, "You're in America, speak English." But Americans speak English overseas so why can't people speak another language here?

Evoking pro-bilingual education discourses in the media about leveling the playing field and preparing students for a diverse world, Enrique added,

> My dad came here as part of the Bracero program, then we came when I was six. I was multiplying and dividing when I got here, but I was put in the back of the classroom to *draw* because they didn't have a bilingual program and didn't know what to do with me. So I lost my edge, I stopped learning in the subject areas. Because of this I'm not going to give up my quest for bilingual education here and now. Our kids need that edge in today's multicultural world.

And many people drew a picture of the conflict as caused by "African Americans'/EOs' " refusal to recognize that immigration and bilingualism were natural and productive elements of the American nation. For example, Crystal asserted,

> Today we live in a global village and our kids have to be ready for that. But *some people* want to pretend that we are still very tribal. There are a lot of immigrants coming, but America has always had immigrants and lots of

languages! They always say we Latinos are taking over their jobs, taking over the country. But they should realize that people from other races aren't willing to work the land in this country. We are. That's what makes the heart of the country.

Like their "African American/EO" counterparts, talk of the other "side's" culture also formed part of "Latino/bilingual" community members' discursive repertoire, as they attempted to describe "the war" to me in ways that gave advantage to their "side." Evocative of the culture of poverty theory, "African American/EO" students were repeatedly portrayed as growing up in dysfunctional homes and, as such, being themselves dysfunctional and resistant to the positive influence of education. African Americans were also constructed as rejecting vigorous participation in the national economy. And parallel to the stories earlier, now "Latino/bilingual" school community members were discursively aligned with an idealized American culture and its essential language practices. For example, when I asked people, "So what caused this conflict?" many responded in ways quite similar to this teacher:

> The demographics are changing. We need to understand migration issues. It is not because the kids are Black, it's because of the lives they lead and what they learn at home. They're malfunctional because of their families. Those African Americans who pulled their resources together moved out. So the ones who stayed in South Central LA are a low quality of folks, and so are their children. We do everything in our power to help them grow up and be open minded, but when they go home they fall back into square one. The Mexican immigrants who came here, they are the ones who can pull themselves together, which got them to the U.S. in the first place.

I interpret the characterizations in the previous two quotes, of Latino immigrants as valuable economic producers for the nation and as prototypical Americans (immigrant, linguistically diverse) to be boldly strategic performative utterances: They attempt to align with certain assumptions and discourses about America that, while historically powerful, were themselves under attack in the mid-1990s. As I showed in the preceding media chapter, the dominant anti-immigrant media constructions of America at the time portrayed immigrants negatively across the board, and Mexican and Spanish speaking immigrants in especially disparaging terms. Regardless of the fact that, geographically, much of America used to be Mexico, that immigrants have been coming to what is now the United States for centuries, and regardless of the historically popular image of America as an "immigrant nation," *these* immigrants were constructed in mainstream media and politics as "alien," "un-American" "invaders." This bred an atmosphere that was quite hostile to communities seen as linguistically, culturally, and racially different from the White, monolingual middle-class. The ideal "America," according to campaigns to limit immigration, to implement Proposition 187, and to enact English Only laws, continued to be a monolingual melting pot where all newcomers were expected to drop their native languages (at least in public and in school) and assimilate. Hence, in aligning themselves with an image of America as the multilingual land of immigrants, these school community members seemed to strategically bypass the fact that this image itself was at the time hotly contested.

As we see, I found that school community members' use of culture of poverty discourses on *both* "sides" of this "war," while different in the details, were constructed in similar terms and brought to bear on school community dynamics in comparable ways. I believe this suggests that these "opposing sides" had more in common than was generally discussed: After such scholars as Piatt (1997), Attinasi (1997), Darder (1997) and Smitherman (1992), I posit that in certain ways important for language, race, and education politics, actors on both "sides" inhabited somewhat analogous positionalities vis-à-vis hegemonic constructions of the ideal American nation, language, and culture, and within the national racial-economic hierarchy. In drawing on these hegemonic discourses, then, school community members could be seen (at least in one sense) to be supporting these constructions and upholding this hierarchy.

Where Should We Go From Here? "Latino/bilingual" Policy Agendas

Given the state of affairs as they were described to me, almost all "Latino/bilingual" school community members I talked with staked out a fractured agenda. They argued that the bilingual program needed to be improved and expanded. However, their vision was one of providing better bilingual instruction *only* for the school's Latino ELLs. Most expressed it like this teacher:

America is changing, and a bilingual program will adapt them for changes we're moving into. Many of our kids are coming from behind, with no English, but bilingualism is the economic passport to future success in the U.S. We prepare them for college, for professions.

But when I mentioned the other "side's" desire for a dual language program, he responded, "Bilingual ed for Black students, too? No, Latino students need that special extra edge. There's already enough out there for English speakers."

I found a delicately balanced double focus in this position. On the one hand, in keeping with national media representations of bilingual education debates, bilingual instruction was rationalized as a way to bring Latino ELLs up to a level (English-speaking) playing field. It was seen as a way to help them master the dominant code they lacked, to enable them to enter the "mainstream." This lent consistency to constructions of America as a monolingual English speaking nation, which made bilingual instruction unnecessary for African Americans who already possessed the valued competency of English. On the other hand, this position challenged hegemonic anti-bilingual education rhetoric by positing biliteracy as a potent advantage in the prestigious public spheres of higher education and the professional job market. This called on constructions of America as part of a global, multilingual community.

I understood this second focus as targeting a strategic, compensatory advantage: While bilingual people would have advantages over monolingual people in these prestigious public spheres, these advantages were not seen as unfair. The argument was that they would create for Latinos a secure niche in the emerging international economy. This niche would coexist along with what were seen as the already (overly) numerous spaces of opportunity for monolingual English speaking people. It seemed, therefore, not at all contradictory or unfair to champion the value of bilingual education and then struggle to limit access to it (see G. Valdés, 1997 for an elaboration of this argument).

Another teacher took a more culturally-based position that a few others on campus also expressed to me. He argued that bilingual education for Latinos was appropriate because Spanish was naturally *theirs* (and, by extension, it was not naturally African Americans'):

> I don't care who you are, if you have no roots, anything can knock you over. So this program teaches kids about their culture, about themselves, through language. I wouldn't worry so much about transitioning [to English]. They'll get there. We need to give the kids the cultural tools first, then worry about transitioning. English is a nice language but give me what's mine. Then I'll succeed.

This agenda for bilingual education as cultural consciousness-building for (only) Latino students led to a very clear description of the knowledge appropriate for educators—and hence to very clear parameters for who should qualify to work at the school.

Whose Knowledge is of Most Worth?

Most "Latino/bilingual" school community members I talked to asserted like this teacher, that first, "We need educators who are native speakers or really strong in the language and the culture." Second, educators needed "the latest training" in the philosophical and pedagogical foundations of bilingual instruction—the kind of training, some pointed out, provided by the LAUSD's District Intern teacher credentialing program. This training, along with the oft-mentioned "energy and dedication of new teachers" (and the new teachers at California Elementary were nowadays mostly District Interns), was contrasted by many with the supposedly pedagogically out-of-date "old guard from the seventies." This "old guard" was described to me as the "older Black teachers," the majority of whom were trained in traditional university education programs. And deeper than particular training programs, some staff members put it like this TA who said, simply:

> If they just knew two languages they'd agree with us. When one EO teacher said she could teach a bilingual class I said, "No you can't. You don't speak Spanish." She said, "With a few years of teaching in a bilingual class we can pick up Spanish. You only need to know a few phrases." A few phrases! With little kids! Is she serious? [groan]

Like those on the "African American/EO" "side" who felt that, "if they just considered professionalism over language ability" we could get along, those on the "Latino/bilingual" "side" tended to feel that, "If they just knew two languages we could get along."

These opposing understandings of the "war," opposing agendas regarding "where to go from here," and conflicting constructions of appropriate knowledge for educators, were presented to me by most school community members as simple and neatly oppositional. But the more I pondered these aspects of the "Black-Brown war" at California Elementary, the more I considered Rosaldo's (1994) reminder that to understand struggles for inclusion, empowerment, and voice—for cultural citizenship—we must be very aware of *whose perspectives* we seek out in our examination of the issues. A quote by author and social critic Toni Morrison came to mind: "Certain absences are so stressed, so ornate ... [that] ... they call attention to themselves" (cited in Pinar, 1993, p. 67).

There were White school community members at California Elementary—I had been one from 1992 through 1994, and there were 17 in 1996. So, just where were they (we)?

WHERE DO WHITE PEOPLE FIT INTO THIS "WAR?"

From the inception of my project I had planned to investigate this question. After all, I am White, and I had been pushed into anthropology by my own drive to better understand where I fit into the politics surrounding the bilingual program in which I taught. Having also heard about the "blackface incident" (perpetrated by a White teacher) before beginning the summer's research, I began my ethnographic inquiry sure that I would hear talk about White/ness. I could not have been more wrong. White people would enter into stories, but their statements and actions were explained as things the "Latino/bilingual" "side" did, or things the "African American-EO" "side" said, depending upon which instructional program they taught in. White people were both very present and very absent.

For example, as mentioned, Scott said at a meeting about the school's discipline problems, "I don't have any behavior problems in my class because my kids are all Hispanic." This infuriated "African American/EO" school community members, while most "Latino/bilingual" staff members chalked the remark up to his harmless "naiveté" about race relations. People on both "sides" characterized comments like Scott's as examples of how this "race thing" had "bilinguals and EOs at each others' throats!" And in the "blackface incident," in addition to the fact that the teacher who painted the students' faces was White (Scott), the teacher who ushered the students on stage (the last gatekeeper of propriety for the performance) was White. Yet, when people summarized the event they called it, "a perfect example of this Black-Brown conflict."

When I asked Latino and African American school community members, "Where do White people fit in this conflict?" some replied like Michael:

> It's an African American/Latino thing. There's natural groups. The older black teachers in a clique, the Latino teachers, the white teachers—no, not the white teachers. They don't really have a clique. Hmmm, no I guess not the white teachers.

In other words, White teachers are simply outside the conflict. When one African American TA described to me where White people fit into all the arguing, she laughed, "White people? Oh, they run for cover!" In other words, White people put themselves outside the conflict. And some replied like this Latina TA: "White people? They can kind of go between the sides, see both sides, try to help everybody." In other words, White people are above the conflict.

Such characterizations could be seen to endorse, to co-construct White school community members' claims to remove. They absolved White people of responsibility and excused them from any complicity in the destructive dynamics that engulfed the community. Extrapolating this to a national context, this could be seen to reflect and even to bolster hegemonic constructions of race relations in the United States that posit White people as naturally outside "race politics," and as innocent of the maintenance of racialized systems of privilege and oppression.

So, just where did White people think they fit into "Black vs. Brown" at California Elementary?

"These People Have a Hard Time Getting Along!": White Constructions of School Community Dynamics

The following quotes exemplify how many White school community members responded when I asked, "What changes have you seen at California Elementary recently?" One EO teacher said,

> OK, there's this debate now between the LEP [ELL] and the EO. Well the thing is, I even have Janice, who is Afro-American, who knows that I'm the only one in the school who's taught both bilingual and EO. I hear both groups and I've tried to push us towards reconciliation. We are both trying to do the same thing, and that is teach the children to be successful. And I've also seen that another thing that prevents that is the overload of crap. If you do everything they say in bilingual and multicultural studies literature you will end up with overexposed, illiterate children, which only allows me in the fifth grade to receive students who may know who George Washington Carver is, but they don't know who George Washington is. They may know who Father Castillo is but they still don't know who Thomas Jefferson is. Now I have a copy of a letter from somebody in my family who fought in the Revolutionary War, and his description of it is very close to what the older books that I studied said. And so, this is a first person account, [and] people in this day and age want to go back and say, "Oh no, what they really were doing was X," and they don't have any business doing that.

The bilingual teacher who had been the stage manager during the "blackface incident" provided these reflections on events:

> Recently, a bilingual teacher, during, what *was* it—the Black American, African, Afro-American History Month program, he had his kids paint their

faces black. And I'm at the door letting people on stage and I see this. And *I* wasn't going to be the one to say, "You guys can not go on now." They were already late as it was. So I said, "OK you wanna do that, let's go, let 'em go!" I mean, I've been dragged into this. Someone said if a person says they don't see color they're lying. Well I felt bad because I don't! But I'm naive. It's hard for me because my Latino kids think they're White! But I don't want to say, "You're not white, you're not like me," because that would just put them down. If they think they're white and all that connotates [*sic*] for them, fine. I don't feel like I fit in, because I'm not for EO because I'm not Black and I'm not for bilingual because I don't speak Spanish. I just found out last year that there is racial strife on the staff! Then I realized, these people have a hard time getting along. It [the "blackface incident"] may have nothing to do with bilingual education but it comes up. I think it's their self-confidence getting in the way there. Every time bilingual education is mentioned this will pop up and it gets exacerbated. But I'm limited to my classroom, so I stay out of other people's crap.

Here we see White school community members employing discursive tropes found to be common in the literature on White/ness: White people are constructed as mediators above the "crap" of racial conflict and multicultural agendas; they are the keepers of the flame of "true" American history, a position legitimized through idealized bloodlines; they are the rational, innocent time keepers during the "blackface incident"; they are blind to and naive of race. They portray perceptions of racism as manifestations of individual, psychological problems ("self-confidence" issues). These discourses can be seen to have the effect of avoiding talk of racism or of complicity in racial oppression through the use of the discourse of color blindness (Frankenberg, 1993; Peller, 1995). The "color blind" perspective assumes that to even notice color is therefore to be racist (Almaguer, 1994; Frankenberg, 1993). One must therefore deny the existence or import of racial difference and hierarchy—even though these teachers quite clearly see color and assign it differential value (one claims her Latino students "aren't White like me," but she cannot tell them because that would "just put them down").

And like their African American and Latino counterparts, these White school community members mixed ideas of language, nation, culture, and race in performative utterances that forwarded a particular version of the issues. Though it was implicit, in the first excerpt this person posited learning about African American and Latino historical figures as multicultural "crap." Yet he himself espoused a deeply cultural-political agenda for learning about history based on *his* ancestry going back to the formative period of the nation state. And, these White people claimed they did not "fit into" either the "African American/EO" or the "Latino/bilingual" "side" because they did not "fit" in either tightly-woven nexus of race/language. Somehow they could not *be* on either "side" as Latinos and African Americans *were* on their "sides." Lending consistency to popular media typifications of how racial issues operate, then, they portrayed this "war" as only involving the school community members who were African American and Latino.

I myself was another example. Some of the issues of cultural citizenship that were hotly contested by 1996 were already beginning to surface in my early years as a teacher at the school. In the following excerpt from my field notes, I reflect on my early days at California Elementary in 1992, in light of what I was learning through research in 1996:

> I remember attending my first faculty meeting. We had to establish our after-school tutoring schedule for the year. A few teachers, I remember some of them being African American, announced their desire to tutor on Tuesdays and Thursdays. I became concerned. If we tutored on Tuesdays and Thursdays, we District Interns might not be able to get to our required Thursday afternoon DI classes on time. I raised my hand and explained this. One African American teacher stood up and objected to tailoring the tutoring schedule just to fit the DIs' schedule. The principal responded, "Well, when I hired these Interns I made a commitment to them so I can't require that they do something that conflicts with their classes." And with that the discussion was closed. What sticks with me about this moment is the frustration I sensed afterwards from many teachers, and how closed my perspective was about what had just gone on. I did not recognize that this decision became, for many, another in an accumulating list of unfair special treatment for "bilingual people." In fact, I didn't even bother to wonder. It was like I kept my eyes closed to the political implications of my actions. I most definitely needed to engage in more critical thought and dialogue about my positionality in the "hot issues." If I had done this, I would have seen why what I said might invite resentment. I would have approached the issue differently. Is my perspective still oblivious to the dynamics I am part of? Probably ... but as much as it was back then? I am working on it, I hope not.

I knew at the outset of my research that I would be confronted with things about myself in relation to this "war" at California Elementary. This did not make them any easier to face, though. As an anthropologist, I hoped that by examining my positionality I could become more critically aware of and proactive in the complex dynamics of race, language, policy, and cultural citizenship that I studied. As a writer, I also hope that by exposing myself, I tip my readers off to the limitations and biases of my analysis. When listening to other White people position themselves through discourses of naiveté about race politics, I had always assumed that those discourses were to some extent cover-ups for biased assumptions that they "*must* have recognized" they harbored. But here I am reflecting back on my own actions and constructions of myself, sounding like other White folks I was critiquing.

Naiveté, color blindness, disengagement, disconnection, being above it, being a mediator, holding a truer key to the "American" past—none of it holds water when we think about our real participation in the everyday life of our communities. I show myself here to have been a contributor to the early tensions that eventually exploded in 1996. White people, and the dynamics of privilege/disenfranchisement woven into the racial hierarchy in this country, are not separate from but part of conflicts over cultural citizenship for all of us, people of all backgrounds. Perceptions of and struggles over equity, voice, belonging, value, and access are experienced and constructed in, through, and between all racial (and linguistic and national and class, etc.) identity and political categories.

Latinos and African Americans Strategically Deploy Whiteness

I and other White people were not the only ones at California Elementary to express the kinds of discourses typically attributed to White people in the scholarly literature on Whiteness. On several occasions during my research, African American and Latino school community members expressed attitudes and employed discourses that have generally been considered in the literature to be "White." I believe that this speaks to intersecting structures of access, agency, and marginalization that we all negotiate. I think it speaks to how aspects of African American, White, Latino, monolingual, and bilingual positionalities in the local and national arenas are "constantly crossed and recrossed" (Hall, 1996, p. 444)—with implications for all of us.

Recent ethnographies of race and education have examined the phenomenon of individuals of color "acting White" in order to draw on specific systems of access, cultural capital, legitimacy, and privilege in the "mainstream" public sphere (e.g., Foley, 1990; Fordham, 1996; Urciuoli, 1996). In these ethnographies, "Whiteness" becomes a metacommunicative symbol, a strategic trope used to create a particular construction of events and power relations. In response to my question about California Elementary, "How would you characterize the conflict?" one Latina TA talked about the TA staff meetings this way:

> If you walk into meetings you see Black and White divided. But I get along with everybody. I interact with all of them. I tend to lean more to their side ["African American/EO"] so they don't think I'm over there [with the "White"]. There is division ever since I've been here. Some African

Americans are "instigators." I think they feel like that because they see me and other TAs stay later working on things, like festivals. I don't know why they don't stay or do. I think that's what it is. But I'm divided in both camps. But I feel some of these issues need to be put behind us.

The first thing that struck me about this was the fact that she characterized the division as "Black and White." She then constructed herself as on the White side, and as the neutral intermediary amidst the turmoil. She seemed to claim a space of remove, able to pass "ideal objective judgment" (MacCannell, 1992, p. 130) on the situation, championing an up-by-your-bootstraps rationale for how "African American/EO" "instigators" could resolve their individual complaints: by working hard like she does.

In a twist on the above claim to White/ness, one African American parent assigned her new Latino neighbors to the category based on their behavior. She explained to me that she was so frustrated with this school and this neighborhood that she wanted to move: "They run around, all those kids, and I can't talk to 'em. They're loud and they knock over my stuff and use my barbecue. They think they're white!" This contradicts the simple "Black-Brown" representations of school community dynamics that most people offered me, indicating a multifaceted system of privilege, symbolized by White versus Black but acted out by Brown versus Black.

In a particularly emotional interview, Janice told me, "We have a race problem here, it's like a hate." Then she added, "But you do have a lot of wonderful Latino people here. I don't look at color. I have a lot of white friends, and Mexican friends. This isn't about color. It's about bilingual versus EO." Similar to accounts of White people employing a discourse of color blindness, I interpreted this as a move to preempt an accusation of a racial bias on her part, given that at many other moments during our conversations Janice had explicitly assigned the culpability for the conflict to Latinos.

Another example of deployments of stereotypically "white" attitudes and discourses was the application of culture of poverty discourses, as discussed earlier. All of the opinions about culture shared earlier in this chapter were quotes from school community members who were African American or Latino. Historically, culture of poverty discourses have been wielded by White scholars, politicians, social critics, and average citizens alike, to naturalize and rationalize the oppression of peoples of color. Peoples of color have been portrayed as culturally inferior to "mainstream Americans" (as gloss for White middle class), and therefore, as "causing their own problems." Here, though, the "discursively white" culture of poverty theory was strategically deployed by Latinos and African Americans to construct each other as superior/inferior to each other.

While I saw these moves as attempts to garner legitimacy and advantage for one or the other "side's" position in the current-day local conflict, they could also be seen to lend consistency to the larger, institutional systems of racial-class inequities that people were trying to challenge through their educational agendas for the future. These moves to strategically deploy typically "White" discourses call attention to the interconnectedness of racial identities and to the complexity of race and language politics. And as we will see across findings from both phases of research at California Elementary (those from the mid-1990s in this chapter, and those from the late 1990s in chapter 5), they were just one way in which dynamics at the school were both very "simply" dichotomous and much more complex than a dichotomy. Pursuing this paradox (Pollock, 2004) and its implications for the politics of language education policy continued to drive my journey towards the next phase of research at California Elementary, which began in 1998.

TOWARDS 1998

I left Los Angeles again in the fall of 1996. By the time I came back in 1998, California was leading the reinvigorated national English Only movement in its passing of the "English for the Children" Proposition 227 statewide ballot initiative. In 1998, I had the opportunity to experience California Elementary's journey through the implementation of this controversial language education policy. This also gave me the chance to trace the politics of cultural citizenship from 1996 to a moment when the supposed main issue in dispute in 1996 (the bilingual program) was (at least ostensibly) removed. What would happen to this "war" that was described as "African American/EO" versus "Latino/bilingual" when the most contested descriptor—bilingual—was effectively outlawed? What would this illuminate about how people understand and construct the parameters of cultural citizenship? How might this further our understandings of language education policy processes more generally?

NOTES

1. This school, like most in the LAUSD, was a year-round, multitrack school. Certain tracks had school year/vacation calendars considered more desirable than others. So, when at the end of each year teachers chose the grade level and track that they would teach the next year it was always desirable to get first pick.

2.   For example, Weinstein (1983), Solá and Bennett (1991), Smitherman and Van Djik (1988), Los Angeles Unified School District (1996b), Labov (1972), Gilmore (1991), Fordham (1996), Baugh (1984), Attinasi (1997).

3.   Levinson and Holland (1996) talk about "cultural production" as "a continual process of creating meaning in social and material contexts" (p. 13). Schools cannot be looked at as sites of seamless cultural transmission, such as in much social reproduction and cultural transmission theory (p. 5; for example see Bourdieu & Passeron, 1977; Bowles & Gintis, 1976; Henry, 1963; Spindler, 1982; Wilcox, 1982). And yet neither are schools arenas of unimpinged agency and creation of social relations. As public institutions, schools are squarely situated between the local and the national (Levinson & Holland, 1996, p. 1), and school community members function within "the interplay of agency and structure" (p. 3). They negotiate differential resources for, and constraints upon, social interaction (p. 3, and see Foley, 1990, 1995; Willis, 1977; MacLeod, 1987; Fordham, 1996; Luykx, 1999; Oakes, 1985; Spindler, 1982). Exploration of the conflict at California Elementary makes this quite clear.

CHAPTER 4

IMMIGRATION, LANGUAGE, RACE, AND EDUCATION POLICY IN THE NATIONAL MEDIA, 1998–2000

Debates Continue

The questions and controversies of the mid-1990s gained intensity in the later years of the decade in the national media. More and more reporters, politicians, and pundits asked, Who are "we" as a nation? and, What will America look like and be like in the twenty-first century (McDonnell, 1996)? It was reported that the coming millennium would bring a "new face" to America (Morganthau, 1997)—by the year 2025, Whites would no longer be the demographic majority. Most notably, by then the Latino population was expected to top 25% (p. 59). And the non-English speaking population was burgeoning. Census Bureau data indicated that between 1993 and 2000, non-English speaking students in public schools increased by 105% (National Education Association, 2003, p. 15). Headlines such as, "Welcome to Amexica: The Border is Vanishing Before Our Eyes, Creating a New World for all of us" (*Time* magazine cover page in

War or Common Cause? A Critical Ethnography of
Language Education Policy, Race, and Cultural Citizenship , pp. 63–80
Copyright © 2008 by Information Age Publishing
All rights of reproduction in any form reserved.

June, 2001) were common. Article after article debated the implications of this coming transformation of America into a "cafe au lait" society.

California was cited as the place where these changes continued to occur first and most dramatically. The state received a full one fourth of the nation's immigrants and was estimated to be the destination of over 40% of all illegal immigrants. Its population was predicted to be at least half Latino by as early as 2040 (Lesher, 1999), and Latinos were expected to make up 25% of the state's legislators even sooner (Balotta, 2000). Statements such as, "Shift in the Mix Alters the Face of California" (Purdum, 2000) screamed from headlines. California, it was said, would be "by far the largest proving ground for what it may eventually be like to live in a United States in which no one racial or ethnic group predominates" (p. A12).

Los Angeles was further singled out as a place where tomorrow's population changes could be seen today (Pape, 1999). Latinos were already close to 50% of the Los Angeles County population (Sterngold, 2000). Between 1980 and 1990, the total population of Los Angeles County had grown by 1.38 million residents, of which 1.24 million, or 90%, were Latinos (and many of whom were immigrants) (Rocco, 1997, p. 103). It is notable that in the same time, the African American population of Los Angeles only increased by 20,000 (p. 103). In this way, Los Angeles and California more generally continued to be the spark for competing imaginations of the evolving "America."

PRO-IMMIGRATION ARGUMENTS

Many saw the transformations at this time as beneficial to local communities and to the country. They told stories about how, for example, immigrant janitors and hotel workers energized the union movement and created a "new language of American labor" (Verhovek, 1999). They reported that Latino immigrants "changed the face" of religion, invigorating shrinking Catholic parishes nationwide (Niebuhr, 1999). They told about recent graduates from a Los Angeles high school who were creating "Journeys Into the New Los Angeles" (Lopez & Connell, 2000).

By 1999 it was an acknowledged fact across political sectors that immigration, both legal and illegal, was fueling the nation's economic boom. Immigrants filled jobs in such physically demanding and geographically widespread industries as agriculture and meat processing. The payroll and sales taxes they paid provided valuable monies for state and federal coffers. The presence of large numbers of immigrants alone was reported to be enlivening withering populations and industries in small towns across the heartland (Regalia, 1999). Latino immigrants in particular were being hailed as "the new American Dream Makers" (Hayes-Bautista, 2000).

Citing this, many powerful governmental and nongovernmental institutions that were traditionally opposed to open immigration began to adopt pro-immigration stances, and even pro-illegal immigration tolerances (G. Rodriguez, 1998, p. 30). For example, Alan Greenspan, head of the Federal Reserve, officially lobbied for the further opening of national borders to immigration. The AFL-CIO reversed its long-time anti-immigration stance in order to support better treatment of immigrant workers, legal and illegal (Medina, 2000). Even federal immigration authorities, while publicly championing fortifications to the US-Mexico border, were often accused of turning a blind eye to businesses that employed illegal immigrants (Uchitelle, 2000).

Politicians took note of the increasingly numerous and powerful Latino/immigrant population: There was a surprising new alliance between Democrats, Republicans, and religious communities that urged the easing of immigration laws (Greenhouse, 2000). In 2000, Senators Reid of Nevada and Kennedy of Massachusetts pushed for federal legislation to allow undocumented immigrants an easier path to citizenship (Reid, 2000). Both Republican and Democratic 2000 presidential candidates took pro-immigration positions, and made more efforts than ever before to woo Latino voters (Linares, 2000). State and county governments, particularly in the Midwest, launched media campaigns and municipal programs to attract immigrant laborers and families (La Opinión News Services, 2000a, 2000b; Regalia, 1999).

The media discourses of these immigration supporters stressed the fact that people came to America in search of what all Americans sought: to earn a good living, to give their children a good education, and eventually to settle into the American Dream in big cities and small towns (Maharidge, 1999). They brought to readers' attention that the desires of immigrants to become full participating citizens actually far outweighed many communities' capacities to accommodate them in pursuing the kind of activities that would help them to realize the American Dream—for example, communities had difficulty providing enough citizenship classes and ESL courses (Leovy, 1999). Indeed, in the late 1990s it could be said that pro-immigration forces were strong.

ANTI-IMMIGRATION ARGUMENTS

However, the strength of pro-immigration forces should not be overstated. The immigration boom was not without its energetic detractors. By the spring of 1999, California's Governor Gray Davis inherited a sticky situation: The judicial ruling on the unconstitutionality of most aspects of the state's 1994 anti-immigration Proposition 187 had been appealed by former Governor Pete Wilson. With Davis now in office, formerly disheartened 187 proponents pressured him to continue on with Wilson's appeal to federal courts. After much debate (see for example Skelton, 1999), Davis took Proposition 187 to mediation, and through that process the measure that became the defining issue of California politics in the mid-1990s—and the spark that woke up the "giant of Latino power" ([my translation] Marrero, 1999, p. 3A.)—went to its legislative death. At the same time, competing imaginations of the nation still swirled around in the media in the form of anti-immigration discourses. By late 1999, a growing push by anti-immigrant groups for a new and even more stringent Proposition 187 began to gain attention (de la Torre-Jimenez & Botello, 1999).

Anti-immigration discourses at this time were strikingly reminiscent of those leading up to and in the mid-1990s that I discussed in chapter 2. A supporter of this agenda was quoted in the *Los Angeles Times* in 1999 as saying that, "People know that illegal immigration is more out of control than ever and that illegal aliens continue to receive taxpayer-funded benefits.... Support for Prop 187 is just as strong as it was in 1994. Illegal immigration [is] a crime" and an even more extreme version of Proposition 187 "is a certainty" (Keeler, 1999, p. B8). "The cactus wall has fallen," said another activist (R. Rodriguez, 2000, p. M1), and America must "cut immigration now" (Collard, 1999).

Immigration foes accused immigrants of all manner of transgressions. For example, they charged that immigrants were "identity thieves," not only figuratively robbing America of its traditional racial and linguistic identity, but also literally stealing law-abiding citizens' social security numbers and lives (Kirby, 2000). They further warned that immigrants brought "rampant" disease such as tuberculosis to the United States (Sachs, 2000), and that they caused smog, over-crowding, and the loss of valuable wilderness (Grober, 2000). Immigrants' presence engendered increased social conflict (Silverstein, 2000) and an ever-threatening intranational "balkanization" (Clough, 1997). And as immigrants infiltrated schools, towns, and workers' unions nationwide, it was argued, they and their Spanish language "conquered" other treasured "American" (read: English language) cultural institutions, such as radio stations (Tobar, 2000).

Akin to Balibar's (1991) explanation of the "immigration complex," Urciuoli (1997) calls such concern with linguistic and cultural "invasion" the "flip side" of U.S. involvement in globalization (p. 1). Immigrants, morphed in popular discourses into an undifferentiated mass of "Latinos," were characterized as "an illicit-nation-within-the-legitimate-nation"

(p. 3), to be fended off by "true Americans" with the proposed "uniting device" of English (p. 5).

More and more municipalities and states began to push for legislation to forbid languages other than English for official business—where simultaneously they were begging immigrants to move to their shrinking towns and to fill their empty factories (Iowa, for example) (Niebuhr, 1999). Some businesses even forbade workers who were hired for their bilingual skills from speaking Spanish during personal break times (Girion, 2000). People also cited incidents of harsh treatment of immigrants accused of being illegal; these victims of INS "inhumanity" often turned out to be falsely-accused American citizens by birth, caught and harassed for "being Brown near the border" (A. Lewis, 1999). By 1999 it was even suggested by broad, vocal political coalitions that incidents of "hunting" illegal border crossers be investigated by the United Nations (Amador, 2000).

During the 2000 presidential campaign the nativist, English Only bent of Pat Buchanan's Reform Party candidacy attracted much attention with its controversial TV ads that featured a White man sitting at his table eating spaghetti. He begins to choke on a meatball when he hears on his television that, "Today English lost its place as the official language of the United States of America." When he picks up the phone and dials 911 he has to listen to a long recording requesting, "Choose your language— Spanish, press one, Korean, press two" In many ways language could be seen as conflated with race and articulated to nation, English standing in for Whiteness and Americanness and goodness, Spanish or other languages standing in for Brownness and Other and danger. This, even as many acknowledged that to take advantage of the growing global economy, businesses everywhere needed employees who could serve increasingly multilingual and multicultural markets (La Opinión News Services, 2000a; Silverstein, 1999).

THE IN-BETWEEN SPACES

It was within these intensifying demographic changes and competing cultural and economic forces that many people were caught in the "*in-between* spaces" through which the meanings of cultural and political identity are negotiated (Bhabha, 1994, p. 4): Take for example states launching public relations campaigns to draw immigrants to populate their shrinking towns while enacting legislation to make English the official language of the state. People found themselves ambivalent about their answers to the question, What can we do now to create the kind of town or state or nation we want tomorrow? People seemed to be searching for the boundaries and contents of the community—for the parameters of cultural citizenship—only to find them slippery and elusive and even internally contradictory. The nation was indeed being (and is, always) actively (re)imagined, constantly "in narration" (Bhabha, 1994, p. 4).

One way to answer the question of how to create a particular kind of "America," Bianco (2003) points out, is to highlight again the dynamic duo of language and education: to make the language/s of instruction "much more strongly than other parts of school curricula, and much more strongly than in the past, [the] subject of discrete policy treatment" (p. 13). In California this manifested in the campaign for the pro-English immersion, anti-bilingual education "English for the Children" Proposition 227 ballot measure.

THE LARGER CONTEXT FOR 227: POLITICS OF RACE

Around the time of Proposition 227, the topic of race also drew much media attention. From one perspective portrayed in headlines, trends in race and equity politics could be seen taking a progressive, inclusive turn. We read about how the world was increasingly multiracial and multicultural. Hence, the old Black/White model of U.S. race relations was no longer relevant. Multiethnic and multiracial coalition building was now "the surest path to political power for a generation to come" (Pape, 1999, p. 26). Diversity and coalition building had become the keys to productivity.

More and more communities were like Walnut, California, it was reported: "Learning to look past race," the community reveled in its diversity and in creating vibrant schools, businesses, and intergroup relations (O'Connor, 1999, p. A1). More and more cities were like Houston where coalition building between Black, Latino, and Anglo construction businesses was necessary to address stiff contract competition (Navarro, 2000). And more elections were like those in Los Angeles, where sets of overlapping community agendas made the dichotomous Black/White paradigm "played out" (Fears & Olivo, 1999, p. A31). In fact, one editorial in the *Los Angeles Times* said, "Everything important in Los Angeles is perceived increasingly through the prism of race.... A real multiracial, multicultural and multilingual leadership [is necessary] to act as role models to inspire kids" (Hayden, 1999, p. B9).

A competing set of discourses that received much media attention at the time portrayed race relations and equity politics in a negative light. From this perspective, the tide could be seen shifting towards trouble and strife: There was increasing racial conflict in prisons (for example neo-Nazi groups were on the rise) (Golab, 1999) and in communities nationwide (for example South Carolinians battled over the future of the Confederate banner on the state's flag). The practice of police racial profiling came under scrutiny (Berke, 2000). A backlash against affirmative action was changing the framework within which industries and institutions did business, according to which school districts implemented busing and attendance policies, and according to which larger and larger segments of society shaped their visions of equality. It was reported that, "Nearly a half-century after *Brown vs. Board of Education* ... [affirmative action] is becoming a pressing issue, as the desegregation orders imposed by the courts decades ago are lifted in more and more areas" (Lewin, 1998, p. A1). In the 1996 *Hopwood vs. Texas* case, the Fifth United States Circuit Court of Appeals determined that race could not be taken into account in any higher education admissions program. And in 1996, California again made national headlines by passing the voter initiative Proposition 209, which outlawed affirmative action in business practices as well as in education.

To some, the U.S.'s increasing diversity equated to decreasing status: A *Los Angeles Times* editorial in 1999 stated that as Latinos came to comprise almost 70% of the population of Los Angeles, the Los Angeles Unified School District (LAUSD) had become "a poor Third World district in the richest of First World cities. The 'developing country,' in this case, is a new United States that will be multicultural" (Hayden, 1999, p. B9).

One journalist, discussing the "simmering racial tensions" in the city (Helfand & Sahagun, 1999, p. A1) reported that:

> Public schools have become the focal point of tensions and conflicts that exist in Los Angeles, particularly the diverse composition racially and ethnically of the city. This has been made evident by the many secondary schools in the city that have exploded with ethnic conflicts during the last five years. Even primary schools ... have had their quota of tension and strife.

In one highly-publicized incident (interesting in the context of this research for its confluence of race and language politics), an LAUSD elementary school principal was beaten unconscious, a newspaper article reported, "by two men who told him they didn't want him on campus because he is White." The attack, it was reported, "may have been related to growing discontent by [the school's majority] Latino parents" over what they perceived as the principal's "efforts to scale back bilingual education" (Blankstein & Luo, 1999, pp. B1, B8).

CONTINUED TYPIFICATION OF BLACK/LATINO/WHITE RELATIONS

As discussed in chapter 2, Shah and Thornton (1991) charge that the "typification" of African American/Latino relations in the media has been "extreme" (p. 133). African American/Latino relations have been presented in an "ahistorical manner" ignorant of group experiences (p. 133). This has had the effect of naturalizing the characterization of Latinos and African Americans as opposing camps, as communities battling each other for resources and jobs. In a popular book titled, *Black and Brown in America* (1997), Bill Piatt also criticizes such typifications, stating that the mainstream media seem to only portray Black-Latino relations as simplified cases of "in-fighting over crumbs" (p. 89). Little attention is paid, he argues, to the issues that Blacks and Latinos have in common in both local and national politics, and little concern is shown for "presenting stories of successful peacemakers" (p. 10).

When I analyzed my hundreds of media clippings with an eye for how African American/Latino/White relations were presented in this time period, I found two distinct sets of discourses. First were a set of discourses like those described by Piatt (1997), characterizing Black-Latino relations as contentious and opposing (e.g., Sahagun, 1999b). In addition to struggles over meager economic and political opportunity, education was presented as a key issue. Said one education columnist, "Black education in LAUSD is in trouble" because "reform must proceed within the Latino-ization of LAUSD" (Aubrey, 2000). This competition for policy, fiscal, and moral "turf" even spread to the pulpit. One church's struggle with demographic change and cultural clash between Black and Latino parishioners, "reflect[ed] those emerging across Southern California" (M. Ramirez, 1999, p. A1): Black parishioners were resentful of Latinos "invading" and "laying claim" to their church.

Second were a set of discourses that tied African Americans and Latinos together around certain issues: African American and Latino students were reported to be increasingly isolated *together* in failing schools, and denied access to good teachers and advanced curricula (Staples, 1999). In this way, the two groups were constructed as one entity struggling against the White power structure and oppression. After the passage of Proposition 209 in California, the number of Latino and African American students in the state's University system plummeted. Full-page ads in the *New York Times* declared that poorly-prepared teachers, overcrowding, segregation, underfunding, and tracking prepared students of color for failure on high school exit exams: "This racially-biased outcome is already evident in Texas. Mexican American and African American students make up 40% of all Texas seniors, but they represent 85% of the students who fail the final administration of the Texas high school exit exam each year" (Applied Research Center, 1999). And achievement test scores for Black and Latino students in California were lagging behind those of White students. Housing discrimination was also reported as an issue that persisted for both groups (García-Irigoyen, 1999).

Throughout these sets of discourses White people tended to be considered as an altogether separate entity from African Americans and Latinos (indeed as a separate entity from all groups that did not seem to fit the stereotype of the "typical American"—White, middle-class). White people as a group tended to be constructed as unconnected to the issues and struggles that African Americans and Latinos negotiated (with the exception of the one strand of discourses I described above that highlighted a "progressive and inclusive" turn in race relations). This left precious little room to build racially, linguistically, and socially diverse understandings of the issues, or to build diverse coalitions around common causes such as education, that are important for *all* Americans. We will see in the next chapter that this was evident in the case of California Elementary.

THE LARGER CONTEXT FOR 227: EDUCATION POLITICS

Debates about Proposition 227 sat within these swirling discourses about immigration and race politics, and within a rising tide of debates about what to do with American schools in general. The era (just prior to the passage of No Child Left Behind) was one of frantic school reform movements nationwide. Plans for how to properly educate the next generation of Americans became so controversial that they were often "deal breakers" in congressional budget negotiations (Hastings, 2000b; Seelye, 1998), and they ranked as "top priorities" for the 2000 presidential candidates (Gerstenzang, 2000).

News about such issues as vouchers and charter schools, the rolling back of affirmative action legislation, and the poor state of urban education were ubiquitous (Ballesteros-Coronel, 2000; Sahagun & Helfand, 2000). News about teacher shortages, teacher training and salaries (Gladstone, 1999), school accountability reform (Groves, 2000a), federal versus local control, instructional innovations such as the implementation of academic standards (Steinberg, 1999), the return to phonics, and debates about structured versus constructivist curricula (Morse, 2000) flooded national publications. Indeed, news of these controversies and reform efforts came so fast and furious that analysts and scholars began to urge that policymakers "take a breather" from mandating more sweeping reforms in order to give schools "a chance to make the existing 'jigsaw puzzle' of mandates work," particularly for public schools' burgeoning numbers of English Language Learners (ELLs) (Groves, 2000b).

In 1998, the issue of education became extremely important to California voters. The state ranked last in the percentage of young adults who earned high school diplomas, and 37th in SAT scores. With its population expected to grow by 18 million (an entire New York state) by the year

2025, people began to see education as a proxy for their more generalized concerns about the future. Leading up to California's 1998 English for the Children Proposition 227 ballot initiative, the national tide had been turning against bilingual education. As mentioned in chapter 2, in 1996 a few districts in California received approval from the state to bypass federal bilingual education mandates and implement their own English-dominant programs for ELLs. Many bilingual education advocates saw the writing on the wall and began to coalesce around the pragmatic counter-position of bilingual programs that limited native language instruction to 2 or 3 years.

THE PRE-VOTE DEBATES: ARGUING FOR OR AGAINST "ENGLISH FOR THE CHILDREN"

California Proposition 227, the English for the Children initiative, was proposed by Ron Unz, a Silicon Valley millionaire and conservative Republican who had recently lost a bid in the California Republican primary for governor. Proposition 227 required that public school instruction be conducted in English. It required ELLs to be placed in intensive "sheltered English immersion programs" (any instructionally-specific description of which was conspicuously absent) until they were fluent in English; the time it was expected that students would take to become fluent was 1 year. There was a provision in the initiative for this immersion instruction to be "waived" in special cases, in favor of an alternative program (such as bilingual instruction). In such cases individual parents/guardians had to demonstrate that their child had a "special need" for a different kind of instruction, and they had to fill out special "waiver" paperwork in person at the school. Proposition 227 also called for the appropriation of $50 million per year for 10 years to fund community English tutoring programs. Finally, it provided parents/guardians with the right to sue their child's teacher, school, or district if they felt their child was denied the opportunity for instruction in English.

Leading up to the vote on Proposition 227, media discourses sounded similar to pro- and anti-bilingual education discourses of the past. Said one columnist (Martinez, 1998, p. 28):

> The topic of bilingual education has all the elements of a hit television drama, with plot lines about innocent children and the alleged abuse of program monies, power driven egos corrupting the ideals of the little red schoolhouse, and a search for the surest, fastest route to the American Dream. Californians are throwing out the first grenades in this new battle over bilingual education.

An article in the *L.A. Weekly*, a major city arts and culture paper, summarized the arguments this way: Proposition 227 proponents charged that, "By any objective standard, the state's bilingual education program has failed … [especially in] L.A. Unified … the nation's premier working laboratory for bilingual education" (Blume & Ehrenreich, 1998, p. 20). Proponents added that even with bilingual education, "the Latino dropout rate is still at least 30 percent…. Bilingual programs have become a sort of curricular equivalent to Black History Month, emphasizing culture and self-esteem, and then declaring the battle won" (p. 25). As in the earlier debates about bilingual education, the personal stories abounded of students who had not succeeded in bilingual education, and of commentators' immigrant grandparents who had "made it" in America without bilingual education. Even LAUSD's teachers' union, which officially opposed the Proposition (though in the face of much internal controversy), printed articles that painted bilingual teachers as "greedy" (because they received a stipend) and teachers in favor of English Only as upholding the ideals of "fairness" (Haguchi, 1999, p. 3).

To the contrary, the measure's opponents argued that bilingual education was largely successful. When done right, they charged, the "results have been entirely respectable," producing test scores for bilingual program students that equaled or exceeded the scores of their monolingual peers (Blume & Ehrenreich, 1998, p. 20) (this certainly was true at California Elementary). And Proposition 227's proposed 1-year program to teach *solely English* until children could understand the language enough to learn content such as math and science, they argued, "may have the practical effect of costing students a year of academic instruction" (p. 21). There was no research, they reminded readers, to "offer support for the idea that in one year, children can learn all the English they need to succeed in school" (p. 25). Representing this side of the debate, also, were the personal success stories—of bilingual program students who did well, and the arguments for bilingual education's role in honoring students' home cultures. There were also the reminders of the national need to create a globally savvy, multilingual workforce. Opined one op-ed columnist (Gurza, 1999):

> Being bilingual may be in, but bilingual education is out, thanks to the English-Only language police…. Proposition 227 … can only make matters worse. So while adults pay thousands of dollars trying to learn a second-language in costly crash courses, our children are being forced to forget the languages they already know…. The English-Only movement [can be seen] as an extension of Manifest Destiny, that delusional American ideology that justifies genocide and invasions. And Proposition 227 is a form of white supremacy … well rehearsed with American Indian and African American children before it was applied to Latinos. (p. B1)

James Crawford, an analyst of language politics in the United States and a vocal proponent of bilingual education (from 2004 through 2006 he served as the Executive Director of the National Association for Bilingual Education), criticized the media for offering slanted, shallow coverage of the pre-vote debates. The media set the terms of the debates quite in favor of English for the Children, he argued, in the following ways. One, they often covered the issue as a purely political story, not an education story or a science story or a story about shifting demographics (Crawford, 1998, p. 8). In political news coverage, said Crawford, "a lot of reporters feel they've done their jobs if they present the charges and counter-charges, quote people accurately, and let the best sound-bite win," instead of digging more deeply for facts.

So, for example, when Ron Unz made the claim that bilingual education had a "95% failure rate," he was basing this on the fact that, on average, 5% of California's ELL students were officially redesignated to fluent English speaking status annually. But rarely was it explained how this data was produced or what it meant: Looking at the entire population of ELLs, one can only reasonably expect a certain subgroup of these students to "redesignate." Within the "100% of ELLs," a certain percentage of them in any given year will have very low levels of English proficiency (for example, newcomers from other countries), a certain percentage will have medium/developing levels of proficiency (for example, those who have been in the country a year or 2), and a certain percentage will have high levels of proficiency (generally those who have been in the country for a longer period of time). It is only this third group of ELLs with the higher levels of English proficiency that should be expected to "redesignate fluent" in any given year (i.e., one would not expect a brand-new student into the country to be redesignated fluent in less than a year). Hence, the group of ELLs that can even be reasonably expected to redesignate each year is a relatively small percentage of the "100% of ELLs." In this light a 5% redesignation rate seems less alarming. Nor was it mentioned in media coverage that only 30% of the state's ELLs were even *in* bilingual programs to start with, and that of those in bilingual programs only 20% had appropriately-certified bilingual teachers (p. 8).

Hence what this "95% failure rate" masked was a deep misunderstanding of the process of second language acquisition and of the educational contexts in which ELLs were served in California. Further, it obscured the troubling truth that, in Blume and Ehrenreich's (1998) words, "The problem was never bilingual education alone, but an entire education system that hasn't delivered." Bilingual education became the latest in a string of scapegoats for a complex set of issues. It became the "official punching bag for politicians and others who attempt[ed] to blame linguistic/ethnic minorities" for the "economic, political, religious, [and] educational [problems] that our country faces on a day-to-day basis" (Antrop-González, 2002, p. 14). But reporters quoted Unz's "95% failure rate" of bilingual education so many times that this became part of the unquestioned, "conventional wisdom" on the issue (Crawford, 1998, p. 8).

A second way that the media tended to set the debate for Proposition 227 in erroneous terms was, according to Crawford (1998), that they routinely treated political opponents of bilingual education as experts—Ron Unz's lack of any background in education was ignored, and his opinions on the topic were taken as fact (p. 10). Proposition 227 was, in fact, based on absolutely no educational research. Reporters simply repeated Unz's charge that educators', linguists' and researchers' *anti-227* positions were either "just more opinions" (p. 11) or worse—bureaucratic, self-serving attempts to save their jobs (p. 12).

And so the details and implications of what Proposition 227 proposed went largely unexposed. One legal policy analyst argued that Proposition 227 was "violative of federal statutes, politically unsound, culturally biased, and pedagogically inaccurate" (Ryan, 2002, p. 487). However, as Crawford (1998) concluded, reporters did not bother to delve into the dense, complicated body of research on, or the decades of experience that practitioners had with, bilingual education. They "saw Unz as good copy" (p. 12), and uncritically took him at his word. In so doing, the media characterized the vote in Unz's terms, creating a common sense, hegemonic understanding of the vote as a choice between the "failing" "ghettos" of bilingual education and the hard-to-argue-against *idea* of English "for the children." Indeed the common question raised in Proposition 227 publicity materials was, "Do you agree that students in California should learn English?" This completely left out a potential second half to the question—How should students learn English? Should students learn English in addition to another language? Should students be able to maintain or develop their first language in addition to English? And so forth.

PROPOSITION 227 PASSES: DEBATES ABOUT THE EFFECTS OF ENGLISH IMMERSION

The measure passed on June 2, 1998 by a 61–39% margin (Ricento, 2000). Then debates about the issue got really interesting. As it turned out, neither side liked the vagueness of the mandate, as it left much to local interpretation. In one section of the official document (California Secretary of State, 1998), it states that students in all classrooms be taught "overwhelmingly" in English. In another, it demands "nearly all" instruction in English. Interpretations of this varied: Some districts interpreted this to mean using 100% English in the classroom. The Los Angeles

County Board of Education interpreted 227 to mean that, potentially, ELLs could be taught in English for 51% of the time and in their first languages as much as 49% of the time. Given these variations in interpretation, then, the law's provision for parents' right to sue if they felt their children were denied a chance for English instruction seemed ludicrous. Teachers' unions and others sued the state, charging that, "The proposition is so unconstitutionally vague that teachers cannot determine what actions are prohibited" (Turner, 1998, p. 2). The provision was eventually upheld by the courts. Many charged that this atmosphere of uncertainty and pressure created a classic example of "chilling" the right of free speech (Lyons, 1998).

The Los Angeles Unified School District, among others, applied for a blanket waiver of 227, to allow it to continue its bilingual programs (Helfand, 1998). Though it was not granted, many believed that the LAUSD still attempted to get around the mandate. For example, regarding parents' right to request waivers to place their children back into bilingual classrooms, principals at each school site in the LAUSD were allowed to interpret this provision (Ramirez, 2000). Some discouraged and some encouraged parents to submit waivers (Anderson & Sahagun, 1998). So not only was there a wide variety in the amount of primary language support versus English instruction, there was variation in numbers of bilingual waivers on campuses across the district. Said one reporter, "227 has hit bilingual education much like a tornado hopscotching through a subdivision, obliterating some programs and leaving others virtually untouched" (Anderson & Sahagun, 1998, p. A32).

Statewide, by 1999 the number of students being served in bilingual programs had dropped from 400,000 (pre-227) to 170,000, while the parental bilingual waivers doubled between October and May of that year. And the READ Institute, a proponent of 227, speculated that "only 15 percent of the 1000 California school districts were in full compliance with 227" (Mora, 1999, p. 6).

Media reports gave vastly different pictures of the effects of 227. Some hailed its success: "At elementary schools scattered across Los Angeles, teachers are delivering promising reports that their students are learning English more quickly than anticipated six months after the implementation of the anti-bilingual education law" (Sahagun, 1999d, p. A13). Others reported and predicted doom: The *La Opinión* Spanish language daily newspaper ran editorials arguing that (Sadek Sanchez, 1998, p. B4 [translation mine]),

Day by day--because of Proposition 227—our students fall behind.... And one day very soon, in March or April of 1999, all students will have to take the same tests—in English: math, science, social studies, language arts. Who will come out ahead on the tests?

A professor at Arizona State University pointed out that in California districts where students remained in bilingual programs, reading scores rose at almost double the rate as in districts that implemented English immersion, and that New York City schools had found similar results. As such, Proposition 227 could be seen as "a dramatic failure" (MacSwan, 2001, p. 8).

Some researchers cautioned that even improvements on certain academic indicators should be viewed with caution. Said one:

> Increases in LEP [ELL] students' scores for SAT-9 [a norm-referenced, standardized test] from 1998 to 1999 need to be considered in light of the overall gains in scores found across the state for all students. LEP students' scores in English-Only programs rose, as they did for LEP students in bilingual programs. And, native English speakers in low-performing schools made gains, as did LEP students in low-performing schools. These gains were probably the result of a combination of things. The fact that schools and districts have gotten used to the test and are taking them more seriously should be considered ... as well as the fact that a variety of other initiatives such as class-size reduction may be taking effect. (National Association for Bilingual Education, 1999, pp. 1, 11)

Reporters even pointed out that in some school districts that had received exemptions from the previously-mandated bilingual instruction years before 227 fewer ELLs were redesignating to "Fluent English Proficient." There were warnings that this "could be an omen of the law's negative impact" (Gittelsohn & Chey, 1999, p. 10).

Indeed, it was very frustrating trying to find out "the truth" about the effects of Proposition 227. English Only advocates and bilingual education proponents presented wildly different statistics on redesignation rates, test scores, and the implications of these (Linquanti, 2001). The president of the California Association for Bilingual Education was quoted as saying:

> English immersion programs [are like] baking bread at a high temperature: The crust gets brown faster [i.e., students learn basic interpersonal communication skills, or "playground" English, faster], but the inside remains doughy [i.e., students' academic English still takes extended periods of time to develop]. (Gittelsohn & Chey, 1999, pp. 1, 10)

Several *Los Angeles Times* and *La Opinión* articles similar to this one quoted English immersion teachers as saying troubling things like (de la Cruz, 2000, pp. 1A, 12A [translation mine]),

[Now] we review writing, reading and math in English, again and again. And we use much simpler concepts. Students get behind in their studies and people send them to special education. Many teachers don't use primary language support at all, and yet they think that when a child falls behind, it is a learning problem and not a language problem.

One fact that was agreed upon in the LAUSD was the controversial nature of the district's continued provision of stipends for certified bilingual teachers. The *Los Angeles Times* ran articles about the "battle" that was ripping apart the 40,000-member teachers' union (Sahagun, 1999c). Of the approximately 4,000 teachers who continued to receive the annual $5,000 bilingual bonus, 2,600 of them now taught English immersion classes. One advocate of eliminating the stipends was quoted as saying that stipends "aren't justified when you take into account Proposition 227, which mandates English immersion." Advocates of maintaining the stipends pointed out that in LAUSD's English immersion classrooms "up to 70% of the content can be provided in the students' primary language," hence the stipends were still necessary to attract qualified bilingual teachers. And a member of the union's bilingual committee warned that "We have a pretty militant committee; mess with us at your peril.... We are prepared to fight for our interests" (p. B3).

It is important to note here that people were not only arguing about the straightforward, "simple" effects of Proposition 227. Its effects and implications also reached far into other high-stakes education reform movements—most prominently, standardized testing and school accountability initiatives. At that time, California was in its first years of using a statewide standardized test (the Stanford 9) as part of a new system for rating schools (the Academic Performance Index), and as an important accountability measure for other programs (for example, the phasing out of social promotion) (Cooper, 1999). Some argued that making "children with limited English skills take tests written only in English and using the results to decide such pivotal questions as promotion or graduation may violate their civil rights" (p. A3). Such debates foreshadowed debates about the No Child Left Behind Act, which I take a look at in chapter 7.

At this time, the California State Superintendent of Public Instruction was quoted as saying that, regarding questions about language education policy, "Right now California is confused" (Cooper, 1999, p. A20). One editorialist put it this way: Given the poor academic achievement of students in general, the very political nature of the Proposition 227 campaign, and the crisis in district management (which I describe below), when it comes to important academic questions like pedagogy for ELLs people are left wondering, "Who makes decisions about these issues during crisis?" It seemed to some that "student needs no longer dictate instruction ... politics does" (Sadek Sanchez, 1999, p. 7A).

Surprisingly to me, given the far-reaching implications of the failure or success of English immersion and bilingual education, and given that 227 spawned several spin-off propositions in other states (Arizona, Colorado, Massachusetts), the topic received what *I* saw as *relatively* little nationwide attention between 1998 and 2000. There was coverage of the moves to launch similar propositions in the other states (e.g., V. Barrera, 2002; Breslau, 2000; NABE, 1999); and of Houston's school board passing a pro-multilingualism policy in anticipation of blocking a coming Unz initiative in that state (NABE, 1999). And we were informed that in September of 1998 the U.S. House of Representatives approved HR 3892, The English Language Fluency Act. The bill repealed the Emergency Immigrant Education Act and converted Title VII federal bilingual education program funds into a block grant to the states, limiting funding to those programs designed to exit children into EO classes within 2 years. In Los Angeles we also heard a lot about our school facilities crisis and our district leadership crisis (between 1999 and 2000 we had three different superintendents, starting with the first one, who was Latino, being deposed in a very controversial and racially-charged atmosphere [Sahagun & Smith, 1999]). Our *United Teachers of Los Angeles* union magazine provided relatively little coverage of Proposition 227 in the years after it passed. This was shocking to me. In *La Opinión* an editorial about the then-incoming superintendent, Roy Romer (a White man), suggested topics that he should address immediately, and none of them included language issues (Slavkin, 2000).

An excerpt from my fieldwork journal in 2000 reflects my reaction to what I saw as a relative lack of coverage of the ongoing issues with the implementation of Proposition 227:

> In the paper today there was an editorial about Roy Romer becoming our new superintendent. They discussed test scores, dividing up the district [into smaller administrative "local districts"], etc., but nothing about language, bilingual education, or 227. It is as if this huge, new, controversial program we've implemented doesn't exist. No need to worry about discussing it, Roy, let's just slog along. It's crazy. It's like in a dysfunctional family when people ignore the alcoholic in the bunch!

This is notable given that some considered debates about 227 to be a serious civil rights struggle, "almost on par with Brown vs. Board of Education" (Breslau, 2000, p. 64). Indeed some called 227 the single most important language policy decision of this last century (Gutiérrez, Baquedano-Lopez, & Asato, 2000). Those on Ron Unz's side characterized the prospect of continued bilingual education on a national scale as, in Unz's (2001) words, "an even greater horror" than "massive deaths from anthrax or suicide bombers" (a bold statement in the post-9/11 world). Americans, he urged, "must remain silent no longer" against the "terror" of native language instruction! And still, academics, policymakers, and politicians continued to urge for increased multilingualism for the benefit of the U.S. economy (Hastings, 2000a).

Amidst these wildly different *arguments* about the facts and import of demographic change and globalism, English Only, Spanish, English immersion, and bilingual education, people at California Elementary *lived* the seesaws between the competing language education policies. In the next chapter I discuss their—our—experiences of the post-227 terrain, reflecting on how these experiences related to debates in the national media and the import of this for understanding education policy processes and struggles for cultural citizenship in diverse school communities.

CHAPTER 5

IMMIGRATION, LANGUAGE EDUCATION POLICY, AND RACE AT CALIFORNIA ELEMENTARY, 1998–2000

Conflict Continues

HOMEWORK

I returned again to California Elementary in August, 1998, just 2 months after Proposition 227 passed. Different from the 1996 research period, this time I returned not only to conduct research but also to teach. For the next 2 years I did all the things a good ethnographer does, and I was also "Ms. Anderson, room 212." I had the exciting, challenging task of educating third graders at a time when California schools were undergoing the massive changes brought by English for the Children initiative.

As part of my role as a teacher I wore several other hats at this time as well: I served on the school's professional development committee and as the school's standards based assessment coordinator, helping to implement the district's new performance assessment system and to coordinate

War or Common Cause? A Critical Ethnography of
Language Education Policy, Race, and Cultural Citizenship , pp. 81–130
Copyright © 2008 by Information Age Publishing
All rights of reproduction in any form reserved.

professional learning for teachers. In an effort to provide our students with academic role models, I established a tutoring program, working with other teachers to recruit students from our local high school to tutor our kindergarten through fifth-graders. At one point we had enough tutors to cover most classes on campus—and a few of the tutors had been students of mine from my earlier days at California Elementary! Coming full circle from when I left teaching in 1994, I also worked as an instructor teaching night and weekend courses in the Los Angeles Unified School District's District Intern Program.

Why did I decide to do all these things, when ethnographic research can be full-time work in its own right? Because this time I did not want to be just a data collector. I wanted this phase of the project to be "homework" as much as "fieldwork" (Gordon, 1998, p. viii [cited in Visweswaran, 1994]). I wanted to ask and answer questions from multiple perspectives (Haraway, 1988), sometimes as anthropologist, sometimes as teacher, sometimes as White person, sometimes as "Latino/bilingual" advocate, sometimes as "African American/EO" advocate." And, I think that a teacher involved in seeking insights into her/his practice is a better *teacher* for it.

This was difficult from the beginning. A few months before the beginning of the new school year I sent my resumé to the California Elementary's hiring committee. Right away, they placed me on "the matrix" (the organizational chart listing all classes and teachers) for the new year, and requested that I submit my paperwork to the district's personnel office. However, a few weeks later I got a call from Enrique, the bilingual program coordinator. He told me that Andrea, the vice principal, was uncomfortable with me coming back to the school. Since I knew her personally from my earlier years teaching there, I called and asked her to share with me her reservations. She told me that it was my research project that worried her:

> This is a different school than when you worked here. We are not doing as well as we should be. So I don't want anything disrupting the staff. I don't want you running around with any surveys. I don't want any of this "he said/ she said" stuff. Our staff is in enough turmoil right now as it is. We don't need anyone or anything disrupting us from the business of teaching kids.

I told her that I understood her concerns. I assured her that I would conduct my research as unobtrusively as possible. I agreed not to do any surveys. I explained that my research would mostly consist of observations and one-on-one interviews that I would conduct with volunteers, at times outside of our required professional duties. I told her that I would not use people's real names or even the school's real name in any writing I did about the project. She responded, "I still don't know, I'm not sure, but in the end I am not the principal. You need to speak with the principal." He was new to the school, so I called him to introduce myself and to discuss Andrea's concerns. He was fine with the idea, even suggesting that I introduce my project to everyone at the first faculty meeting of the new school year and solicit volunteer interviewees. My place on the matrix was secure, he said. Everything seemed set.

Just before I arrived in Los Angeles, I got a call from one of my friends. She said, "Andrea took your name off the matrix and she recruited someone specifically for your spot before she filled any of the other positions that were open!" So I called the principal and asked him if it was still possible to place me in a position (any still-open position). He agreed. When I arrived at the school the following week as a third-grade teacher on staff I felt welcome, and neither Andrea nor I ever mentioned the incident.

My first day, I was so happy to be back. I had missed teaching kids, I had missed my friends. I was anxious, though, too. How would it go? I had prepared by studying my curriculum materials, planning my lessons, spending lots of money at the teacher supply store, readying my fieldwork notebook, buying batteries for my tape recorders, and finalizing my interview questions. Could I be a good teacher *and* a good anthropologist simultaneously?

At the first faculty meeting the principal asked that I introduce my research project. I explained that the continued focus of my research (for those who remembered the research I did during the summer of 1996) was *us*—the adults at California Elementary. How did we define ourselves and our relationships now, in this "Proposition 227 world?" What was on our minds as educators, professionals, community members? How did our lives at school relate to trends in national-level politics? And how did this inform our work to improve the education of our students?

Throughout that 2 years, I explored how EO instruction, bilingual instruction, and English immersion looked and felt from multiple subject positions at California Elementary. I traced the "multiplicity of socio-material concerns" that people expressed, and the different personal, political and material outcomes that they experienced (Rosaldo, 1994). I sought to unpack the "collective fictions" that we told about ourselves and others to claim cultural citizenship in the community—our sense of belonging, recognition, entitlement, agency, and voice (Flores & Benmayor, 1997; Rosaldo, 1994). And I sought to carefully map out how this groundbreaking statewide language education policy took shape at our school, and with what effects.

A SCHOOL COMMUNITY STILL IN TRANSITION

Demographically, the trends I described in chapter 3 had continued: By 1998 the LAUSD student body had risen to 681,505, with 68.5% being

Hispanic/Latino, 13.8% African American, 10.9% White, 4.3% Asian, 1.9% Filipino, 0.6% Indian, and Pacific Islander (LAUSD, 1998e). The Latino population continued to be the fastest-growing. By 1999 on our campus Latino students comprised 91% of the student body, African Americans 9% (California Department of Education, 1999a). At the end of 1998 and going into 1999, among all adults including teachers, administrators, and other staff members, 53% were Latino, 24% were Black, 21% were White and 2% were Asian. Amongst the faculty and staff, I counted lots of old friends and colleagues. There were also many new faces. Our school, like many in the vicinity, had a high turnover rate and each year brought a number of new teachers.

I was never able to gather reliable data on what percentages of people on campus actually voted for and against 227. A few of the people I interviewed did not share with me which way they had voted and I did not administer a survey requesting this sensitive information, given the concern that the idea of a survey had raised with the vice principal. However, many people told me that the vote was just as controversial at California Elementary as it was across the state. There had been petitions circulating and debates were frequent and heated.

As discussed in the previous section, districts and schools implemented English for the Children differently due to the great latitude allowed by the vague wording of the initiative. Everything seemed to be left to interpretation: from what kind of instructional programs would qualify as meeting the guidelines, to whether or not a school *had* to offer parents the "waiver to bilingual instruction" option, to what exactly a student had to do to demonstrate "reasonable fluency" in order to transition out of an immersion class into an EO class. Even the very crux of the initiative—exactly how much primary language support was allowed in immersion classrooms— seemed up for grabs. The great irony of this initiative was that it purported to seek statewide uniformity and improvement in the teaching and achievement of English Language Learners (ELLs). Instead it ended up fostering, from my perspective as a teacher and in reading media reports, more variety in instructional approaches than before, and even greater amounts of uncertainty about what was working and what was not.

Rumors circulated at California Elementary about all manner of scenarios of school, classroom, and instructional reorganization that would take place when we implemented the mandate. We were held in suspense until just days before the district's 227 plan was to go into effect.

The LAUSD's Proposition 227 implementation plan comprised two structured English immersion programs, called Model A and Model B: Model A consisted of "instruction *in English* using special methods in English with support of the home language" (LAUSD, 1998a [italics added]). We were told that this meant we taught all in English, only helping students using the primary language *one-on-one* if we had already tried all other ways we knew to convey understanding. Model B consisted of "instruction *primarily in English* using special methods in English combined with the home language used by the teacher to develop academic concepts" (LAUSD, 1998a [italics added]). We were told that this meant we could "preview and review" the concepts in Spanish but that the meat of the lesson was to be in English. Primary language support could be used with groups of students as necessary.

Because the immersion programs allowed some use of students' native languages, Model A and Model B teachers with bilingual qualifications continued to receive bilingual stipends of up to $5,000 (depending on which fluency tests they had passed; I received the full amount). And the district continued to actively recruit bilingual teachers in Spanish, Armenian, Cantonese, Mandarin, Farsi, Japanese, Korean, Filipino, Russian, Samoan, Serbo-Croatian, Spanish, and Vietnamese. The district also specified that dual-language bilingual programs could continue in the limited number of schools where they had previously existed, but these once acclaimed programs fizzled, dropping from 10 to 4 by the spring of 2002 (Blume, 2002).

Schools across the district had widely varying numbers of students in "waiver" (bilingual) classrooms post-227. For this to occur, as I have described, parents had to fill out "waiver" paperwork. There also had to be at least 20 waiver requests at the same grade level (i.e., enough to generate funds for a teacher to dedicate to the class). As such, critical masses of parents could ensure that bilingual programs would continue in their school—that is (according to the district) *unless "the school administration determines* that the alternative program requested would not be beneficial for the student" (LAUSD, 1998b, [italics added]). Wording the policy this way really meant that ultimately the decision on granting waivers could be made by each school's principal, not the parents. At California Elementary there were several public meetings held to inform parents about all of their programmatic options—English immersion (Model A or Model B), "waiver" bilingual, and EO. Largely, though, it fell to us individual teachers to speak with parents on a one-on-one basis. After sending the paperwork home, I called my parents to discuss it with them. Most chose one of the immersion options, a few chose the waiver bilingual option, and a couple chose to place their children straight into EO. Before making these decisions, however, most parents had lots of questions for me. What did I recommend, they wanted to know?

In this nervous time, teachers even had to be careful about how we worded our "recommendations" to parents. We could not be seen to be advocating either for or against bilingual education or English immersion. In the midst of implementing one of the most politicized education policy measures in recent memory, advocacy on our part was seen as "too political." In the September, 1998 *Spotlight Newsletter* for LAUSD employees, the official directive from the Superintendent was, "In short: Advice, Yes; Advocacy, No" (LAUSD, 1998c). I advised parents that if they wanted their children to attain literacy in Spanish *while* they worked towards literacy in English, I recommended a waiver for the bilingual program. I shared with them my previous experiences of success with the program. I advised them that if they wanted the total focus to be on English literacy (utilizing Spanish only as a minimal aide along the way), I recommended English immersion (and given research showing the benefits of using the primary language in second language acquisition, I recommended Model B, which allowed more first language support than Model A). I advised them that if they wanted the total focus to be on English literacy, with absolutely no primary language support, they should opt for EO. As many of my colleagues also found, some parents in my room seemed to value a sense of consistency for their children in their relationship with their teacher as much or more than they valued a particular language instruction model—they wanted their children to stay in my class regardless of what program choice that meant.

HOW DID THE IMPLEMENTATION OF 227 GO? "IT WAS CHAOS"

At California Elementary, being a multitrack year-round school, the track that began the school year "off-track" (on vacation in July and August) began implementing Proposition 227 when they started school in September. The two tracks that began school in July, however, continued their regular programs and classroom compositions through the first "on track" sessions (until winter holiday break). I was teaching on one of these tracks. So, I taught my third-grade bilingual program class up through winter break, and when school opened after the New Year we began 227, going cold turkey to a mandated 30 days of 100% English instruction. After the 30 days, parents advised us of their choice to place their children in Model A or Model B English immersion, into the "waiver" bilingual program, or straight into EO.

When we switched to the 227 organizational models, for many of us our classroom rosters changed. Many teachers now had mixed classrooms with Model A and Model B students. Noting the stipulated differences for first language use in the two immersion programs, we wondered aloud, "What do I do if I want to preview a lesson in Spanish for my Model B kids? Tell my Model A kids to put their hands over their ears?" Those of us who now had combinations of "waiver to bilingual" students *and* Model A *and/or* Model B students (yes, some of us had all three models in our classroom), were even more apprehensive about this question. We were apprehensive because we received only 2 days of training on the nuts and bolts of implementation, and we perceived mixed messages during this training: We were told verbally that we were to focus on teaching the English vocabulary of the content areas and to worry less about the content material itself, that is, teach the *vocabulary* of math, science, and so forth, and worry less about whether students understood the *concepts* in math, science, and so forth. Yet the written documents outlining the Proposition 227 immersion programs that we were given stated that the students' first language could be used by the teacher or teacher assistant (TA) to ensure students understood the *content* of the material (LAUSD, 1998a). We were left unsure about what to really focus on, and how.

Neither the district representative nor our administrators had definitive answers about many of our detailed implementation questions. They guessed what proper immersion instruction might look and sound like. This was incomprehensible to us as teachers. Just what were we responsible for? Would we be monitored and sued if we used one too many Spanish phrases? We were frustrated and even afraid. Not only was what we knew about effective instruction for ELLs being turned upside down, but we were worried that we would never be able to teach well what we did not understand ourselves.

Proposition 227's organizational changes not only affected bilingual program teachers and students, however. We were all impacted. Bilingual classes *and* EO classes at California Elementary had to be reorganized to accommodate parents' choices of programs. The full range of English materials then had to be distributed to formerly bilingual classrooms, and many did not come right away. In the meantime, some of us had our students' Spanish textbooks taken out of their desks and carted away as students, "traumatized" (in the words of one colleague), looked on. One of my February, 1999 field note entries reads,

> On January 4th we began 227, the 100% cold-turkey 30 days. I did not know what to expect, really, from my students. We discussed it before vacation, that we would do a lot more English when we came back. They seemed a little scared. But in January they seemed ready to go, and actually rolled with the punches pretty well. We have to do a lot of hands-on activities, I repeat more, we do problem solving together. But there were no big incidents as some teachers had worried. Last week they let us know that on Friday we would switch, because the mandatory one month of 100% all English was ending. Up until the last minute Enrique was working on the new class rosters. On Thursday he came to me on our way in from lunch recess and said, "Kim, which class would you like? The third grade waiver bilingual class or the third grade modified (15 Model B, 15 waiver bilingual) class? You have to decide now, right now." So right there in the hall with 20 kids fidgeting in

line behind me, we decided I would have the modified class. Such a big decision, almost like a coin toss. I would lose five students and get five new ones.

After that first reorganization of the entire school came continual reorganizations of students throughout the semester, as parents changed their minds—some multiple times—about which program they preferred. I got worn out by a seemingly endless process of integrating new students into my class, of bidding students goodbye as they switched to new teachers, and of trading students' records, report cards, and work samples with other teachers.

Things settled down eventually, though, and going into the 1999-2000 school year our matrix listed the following class compositions:

- immersion: Model A, Model B, or mixed A and B: 25
- waiver bilingual: 12
- mixed waiver bilingual, Model A and/or B: 13
- full EO: 3
- EO mixed with Model A, Model B, and/or waiver bilingual: 9

By June of 2000 our 2000-2001 matrix listed the following expected class compositions:

- Immersion: Model A, Model B, or mixed A and B: 18
- waiver bilingual: 16
- mixed waiver bilingual; Model A and/or B: 7
- full EO 1
- EO mixed with Model A, Model B, and/or waiver bilingual: 19

So we see that waiver bilingual classes went from 12 to 16, and classes with *at least partial* waiver bilingual composition went from 25 in 1999–2000 to 23 in 2000–2001. Full EO classes went from 3 to 1, and classes with *at least partial* EO composition went from 12 in 1999–2000 to 20 in 2000–2001. All in all, these were somewhat contradictory programmatic outcomes given that the philosophical goal of the authors of the English for the Children policy was to put an end to bilingual education and go all English for everyone.

While people on our campus felt differently about the ideals behind English immersion and bilingual education, one thing that most agreed on was the difficulty and confusion we all went through those first two years. People across the school community used the word "chaos" to describe the instructional, organizational, and social environments at that time, and many people confided to me that this made it difficult to "just get through the day." Others who have chronicled the implementation of the initiative statewide have also called it "chaotic" and "frenzied" (e.g., Attinasi, 1999; Valdez, 2001). One bilingual-turned-English-Immersion teacher reminisced at the end of that first year of 227,

> My class was destroyed. Every couple of weeks I traded multiple students. I ended up with a total of 4 students from my original class by April 28, when [standardized, Stanford 9] testing began. And on that day I had a whole group of students who were brand-new the week before the test. So much for accountability! It wreaked havoc—and the district still doesn't know what the curriculum is going to be! 227 wasn't *implemented* [sarcastically] in my classroom. It was just constant chaos.

The teacher who took our Title I coordinator position after Roslyn left said, "I think that we did the best we could but it was probably a disaster. We didn't have the materials, the training, or a curriculum, we didn't have anything but the law to go by." Our bilingual program coordinator who took over after Enrique left in 2000, shared with me, "Well, as you know, because you are teaching it, there is no actual set program. I mean we don't really have, all we have is [he pauses, searching for words], you know what I mean?" This, from two people in the school who were charged with monitoring policy implementation and compliance.

We did not get any firm curricular guidelines until the beginning of the 1999–2000 school year, when we began to discuss grade level English Language Development (ELD) standards, but even still these were skeletal. Many of us felt, for a long time, like we were wandering on our own in uncharted territory, with only our instincts to guide us. Even several "African American/EO" staff members who had expressed anti-bilingual education sentiment in the past said, similar to Michael, "If I had known the chaos 227 would cause at this school, I would not have voted for it."

In this context of massive programmatic changes, unclear curricular guidelines, frazzled staff members, and confused parents, consistent quality teaching was a challenge. Unquestionably, our academic environment was affected drastically, and in many ways negatively.

CONTINUING DISPARITIES IN STUDENT ACHIEVEMENT

As in 1996, in 1998 through 2000 student achievement data sparked many conversations about equity. In 1999, California Elementary's Academic Performance Index (API) statewide rank was a 1 out of 10. Our 1998–1999 scores on the Stanford 9 standardized test showed that overall only 9% of our students were reading at or above the 50th percentile, and only 43% of our students scored at or above the 50th percentile in math. (California Department of Education, 1999b). (California Department of Education, 2000). And within this alarmingly low level of average school-wide student achievement, there were further disparities. Stanford 9 reports in 1998–99 and 1999–2000 showed the following trends: Latino ELLs scored similarly to the EO students, somewhat higher or lower depending on the grade level. Latino students who transitioned from ELL status to Redesignated Fluent English Proficient (RFEP) status (exiting either the bilingual or English immersion program) scored the same as *or up to more than twice as high* in reading, language and math as the mostly African American EO students and they did this in their second language.

With the increased focus on ELD in the Model A and Model B classes, and the increased push by the district to redesignate those students (from ELL to RFEP), the redesignation rate at California Elementary took off: The principal reported in June of 2000 that we had gone from redesignating "only 3 or 4 students" in 1997–1998, to 100 in 1998–1999, to 170 in 1999–2000. In 1999–2000 the school underwent a state-mandated program quality review (PQR) (all California schools cycled through this review every 4 years). Administrators shared with teachers that the PQR process identified the major improvement criteria for our school as closing the achievement gap between our generally lower-scoring African American/EO students and our generally higher-scoring Latino/bilingual/immersion students.

KEY TERMS ENDURE:
AFRICAN AMERICAN, EO, LATINO, BILINGUAL

Urciuoli (1996) reminds us that the words people choose to describe their reality tell "a great deal about how their world is put together, particularly its power relations." Hence a focus on semiotics is important: "How people talk about language, race, and class must be interpreted in terms of their social location[s]" (pp. 1, 2). After Peirce (1956) and Silverstein (1976), she urges us to pay attention to the pragmatics of metacommunicative discourses—they can be seen to index connection, causality, social location, and strategic performance (Urciuoli, 1996, p. 7).

In chapter 3 I examined how, in 1996 as people described politics on campus they used several key terms interchangeably. They mapped linguistic and programmatic categories onto categories of race and nation: African American and EO; Latino and bilingual; with both sides constructing themselves as quintessentially "American." How they did so provided a window into power relations and struggles for cultural citizenship, as well as into the fluidity of identity/political categories of language, race, and nation (Harrison, 1998; Ong, 1996). This shed light on the different dynamics at play when people either advocated for or fought against a particular language education policy—or why they might do both simultaneously.

Returning to California Elementary, I wondered if I would find shifts in the language policy environment reflected in the ways people talked about politics on campus. For example, would new terms like "227" and "Model A/Model B" become hot button symbols like "bilingual" and "EO?" Shore and Wright (1997) argue that shifts in the semantics or pragmatics of a key symbol become "fingerprints for tracing more profound transformations" in human relations (p. 19). Similarly, Roediger (1991) states that a "change in signifiers itself signal[s] a new set of social realities and racial meanings" (p. 15).

What I found was that instead of changes, there was *continuity* in the terms themselves. "Latino/bilingual" and "African American/EO" continued to be the terms that demarcated difference on campus. These terms continued to be used interchangeably and continued to be popular "key symbols" through which different groups of folks meaningfully disagreed (Woolard, 1989). What shifted was the *content* of these terms: They expanded to fit the new policy context. "Latino" and "bilingual" continued to—interchangeably—refer to school community members who were or were perceived to be in favor of Latinos, the Spanish language, or bilingual education, *and* this now also included those who taught in the Model A/B English immersion programs. (Though like before, "Latino/bilingual" was actually an internally heterogeneous group— there were some on this "side" who were White or Black, and some who were not in favor of a bilingual policy agenda.) "African American" and "EO" continued to—interchangeably—refer to school community members who were or were perceived to be in favor of African Americans and EO education. (Though similarly, there was actually quite a bit of diversity within this group. There were some "African American/EO" people who were White or Latino, and who taught in a Model A/Model B class.)

I found this over and over, people referring to Model A and Model B staff members as "bilingual," and people referring to African Americans as "EO" even if they taught Model A and Model B. For example, Frank put it bluntly: "I consider Model A and Model B to *be bilingual*. It's all the same to me." And one day, as we talked about classroom reorganization, the principal shed a clear light on the enduring quality of the discursive language-race conflation, and how Model A and Model B fit and even continued to fuel the earlier dichotomy:

The big problem at California Elementary is that language here isn't just language, it's also race. If you organize classrooms based on language you end up organizing them also by race. I think that's something people thought was going to get solved by 227. It didn't, really. We still organize by Model A and Model B on one side and EO on the other; we're still not really integrating classrooms. And I think if the school had gone with 227 the way some people thought, then they probably would be integrated, everybody together.

The fact that there was little change in the way people experienced and constructed relationships to each other across a dichotomous "Latino/bilingual," "African American/EO" divide, and the fact that new pedagogical practices and terms fit into this old mold, speaks volumes about the importance of understanding policy as both received mandate and as locally-created cultural resource. It highlights the importance of understanding policy changes both as changes in official institutional directives and as practical and social shifts within which local actors continue to shape enduring struggles for cultural, material, and professional capital.

As I examine the constructions of post-227 cultural citizenship at California Elementary, I keep in mind Levinson and Holland's (1996) assertion that the supposedly essential categories, discourses, and symbols deployed in struggle are actually open political categories (p. 11). Rather than static givens, the contours and content of these categories are negotiated "in struggle" (p. 11). Finding out why Model A/Model B "meant" bilingual to many school community members, for example, can help illuminate how social and political relations were shaped as they were (Giroux, 1992). Therefore I keep the "Latino/bilingual" and "African American/EO" terms intact as I describe school community dynamics post-227, because I found that people at California Elementary, my colleagues and I, did so.

This general stability in the key metacommunicative discourses on campus illuminates a major finding from this phase of my research: The dynamics of the 1996 "war" did not seem to change very much. Even though 227 was meant to dismantle the supposed central issue of the earlier conflict—the bilingual program—it did not do this at our school (we had many "waiver to bilingual" classrooms, not to mention the fact that the immersion classrooms were often seen "to be bilingual"). I found that 227 simply shifted the intensity of the conflict. The all-out combat of the earlier years became what might be characterized as a series of decentralized skirmishes post-227—heated conversations, for example, in the lunch room, in the parking lot, at school leadership council meetings, and in interviews with me, amidst the chaos of drastic, rapid programmatic change. Many people felt that "their own" students, parents, and teachers still ended up on the wrong side of the answer to the old question, Who are the valued members of our school community, and what does that say about us? I still heard whispers of, "I would work harder on this," and "I would go the extra mile on this, if *they* would act right," or "if *they* would address our issues." I saw many opportunities for collaborative projects to improve the school lost. Morale was still low. Student achievement was still abysmal.

There were, however, a few people I spoke with in 1998 through 2000 who held a different opinion of campus politics. They contended that the 1996 "war" was either a part of the school community's history that they did not know, or a relic of the past that should be kept in the past. I discuss these different impressions of the campus dynamics post-227 as this chapter progresses.

Before diving further into school community members' descriptions of goings-on at California Elementary in 1998 through 2000, in the next section I provide updates on some of the key voices from the earlier years, and introduce some new ones.

KEY VOICES IN THE POST-227 CONTEXT

"African American/EO" Key Voices

Three key voices from the pre-227 "war" continued to be key voices post-227. Janice continued to be an outspoken, passionate voice for the "African American/EO" teachers, students and community, though she now taught students in the EO and Model A programs. Michael continued to serve on the school's LEARN committee, and as a classified employees union representative. He was still a vocal advocate for Black students and staff members. Post-227, however, he worked as a TA in a classroom with EO, Model A, and Model B students. Eleanor also continued to work as an educational aide, with EO and Model A students. She continued to be an active, popular member in the school community and continued to be a leading organizer of holiday celebrations, Career Days, and other campus activities.

"African American/EO" Border Crossers

Now more people than ever seemed to cross the line between "sides," even though most people recognized (and actively constructed) a continued dividing line between "African American/EO" and "Latino/ bilingual" interests on campus. As Roslyn put it, while the conflict definitely still simmered post-227 she could see that,

> There was this faction and that faction, you know, but you could belong to different factions. I was in the Black faction, and I was also in the new

teacher-pro-bilingual faction. And sometimes they crossed and there were different interests.

The "battles were kept low" post-227 because, "I couldn't be battling with somebody that the next moment I was aligned to on another issue. But that was just me. Some of the hard-core people never crossed lines." At the beginning of the 1998–99 school year Roslyn was still in her coordinator position, but half-way through the school year she transferred to a district-level position.

Frank continued to teach, teaching mostly Model A/Model B classes. Elizabeth also continued to teach, with mixed immersion and EO classes, until in 2000 she was chosen to take an out-of-the-classroom instructional coach position. While she had been recognized as an exemplary teacher of "African American/EO" students, she was encouraged by staff members of all program groups to take this position that would have her working with upper-grade teachers and students in all classrooms.

A new vocal force for this "side" was Mary. Mary, who was White, began working at California Elementary in 1994. In 1996 she did not emerge in interviews or in my observations as a key voice, but by 1998 she sought out any opportunity she could to express to me and to other colleagues—at the lunch table, in whispers during professional development sessions, in social settings—her opinions about the inequities between "African American/EO" and "Latino/bilingual" education at the school. Others also now cited her in interviews as a representative of this "side's" views.

"Latino/bilingual" Key Voices

Enrique continued to work as California Elementary's bilingual program coordinator in 1998, but the next year he moved to a different school. During the time he was at California Elementary in the post-227 context he was still a vocal supporter of bilingual education, even while his job now also encompassed coordinating the English immersion program (which he officially, professionally supported). Many on the "African American/EO" side still considered Enrique to be in part responsible for what they saw as the neglect of African American students, the favoring of Latino students, and incomplete compliance with Proposition 227. Even after he left, his name would surface in discussions about issues on campus.

By 1998 Crystal had transferred from a position as TA to one as an office administrative assistant. As such, she was highly visible to all stakeholders as they interacted with the school administration. She could often be heard speaking Spanish with her sister who worked on campus, and with many of the bilingual TAs.

"Latino/bilingual" Border Crossers

Scott had left California Elementary by 1998. Some people said it was because he felt unwelcome on campus after "the blackface incident"; others surmised that, "he just wanted to do something different." Linda became an English immersion teacher in 1998. Early on that year she made no secret of her distaste for Proposition 227. She was vocal about her continued support for bilingual education. A few months into implementation, however, during interviews with me she shared her pleasant surprise with how fast children seemed to be learning English. She went so far during one interview as to chastise the teachers who had full waivered bilingual classes, charging that they were holding children back by going against the rest of the school. She still vigorously defended the district's bilingual teacher stipend (which she received).

Andrea was still assistant principal in 1998 and through 2000. Throughout she was officially, professionally supportive of 227. Still, she often expressed in personal interactions her philosophical dedication to bilingual education.

A new "Latino/bilingual" border crosser was Amy. She joined the faculty as a District Intern just after my 1996 research. She was politically active in the anti-Proposition 187, 209, and 227 campaigns in Los Angeles. Very pro-bilingual, she taught a full "waiver bilingual" classroom both years, 1998–2000. She was often mentioned by others as either an inspiration in the fight to "save" bilingual education or as one of those who was "cheating 227" by not implementing the mandated immersion. Amy was White.

MEXICAN MOTHER'S DAY

Imagine this scene (excerpted from my field notes, 2000):

It's a hot, sunny Wednesday in May, 2000. For two weeks students have been preparing Mother's Day gifts—cards, paintings, tissue paper flowers with pipe cleaner stems, and jar-top picture frames. The Mother's Day celebration committee, a small group of volunteer staff members and parents, solicited teachers to volunteer their classes to give a presentation at an assembly. Invitations were sent out to all the parents. I had signed up my class to recite a poem, so on this day we stopped our lessons early, practiced our poem, "Mothers," one more time, grabbed our gifts and headed excitedly for the yard. As we opened the double doors out onto the yard we saw the entire playground festooned with decorations. Merengue music was blaring over the speakers. Classes lined up facing each other with a large performance area in the middle. At one end of the lines was the sound system. At the other end were the parents, around 60 by my count; my quick "eyeball assessment" noted mostly Latino parents and less than a handful of African American parents. The celebration committee

chairperson (and the school's official parent representative), a Latina, gave a wel-
come speech, speaking elaborately in Spanish and briefly in English. Then came the
presentations. Traditional Mexican folk dances were danced, current salsa hits cho-
reographed, and traditional Mexican songs sung. The entire 40 minute extrava-
ganza included only two presentations in English: one class lip synched and danced
to a Jennifer Lopez song, and my class recited "Mothers." At the conclusion of the cel-
ebration, several mothers of my students approached me with thanks and praises.
They felt so appreciated, they told me, and this made me feel great. But I wondered,
how must the Black parents feel—both the few who attended and the many who
didn't? I approached one of the planning committee members later that day with
questions. I found out that so many class presentations were in Spanish because,
"that's what teachers signed up for." I found out that the celebration was on that par-
ticular day of the week, Wednesday, and not on Friday (Friday being chronologically
closer to what was on the US calendar as Mother's Day—Sunday), because Wednes-
day was the day when Mother's Day was celebrated in Mexico. "It just made sense" to
schedule it that way, she told me. And as for the disproportionately low number of
African American attendees? "Well," she said shrugging her shoulders with an air of
frustration, "we invited everybody. I think it went great!"

The "Mexican Mother's Day Incident" (as I call it) in the post-227 context was similar to "the blackface incident" in 1996, in that both were major
school community events. Both events had been planned as public recog-
nitions of school community members. And in both cases the meaning of
the event was up for interpretation. However, unlike "the blackface incident," which became a hotly debated symbol of "what was wrong" for both
"sides" of the "war" in 1996, the Mexican Mother's Day incident did not
become a flash point for conflict in 2000. I wondered if it might have been
more welcoming to all our school community members (and more reflective of our greater focus these days on English) if there had been a more
equal amount of Spanish presentations and English presentations. But
there was no public discourse about it afterwards—there were no arguments in faculty meetings, in the lunchroom, or in the parking lot. There
was a routine note in the "Special Thanks" portion of our staff weekly bul-
letin the following Monday recognizing participants and organizers for a
great show, and that was the last I heard about it. Below I discuss school
community dynamics post-227, returning later in the chapter to discuss
why this event might not have sparked public controversy, as well as the
implications of this lack of debate for understanding how policy processes
inform and are informed by both local and national contexts.

"LATINO/BILINGUAL" PERSPECTIVES ON PROPOSITION 227

"Latino/bilingual" school community members constructed the post-227
terrain in varying ways. The majority I spoke with expressed the opinion

that 227 was a kind of "backlash pedagogy" (Gutiérrez, Asato, Santos, & Gotanda, 2002)—part of state and national cultural trends of anti-immigrationism that adversely affected and demonized Latinos, bilingualism, and immigrants. They experienced and constructed Proposition 227 as a professional attack, as racism, and as yet another example of a situation that "the other side" would use to satisfy their greed and grabs for power. For these reasons, people told me, "Latino/bilingual" students' achievement, their programs and the people who served them required extra care and vigilance now more than ever. A few, however, had a different opinion of politics in the era of 227: A few characterized the coming of 227 as largely resolving the "war" of previous years. I explore both perspectives in the following sections.

Proposition 277 Experienced as Policy Backlash

Describing to me the feeling of coming under attack by a kind of backlash (Gutiérrez, Asato, Santos, & Gotanda, 2002), or a kind of "attack by policy," many "Latino/bilingual" school community members described it in terms of experiencing an imminent threat on school grounds. One TA told me that at the time of the statewide 227 vote,

> A lot of us were upset. There was a lot of anger and questioning. Nobody knew what to do or what was going to happen. We didn't know, Can we talk to the kids, can we not talk to the kids [in Spanish]? Are we going to go to jail [if we speak in Spanish]? We didn't know if they would have tape recorders in our rooms trying to tape record us. We wondered if they would fire us if we said anything in Spanish. We felt helpless, like we couldn't do anything. We were scared.

At this time as well, people mentioned what could be seen as an attack on the cultural capital and power of Latinos and bilingual education proponents in the LAUSD: The superintendent, a Latino and a supporter of bilingual education, was pressured to step down. After months of wrangling, it was decided that his contract would be bought out early and a new superintendent installed. Large numbers in the Latino community protested, asserting that the move was an attempt to strip Latinos of power. At the controversy's height, petitions were circulated asking the state to take receivership of the district due to the blatantly unfair nature of the move. This frequently made the news in English and Spanish, with most coverage highlighting the racial tensions behind the controversy. Many reports connected it to the issues of anti-immigrationism and racism against Latinos that also permeated national debates about Propositions 227, 187, and 209.

Articulating to National Media Discourses

People on this "side" of the ongoing conflict at California Elementary felt that our school and district politics articulated to cultural debates—and to an anti-immigration backlash—nation wide. In the words of one teacher,

> I think California has always had a problem with education. Maybe it has to do with the states down here that have the most immigration—Texas, New Mexico, California. We're always trying to figure out how to meet the needs of these kids. Our government doesn't want a lot of immigrants pouring in as we're so close to Mexico. The goal is to keep them out, most of the time. But people come here thinking they're going to have a better life and then they wonder when they feel unwelcome, "What did I do?"

Drawing on national discourses about public education as a tool to level the socioeconomic playing field, another teacher reflected similar sentiments when he said,

> I think a lot of people were wanting to get rid of Affirmative Action. They felt that it was really helping them [Latinos], you know, get ahead. And I guess that really drove people to vote for 227. And then there's the argument, "I did it [English sink or swim], why can't they?" Those people had a lot of advantages over these kids. So they say everyone's equal, and unfortunately I don't believe so. You know these kids start off with a lot of disadvantages. So I don't see how individuals think they can put someone on the same playing field when these kids don't start off with the same opportunities that other kids have.

Hence this teacher, like others, told me that to level the playing field, more Spanish language support than that given in Model A/Model B was needed. And another characterized the anti-immigration theme in the debates over 227 debates over 227 as, "Latino vs. The World, you know like the English-as-first-language population."

It was hard for staff members who were pro-bilingual education not to experience the daily practicalities of 227 policy implementation as an assault on the quality of the academic environment that we had been striving for in the bilingual program. As I've mentioned, the term "chaos" was commonly used. One teacher told the story this way:

> I started here in 1992 teaching bilingual. 227, God it was terrible for me. We got nothing [no curricular guidelines, materials] last year. I had to create something from nothing. I had a bilingual class and in January of last year for 30 days I could not speak Spanish to them, and then after 30 days half of my class signed a waiver so I had a half bilingual, half Model B class. It was

terrible because you were short-changing the bilingual kids because I had to tone down the Spanish. At the beginning of the year certain pro-227 teachers were like, "Oh this is great, my kids are learning so much English, it's amazing." But now we are a year later and they're like, "Oh my God these kids can't read or think for squat!"

Even teachers who retained full bilingual "waivered" classrooms felt that 227 created chaos for them. Amy argued that the push for 227 caused the district to abandon support for the bilingual programs that did survive through the waivers:

> 227 is terrible. There are no directives, just chaos. And bilingual education here is in chaos, too. There are no directives and the district is not supportive of it, it's phasing it out. The parents want bilingual education here, they're filling out waivers. I think that the waiver is the only way to save our kids, but it's getting harder.

One of my own fieldwork journal entries from February, 1999 reflects the confusion that we felt as we implemented these drastic, untried English immersion programs amidst other changes going on:

> Things are basically chaos. Today we were talking at a grade level meeting about integrating the new [California student learning] standards into our grade level curriculum pacing plan, and we do not know if we should do a Spanish/bilingual version as well as an English version, and should we do an interim/temporary immersion version?? Or, how to do it once we decide what to do—and we don't understand how to even decide.

Enrique lamented to me that with so much general confusion about 227, many bilingual teachers misunderstood the intent and the pedagogical differences between the bilingual and the immersion programs. This led to grave injustices done to children, he said.

> Many bilingual teachers are misinterpreting 227. They think that it's some kind of advanced program and that waivering a kid to stay in bilingual ed. is like remediation. They are recommending to parents that the 'bright' kids go to Model A or B, and the low kids stay in bilingual. People don't understand what the bilingual program was aiming for, I guess—two languages, not just one. So people are not recommending correctly what child might do best in what program. People don't understand the difference between bilingual and immersion. So it's not giving the kids placed in immersion all the advantages that they deserve and that they otherwise could have access to. They don't understand the bilingual program and they don't believe in it.

The chaos created by 227 was only compounded by the forces and pressures of other controversial initiatives of the time (mentioned earlier—a new state accountability program, new academic standards, the phasing out of social promotion, and a district leadership crisis). It is easy to see how together these issues could weave what Mora (2002) calls a powerful "policy web"—a set of intersecting directives and forces that made it hard to know what to prioritize or who had the answers, to bring some order to the chaos.

"They Got What They Wanted" but "They Are Still Causing Conflict"

Many people who felt that the environment on campus was chaotic and still hostile to bilingual education and Latinos told me their opinion that the "war" should have ended with the implementation of 227 because its mandate for English immersion (at least theoretically) removed *the* issue in that conflict—the bilingual program. Explained Linda, "The Black teachers don't have anything to complain about now, *they got what they wanted*. We're all using English." But, she said, "some EOs still like to whip up the race politics—I don't know why, we are all doing English!"

Many explained that money, as a fiscal resource and as an expression of value in the community, continued to fuel the race politics. A TA opined, "Some EO people are still complaining. It just has to do with greed, with people wanting what other people have. They just want the bilingual resources." And while we all knew that large sums of money were still spent on materials in Spanish and materials designed specifically for English as a Second Language (ESL), two staff members stated to me that even so, "African American/EO" students benefited from plenty of materials while "Latino/bilingual" students did not receive their deserved share: Said one, "They said that the Spanish kids get everything but what do you mean? You go into the IMC [Instructional Materials Room, where supplementary resources were stored] and everything is in English and I'm like, what are you talking about, what school are *you* going to?" Our Title I coordinator in 2000 told me,

> Teaching English to native speakers is not the same thing as teaching immersion to English Learners, and I think we need special techniques, we need special materials, we need special staff development. We still need specialized everything and I think there's still a bit of that resentment from the EO teachers that we even need those things; that we can say as bilingual educators, "Well, you know, I cannot use those materials with my English Learners. I need such and such and such." You know? I think they resent that because they know we're still buying those materials for our kids, still spending the money.

And in the summer of 2000 another teacher added,

> The teachers who teach the EO kids, I think they think that all the money is going toward the special programs to accommodate the ELLs, whether it be the ESL program and materials that we got, or how the school has done things to change, like there is now a universal ESL time. During 1:00 to 1:40 the entire school teaches ESL. So at first we would hear complaints from the EO teachers. They would ask, "Well what are we supposed to be doing during this time?" Well, my opinion was that those EO students they still need help anyway. They benefit from ESL regardless because their writing is still very poor.

Discourses of culture also still played a role in school community politics post-227. A few of the "Latino/bilingual" school community members cited differences in culture as a cause of continuing strife. A staff member explained it this way:

> I think that there are many, many, many socioeconomic factors that enter into the African American family structure in this community that do not happen in the Latino community, and this causes problems. I think there is a large population of single mothers, it's more rampant in the African American community. And I also think drug use is more, you know, widely used. I think that alcoholism is a problem in both communities but it seems to me that the fact that the African American grandparent is the parent, um, I think that I see people that have come to know the system. You know the Latino community, the immigrants, they come here to work. They really don't, you know, use the social services like welfare.

Almost identically to how school community members spoke in 1996, this staff member draws on the culture of poverty discourses about dysfunctional families (poverty-perpetuating lifestyles passed down family lines), and about withdrawal from the American mainstream ideal of hard work leading to success. A parent of one of my students responded similarly to my question about relations between Black and Latino parents, highlighting the culture of poverty tenet of laziness: "We Latinos are doing well. The Black people don't like us. They don't want to come and work in the meetings. I don't know why. They don't want to get together with Latinos." I responded, "I have heard that some parent meetings and workshops are presented in Spanish with no English translation. Might their lack of involvement have to do with language?" "It doesn't have to do with language," she responded:

> They do a lot of stuff in English and I don't speak English but I come to meetings. It's not language. The school is all of ours. They say we are taking over the school but they don't come. They don't support anything, they

don't help with anything. The administration treats us well, they have good meetings, beautiful meetings. I think we have a great principal now. He listens to us.

I followed with the question, "Do you think Black and Latino children get an equal quality of education here?" "Yes, they all do," she stated, "but they [African American parents] don't want to work as hard. We are out working at jobs, to make $200 a day. They aren't."

A TA also described the ongoing conflict to me as caused by African Americans' refusal to participate in today's ever-more diverse local and national culture. She argued,

There are a lot of Black parents that get upset about the number of Latinos here. But this is a new world, we are living together. If you want to go to an all-Black school you should go look for Martin Luther King. We have to deal with all kinds of people now. Get used to it. This is the real world.

Further Connections to National Media Discourses

These "Latino/bilingual" school community members' constructions of African Americans' cultural dysfunction, lack of participation in school activities, laziness, and even anachronistic segregation-era culture contrasted with their constructions of Latinos' work ethic, up-and-coming socioeconomic status, and participation on campus and in the increasingly diverse American cultural climate. In posing this contrast they articulated their position to powerful media discourses—I described in the preceding media chapter that it was hard to pick up a newspaper, watch the TV news, or listen to the radio from 1998-2000 without finding stories about immigrants making more and more inroads to jobs previously abandoned by American workers, many of whom had been African American. Latino culture(s) and the Spanish language were changing industries, governments, schools, social norms and whole communities small and large. The 2000 census revealed that Latinos surpassed African Americans as the largest minority group in the nation, and that *García* was the most common name of new homeowners in some cities. Latinos were often portrayed as the new "American Dream makers." In drawing on these discourses, these "Latino/bilingual" school community members' arguments could be seen as strategic, performative utterances. They had the effect of freeing "Latino/bilingual" school community members from a role in or responsibility for dynamics at the school that narrowed opportunities for "African American/EO" students and adults. From this perspective the conflict was rationalized as "caused" by "them" because "they" wouldn't "work hard" or assimilate to the new "real world."

Whose Knowledge is of Most Worth?

Now that English for the Children was in effect, there seemed to be an uncertainty for many bilingual and immersion teachers about their worth and their skills. We still used our Spanish language skills with the students in the Model A and Model B classes (though, granted, to a lesser extent than in the bilingual program), and we still used Spanish with the parents. But many teachers felt that their worth was being devalued by the fact that the bilingual teacher stipend was now under attack. At both our school and in the district, people questioned its legitimacy. The teachers' union went into negotiations with the district about the stipend's future, and no one knew how long it might last.

In response, some teachers expressed resentment. More than one put it like this new teacher:

> I think the school and teachers and the district should have to see what is in the best interest of the kids. And for me, I hate to even say it, but the money, too! It bothers me that I'm getting my credential in bilingual, I'm getting BCLAD [Bilingual, Cross-cultural, Language and Academic Development specialist certificate] and I might not get paid for it. So then there is no benefit for me being able to discuss with the parents, write my own letters home. I could just speak to them in English if I wanted. I just feel like I might not get paid for my services.

Other teachers took a "get it while you can" attitude: "I have eight students who are on grade level in English," admitted Linda at a meeting of grade level chairpersons, "but I'm not telling anyone they are ready to redesignate yet [out of ELL status], because then I wouldn't have enough LEP students in my class to get my stipend, and I want it." As other teachers listened to this, some (including me) with wide eyed looks of surprise, she continued, "I'll tell their next year's teacher that they are ready. They can redesignate them. But I want my stipend this year." And so emerged the competing, contradictory motivations for immersion teachers: On the one hand there was the policy pressure to bring students to English fluency as soon as possible. On the other hand there was the competing policy offering financial incentive to maintain students' ELL status long enough to get one's stipend. This "get it while you can" sentiment became very controversial. (I will return to this in the next section.)

Most "Latino/bilingual" teachers I spoke with argued, along with the pro-bilingual education stories in the media, that a major weakness of advocates was that they did not possess the appropriate professional knowledge to decide what instructional policies would meet the needs of ELLs. In the words of one teacher, "The people who felt that 227 was good" were "all English-speaking teachers. They didn't have a bilingual classroom and they didn't know anything about bilingual students and what their needs are." Only a few "Latino/bilingual" teachers even mentioned to me that "African American/EO" teachers might have expertise and materials that could be a resource for teaching English immersion (even though several "African American/EO" teachers had state Language Development Specialist certificates and many years experience teaching ESL). One did mention two EO teachers as colleagues from whom she had learned valuable ESL techniques. These two teachers just happened to be White. Wondering about this, I poked around a bit: I asked if Janice was a teacher such as these, who possessed ESL knowledge this teacher might draw upon. The teacher responded; "No, Janice has Black kids, she never has to transition them." I found it interesting and disturbing that "having Black kids" was meant to signify that one had no knowledge of how to work with ELLs in English. Not only was Janice teaching a mixed EO/*immersion* class that year; she had taught and successfully redesignated ELLs in her EO and modified bilingual classes for many years.

Here we can see that race—both the race of the students and of the teacher—seemed to override program participation as a factor in people's assumptions about the knowledge others had, as well as the value of such knowledge. African American continued to denote EO and vice versa. Even though now more than ever, faculty members of all backgrounds had sets of knowledge and skills that could be useful across programs, race continued to perpetuate the division between those who were seen to be knowledgeable and, therefore, "on one's side."

A Different "Latino/bilingual" Perspective: Proposition 227 Seen as Resolving the Conflict

Among others' talk of attack, chaos, and continuing conflict, a rare few "Latino/bilingual" school community members presented me with a different picture of the post-227 terrain. They portrayed the lines between racial-linguistic communities on campus as dissolving: Out of all the people I spoke with over those 2 years, six on this "side" told me at one point or another that they thought English for the Children resolved the "war" of 1996. With one stroke of the policy pen, they told me, the focus on English changed division and exclusion to unity and inclusion on our campus, and improved "Latino/bilingual" students' attainment of English.

Interestingly, three of these six people were White. For her part, Linda argued that, quite simply, "English, English, English has us all in the same boat and we get along better now because of that." Showing a change of heart in her policy stance (she had been a vociferous advocate for bilingual education pre-227), she even maintained at one point that the teachers who still had waivered bilingual classes were "doing a disservice" to the students by going against the direction of the rest of the school, district and state. Andrea (who didn't want me to do research at the school in 1998 because she didn't want me to document ongoing conflict) explained the shift towards English as encouraging a mending of fences:

> There was a push in the past to hire bilingual staff members, and that caused problems. But now we're hiring everybody, despite their language abilities. We still need bilingual teachers, but we also need teachers who are good monolingual English teachers. I have personally hired a number of good African American teachers. I think many of the people who were disgruntled racially have gotten to know each other better. They can see we're moving in a positive direction, that we are including all people.

The third White school community member who maintained that conflict had diminished said that it did so because, given new data showing gains in ELLs' test scores, her "Latino/bilingual" colleagues could no longer justify an argument to save bilingual education. She said,

> I believe in bilingual education when it's done right. I've taught transition [bilingual] classes, but I don't think that the way the district has done it has been done well. I think that [the implementation of 227] went really well. When the Stanford 9 results came back [from last year, our first year of 227] and we had higher scores, I think that shut a lot of people up because they really couldn't argue with the fact that students were performing better. Kids are learning English now. I don't hear a lot about bilingual education anymore.

These staff members who told me that 227 was good for the school as a whole shared a similar evaluation of the English immersion program in their classroom—two teachers even used exactly the same words to answer my question, "How is 227 going in your classroom?" They said, "Oh my God, my kids are learning so much English! I'm so surprised!" Seeing that their students did not fall apart in an immersion setting as some had predicted was proof enough, they told me, that English immersion was OK, maybe even better than bilingual education. And another colleague confided, "My kids are learning so much English! I guess we weren't expecting enough of them in bilingual education! Now I see the EO point of view—just teach English and they learn!" (I wondered if these teachers ever taught ESL in their *bi*lingual classrooms, where the policy goal was to build and utilize first language literacy in order to transition students into EO classrooms.) And even as Enrique maintained that race and language divisions still existed at California Elementary, he made a point about the dynamics of cultural citizenship, suggesting that some of the tensions might have lessened because 227 redistributed voice, value, and access to the power structure to the "African American/EO" community. He reflected, "227 was almost like a safety valve. By its passing it relieved a lot of the aggression from the people who were fighting the bilingual program. So they were kind of like, 'Whew! Now we're winning.' "

With these varying experiences and constructions of the impact of Proposition 227 came varying agendas for how to serve our children better and how to realize full cultural citizenship for the adults on campus.

One "Latino/bilingual" Policy Agenda: Save Bilingual Education

Of the "Latino/bilingual" school community members who characterized 227 as a destructive policy development, and the "war" as ongoing, several upheld the call to save bilingual education. They articulated their stance to pro-bilingual education discourses in the media. They stressed the need for students to be successful participants in an increasingly diverse world, and the need to save them from the xenophobic, anti-immigrant English Only backlash movement. They also maintained their support for the research behind, and their own experiences in, effective bilingual programs.

Teachers who still hoped to save bilingual education were clear that the effort now depended on individuals willing to swim against the powerful English immersion tide. While the administration provided parents basic information on all of their programmatic options, it was individual teachers who spoke with individual parents about their recommendations for particular students. One teacher put it this way:

> There are a few teachers who really know what they're doing and who have successful programs and who were able to convince—that is, professionally advise—parents that it would be good for their children to keep them in bilingual ed. for the rest of their primary education. So there are still a good number of classes that will be fully bilingual and that actually will probably do well.

Amy told her own story of resistance this way: She actively sought out parents to discuss the benefits of a waiver because,

> I think bilingual education's great. I was involved with the anti-227 and the anti-187 and -209 efforts in LA. It's all so scary. The parents want bilingual education here, they're filling out waivers. My whole class is waivered. I think that the waiver is the only way to save our kids. I am protecting them,

keeping them ahead. They will get ahead in this multilingual world with bilingual education. My kids are doing great.

It was not just people opposed to English immersion who championed bilingual education, however. One of the Latino teachers mentioned in the previous section who shared his opinion that 227 had had a positive effect on the community actually espoused a paradoxically pro-bilingual education agenda for the future. He said that, were he to have things his way, he would "reinstate more bilingual education" because it would offer a counterforce to dynamics of anti-Latino racism which he saw as undergirding the English Only movement. In this instance, we may be seeing another moment when the "Black-Brown" aspect of community tensions became more salient than the "EO-bilingual" aspect. Bilingual education as a social agenda for Latinos was accorded more weight than the unifying force of English immersion as an instructional policy. Again, we see the context shaping the ways in which this dynamic plays out: In the local context this teacher saw 227 as a positive policy force, and he praised it. At the same time, within the national context he advocated for bilingual education as a political counter to racism. The fact that there were some White teachers within the "Latino/bilingual" "side" of the debate who felt that 227 was a good thing but who did *not* harbor a future agenda for bilingual education may speak to the general remove that White staff members still inhabited in the community. They did not feel connected to the "Black-Brown" aspect of community tensions and so easily disconnected from the Latino-oriented social agenda aspect of a pro-bilingual education stance.

Another "Latino/bilingual" Policy Agenda: Stick With English Immersion

For the few who argued that English for the Children ended the "war" at California Elementary, the answer to my question, "If you could dictate our language education policy in the future, what would you do?" was clear: continue with English immersion. These people explained their support for this agenda in strikingly similar, simple terms: In the words of one, since immersion students were "learning so much English" and 227 was "the way everybody's going," we "should just stick with it."

"AFRICAN AMERICAN/EO" PERSPECTIVES ON PROPOSITION 227

"African American/EO" school community members painted a varied picture of the post-227 terrain, like their "Latino/bilingual" counterparts.

Most maintained that the 1996 "war" still raged, and they generally cited the following points of contention: a lack of concern for, respect for, and resources for "African American/EO" children and adults; "cheating" in the implementation of the 227 policy to the detriment of "African Americans/EOs"; racism; and unfair moves to maintain money and power by "Latinos/bilinguals." However, a few school community members on this "side" had a very different opinion of politics in the era of 227: These few characterized the coming of 227 as largely resolving the "war" of previous years. I explore both perspectives in the following sections.

Things are "Still the Same" Under Proposition 227: The "War" Continues

Most "African American/EO" school community members that I spoke with at this time shared with me the opinion that "things are still the same": there was great division on our campus. The major reason cited for continued conflict was a lack of concern for, respect for, and resources for Black children and adults. Proof enough, they argued, was the fact that "African-"Latino/bilingual" counterparts on high stakes academic assessments without producing a major campus uproar. On many occasions, I heard stories similar to this teacher's:

> I have heard, I'm not going to say only from Latino teachers or white teachers, but from teachers, that they don't think there's a problem, um, they see that, [sighs] it's hard to say. [sighs] For example, the Stanford 9. They see that the Hispanic kids are scoring higher than the Black kids. And it was asked, "Do you really think it's a problem?" And this person said they really didn't think it was a problem. I'm serious, Kim. I'm not going to even tell you who said it but I heard it. It's awful. They don't see it. And they're in a position of leadership, Kim, they set the tone. It's awful.

The achievement gap between African American and Latino students at California Elementary was of concern to the district. As mentioned earlier, a finding of the school's PQR in 1999 was the need to narrow this gap. Our African American students were scoring much lower on the Stanford 9 test than were our Latino students who transitioned from bilingual or immersion classes into EO classes; and our bilingual program students were scoring high on the Aprenda (Spanish-language standardized test), while our Latino students who were transitioning from bilingual or immersion classes into EO were scoring in the 60th and 70th percentile; and our bilingual program students were scoring high on the Aprenda (Spanish-language standardized test). From my perspective as a teacher at the school, I perceived that addressing this issue was not a priority of the school administration—we never addressed it as a whole school community, in a coordinated fashion, or with any urgency.

The academic achievement of "African American/EO" students was not the only aspect of their growth with which people were concerned. Many charged that African American students were culturally marginalized at our school. For example, in February of 1999 Michael shared with me his objections to how students were grouped on tracks in the year-round schedule:

> The majority of the Black children are on one track, track A, which doesn't make sense to me. Not only am I going to say it looks bad, it is bad. I mean, this is Black History Month. When we're talking about the Black heritage, they're off-track! So who's listening? I must admit that I felt, I feel this now too, it seems there is much more emphasis on bilingual education as opposed to EO education because the majority of the school is Hispanic.

Janice told me, "I have tons of materials on African American History Month and Kwanzaa that I put in people's boxes. No one asks me about it. No one even uses it." And another teacher stated,

> We're still dealing with racial issues. I've heard bilingual teachers say that they don't want to teach "those kids," "those" African American kids. They're scared. It's racism any day of the week but people don't want to address it. It's just too hot of an issue and people might get a chance to vent their frustrations and then what? Our administrators have steered away from it because it is still seen as a hot button issue—you're going to scratch the surface of it and aaaaah [sarcastically]!

Regarding adults on campus, a few people pointed out to me that just looking at our administration told the story: Our principal and vice principal were known to be very pro-bilingual (they were both White), and after Roslyn left our Title I and bilingual coordinators were Latino. Experiences of personal and professional marginalization and disregard were plentiful. Eleanor told me that the principal set the tone for this. She recalled,

> [The principal] did not speak to us in the hall. I questioned him about this, I brought it to his attention and he has tried to be better but it's not right. And some Latino teachers only started speaking to us around Christmas but their looks are like, 'What are you doing here? You don't need to be here.'

And, she continued,

> I have asked for supplies before but they won't give me the key to the supply room. But they have these kids who come in off the street [high school

students who are "off-track" who do volunteer work for the office staff] who they don't *know* and they give *them* the key. Enrique once would not give me the keys, he asked [a Latino TA] to take me up to the room. It's like, I don't want this stuff! What is it that you are trying to keep away from somebody? California Elementary has never been this way. This is not California Elementary. It's not supposed to be this way, we are all grown-up and supposed to be professional, we're supposed to love the kids. It's still like, "The more Hispanics we get in here the better it's going to be for us." You [referring to herself] don't say anything because you really don't have a *word*, but [voice trails off, looks away, does not continue].

A school security aide told me this story: She explained that the several-person campus security staff had only two Black members, herself and one other. When she recently asked the vice principal about the next security staff meeting, "She told me that *we* did not have to attend. Aren't we part of the team? Don't I sit at the door and help keep the school safe?" She went on to give examples of times that she and the other Black security staff member had actually prevented security breaches, as well as times when particular Latino security staff members had not been present to help prevent them. Then she reflected, "That's discrimination to me." Another teacher added her perception that "African American/EO" people were not even part *of* the community:

You know, when I walk into the cafeteria and they're speaking in English they switch to Spanish and stuff like that. I mean, you feel neglected. You feel like what you say isn't important. You don't feel *a part of*.

In my field notes in June, 2000 I reflected on feeling this dynamic:

We had the Juneteenth celebration on the 17th. I noticed Monday morning during the assembly announcements [held each Monday, the whole school is present], that the principal only mentioned it briefly, saying that if students did not know what Juneteenth was they "should ask their teachers." That was it. He did not say anything about why it was important or anything. And our "celebration" was only a pot luck lunch for the staff. No school wide program or celebration for students and parents. At the Cinco de Mayo celebration, which was huge and for *everybody*, we had a review of the history and why it was important at the beginning of the program. For Juneteenth it was up to individual teachers to address the topic in class. The students—we all—got short changed.

Parent representation and inclusion had been a challenge for California Elementary since I had first worked there. The task of meeting everyone's language needs, for instance, always had to be carefully planned. Our bilingual coordinator told me the following story in 1999, which to me crystallized the "African American/EO" side's argument that Black school community members were systematically denied full cultural citizenship. Several months earlier, he told me, the district sent representatives to the campus to run a parent training institute. The principal was on vacation that week, and "he had not told any of the other administrators that the meeting was scheduled. So all of a sudden that morning the auditorium was filled with parents and it was crazy." He (the bilingual coordinator) was sent on a run to procure some refreshments and then to represent the building administration at the institute. The presenters began speaking in Spanish, and African American parents asked what they were supposed to do to understand. The presenters responded "by telling them to go to *the back* of the auditorium where they could receive translation." The "translator" ended up being just one of the bilingual parents who happened to be in attendance (this person had not come prepared to translate). People were furious and left. At the next institute the presenters tried to compensate for their blunder by moving the African American parents to the front, which, in the California Elementary auditorium meant up on the stage— *behind* the curtain. Since then, the coordinator told me, "not a single African American parent has come back for a parent institute."

These kinds of experiences led to pressure from some to rethink the way the administration provided for parent representation in community life: Just like in 1996, the race of the school's official parent representative became an issue. The school's LEARN Council (as described in the earlier chapter, the LEARN Council was an important decision-making committee) had the power to hire a parent to coordinate trainings and meetings for the community. The makeup of the Council varied depending on which tracks were "on" and which were "off" (on vacation) at any given time, but a typical roster (from March, 1999) included seven teachers— three Latino, one Black, and three White (including Linda); one classified employee representative (African American, Michael); 2 parent members, both Latina; and the (White) principal. From the perspective of language education programs, two of the staff members on the council were associated with the EO program, five were associated with the bilingual and/or English immersion programs, and the principal was widely considered to favor bilingual education.

Some members of the LEARN council felt that having one parent representative was sufficient. The current parent representative was a Latina, and they argued that she could effectively reach out to both communities, Latino and Black. Yet some members, the most vocal of whom was Michael, felt that two representatives were necessary, one to reach out to each community. For months the Council was deadlocked. By May of 2000, when the council still could not come to consensus, they postponed the discussion. "It looks like we will just keep [the current Latina representative], for now," one member told me. "We will just talk to her to make sure she tries to reach out to everybody." Michael and others expressed doubt that this would ever happen.

In addition to these perceptions of racism, lack of concern for the academic and social growth of "African American/EO" students, and lack of regard for "African American/EO" adults, many charged "Latino/bilingual" school community members with blatant bias—even cheating—in the implementation of the Proposition 227 policy mandate. Mary explained the cheating in terms of bilingual teachers improperly "advocating" (not "professionally advising") parents about the bilingual program waivers, in order to retain their stipends, and she simultaneously raised the issue of concern for her own material well-being:

> I have spoken to teachers who are not bilingual teachers and they are very angry. Proposition 227 is not being implemented. I am angry that several people who, although they were told not to coerce their parents, they did so anyway. They just want to keep their bilingual benefits. They persuaded the parents to do the alternative, the waiver. I think it is a disservice to the children because a lot of those children are speaking English very well. My feeling is, I'll do anything to help a kid. But when it hinges on the fact that I'm not going to have a job because there are only bilingual positions, then you are messing with my livelihood.

Another charge of "policy abuse" surfaced in questions about the use of Spanish in immersion classrooms. Enrique told me at one point that even though he thought he had made everyone aware of the sanctioned (limited) use of students' first language in the immersion models, "They still asked me, 'Why are people still using Spanish with the kids? Isn't that illegal now? We have 227 and we should be teaching in English. Why are people cheating?' " A teacher expressed it this way:

> I think that the reason 227 isn't helping the politics here is because teachers like yourself might be implementing it, Kim, but I don't think that everyone is implementing it. I think they're still teaching in Spanish. I was never really in a class where that bilingual stuff was going on. I don't know what you guys were doing. I don't know if you were teaching in Spanish all day long, half the day, part of the day, I don't know. But my partner teacher next door I *still* hear him all the time speaking in Spanish! He's writing in Spanish, the kids are speaking to him in Spanish. If he's doing it behind closed doors I think other teachers are doing it behind closed doors.

The partner teacher she was referring to had a waivered bilingual class that year. But in the early days things were so chaotic that it really was hard for anyone to tell who was doing what, who should be doing what, and hence who might be doing something against 227 policy.

Another "abuse of policy" that I heard about on more than one occasion from Janice was the perceived refusal of the bilingual coordinator to process the paperwork to officially redesignate students from Limited English Proficient to RFEP. In early spring, 2000 I was working in my role as standards based assessment coordinator, helping teachers prepare for the district's upcoming performance assessments. We had to confirm which students were and were not ELLs, as only students fluent in English were mandated to take the test. Janice pointed out students on her roster whom I had not considered eligible for the test because our database indicated they were ELL. She said that she had told Enrique that those students needed to be reclassified in the school's database but, "It's a joke. These kids have *been* redesignated. I have been waiting since last year for them to change this. It's a joke." And at another performance assessment preparation meeting, three EO teachers and I sat, shocked, listening to Linda basically confirm suspicions that there was an intentional dragging of feet in the process of redesignating ELLs to RFEP. As quoted earlier in this chapter, she exclaimed that she would not report the fact that she had students ready to redesignate because she wanted to maintain enough ELLs on her roster to receive her bilingual stipend.

Such an "abuse" of sound instructional practice led many to perceive a blatant neglect of the instructional needs of "African American/EO" students. Elizabeth shared with me at one point that,

> EO teachers are on fire! Racial tensions have not gone away. Black students are still treated totally differently, and Latino kids are still favored. For *years* we [EO teachers] pleaded with the administration to get us phonics materials and they never did. Well, now with 227, now that *Latino* kids have to learn English, we're getting more phonics books than we know what to do with. The Black kids weren't important enough on their own to buy it for. And then when you go to the upper grades many of our EOs just aren't reading on grade level. So what happens is you lump them in with the kids who are just learning English, using their story books, using their phonics books, and we really don't know if it meets the needs of the EO kids. But that's what we do because that's the resources we have.

Looking at budget figures proposed for 2000–2001, one could see this discrepancy in numbers. While huge sums of money—many tens of thousands of dollars—were allocated for instructional resources for school wide use (for example, the phonics materials mentioned above) or specifically for ELLs (ESL materials), only $3,000 were set aside for material specifically geared to EO students (the Proficiency in English Program, a language development program for speakers of nonstandard English). While "African American/EO" students were certainly a smaller percentage of the student body than "Latino/bilingual" students, this extreme monetary discrepancy reinforced the opinion held by many that Black students were still undervalued and underserved.

Whose Knowledge is of Most Worth?

Unequal compensation for adults was also an issue, just as it was in 1996. Many people expressed feelings ranging from disappointment to anger and resentment that the knowledge and skills of "African American/EO" staff members were not perceived as valued—financially or professionally. That teachers in Model A and Model B classrooms still received hefty bilingual stipends was a huge point of contention. And further, the ESL skills of many EO teachers were considered to be undervalued. Many "African American/EO" teachers had a California Language Development Specialist (LDS) certificate, recognizing their training in teaching ESL in the mainstream English classroom. Elizabeth explained,

> Now that we have 227, you would think that there would be an emphasis on people with skills to teach ESL. But no, the LDS certificate is hardly worth anything now. They took our LDS stipend. It used to be $2,500, now I think it's $750. But the bilingual stipend is still in place [$5,000]. Kim, you have your immersion class because you are bilingual. I have my class, all transitioned kids, because I have an LDS, but I am not compensated for it. I mean not that you would do anything different in the one class from the other basically, but the one stipend is still in place and the other is not. When 227 came you had bilingual teachers who said, "I don't know how to teach English. I don't know how to teach reading in English." As if it was a foreign thing!

I told Elizabeth that I had also heard this from some teachers. We wondered out loud together whether they had ever taught anything in English in their *bi*lingual classes. Hearing this admission from bilingual teachers was all the more frustrating to EO teachers because their expertise was not tapped. Said Janice,

> None of the bilingual teachers have come to me asking for help, even though they know I have been teaching *English* Language Arts for 20 years. I have a million supplies, and now they need us because we have the expertise, but they're not coming to ask.

When it came time to "do the matrix" (when teachers select which grade level and track they will teach the following school year), this perceived mismatch of value to skills rose to the surface again--just like in 1996. In April of 1999, I wrote in my field notes,

We did the matrix for next year today. There were all kinds of crazy class makeups, many classes a mixture of Model A, Model B, bilingual and EO! So the qualifications were confusing—did you need a BCLAD? LDS? [One teacher] did not know which classes she was qualified to teach, and she kept asking questions. It ended up that she couldn't get what she wanted because she did not have a BCLAD. [A few "African American/EO" teachers] sat behind me and kept making comments quietly about how experience should count in class selection, not language ability.

Mary explained it to me this way:

I'm not against bilingual education by any stretch of the imagination and I disagree with 227 but I think there are times when we need it. The reason that bilingual education failed, you know, quote unquote "failed"—and I don't think it failed completely, but broke down—is because we did not have the proper teachers teaching ESL. The people who were teaching ESL were teaching with a Spanish, or Armenian, or Korean accent. In linguistics, we know that all the inflections that go along with phonemic awareness of the language are lost because they don't know it themselves. And I went into a lot of classes in our school where the people who were teaching learned English as a second language themselves, and they had things that were on the board wrong, dramatically, spelling and everything else. I am an English major and a sociology major, a double major, and I minored in education. So I know English. I speak it properly, but am I valued? No. I don't want to see this bilingual program pull everybody apart again. You know, it could! Some people are very angry.

And Elizabeth shared,

I took Spanish in high school and college. I never really held onto it, though, and then I started working here. They needed bilingual teachers and I wasn't, but they gave me a bilingual and multi-grade classroom anyway. So you pick it up. Then I was teamed up with a person who was bilingual and we started planning together and it got to the point where I wanted a bilingual class. By then I had taken two more years of Spanish at the college. I wanted to be in the bilingual classrooms so I could use what I learned and become proficient at it. And then I was denied because someone else was Level A [the district's desired fluency level to teach in a bilingual classroom]. I was *denied*. And since then I haven't taken one more class of Spanish. You know, when they needed me it was okay but then when I wanted it and they didn't need me, too bad. That used to anger us. Your skills that once were valuable, now they didn't have any value.

Reflecting on the value of the experience and expertise of EO teachers as it could have been with 227, the principal told me:

I think if 227 had passed the way a lot of people thought, we would be teaching everything in English, and instead of separate classes you'd have everybody together. It would be integrated. If that had happened we'd be like one school. But because it didn't we still have the matrix and everything, and I don't know, there's probably a certain amount of prestige in being bilingual, you get paid more and you get first choice in the matrix, and so there should be prestige attached to the teachers that can work with the predominant EO classroom and manage those students and make them learn and deal with discipline and all that, and that is harder. And there are teachers who can do it wonderfully. And I think if the school had gone with 227 the way people thought, then they probably would be recognized. And I think people don't want to talk about that. You know you say something like that and you're in danger of being branded a racist. But its true.

So we see again that there was disagreement across "sides" of this conflict about what sets of professional knowledge and skills were needed in this post-227 environment, and which should have been highly valued. Now more than ever, faculty members across the school community had--and needed—sets of knowledge and skills and materials that were useful across language education programs. However, because of the volatility of the race divisions embedded in the conflict there was reticence to address publicly our need to collaborate across programs. Certain discrepancies in monetary compensation were controlled by forces outside the school (e.g., district and state policy on bilingual stipends), but other dynamics were in the purview of local actors, and might have been addressed head on to increase collaboration. For example, there could have been professional learning opportunities scheduled to share the high levels of expertise in ESL and language acquisition techniques that faculty on both "sides" of the constructed line of division possessed. The recognition of each others' skills and shared participation in each others' professional learning—not to mention an opportunity to discuss openly the issue of racial tensions— might have gone a long way towards nurturing collaboration and cultural citizenship across the community.

Articulating to National Media Discourses

Often when describing these dynamics to me, people echoed particular discourses from the national media: immigration, Latinos, and the Spanish language were constructed as creating division and inequity in the government, in social services, and in American culture. America was constructed as an English-speaking, assimilationist melting pot. People employed discourses about a Latino "invasion" changing the face of

America. They echoed discourses about the Spanish language and Latino culture(s) tilting the landscape of social services and resources away from "Americans" and towards immigrants. They articulated media discourses about Los Angeles becoming "Latino-ized," causing racial strife and inequality that had to be addressed for the institution of public education to fulfill its charge of providing all with a quality education.

Sitting with me on the playground benches one day after school, an African American parent told me about how his daughter had to enroll at a neighboring school instead of California Elementary because of over-enrollment. This caused his family transportation and schedule difficulties, he told me, and it was due in large part to the continuing explosion of Latino immigration to the area. "Mexicans are taking over," he said,

> and the United States is not dealing with the issues. They are throwing it up under the table. They don't see it because all our assemblymen are Latin. It is a Latin machine that is winning, that is pushing forward regardless of what anybody else says.

And Mary explained it this way:

> Kim, if you are a bilingual teacher you don't understand the position that we're going through because we are being discriminated against. Look, I had to do things in English and Spanish in my modified bilingual class [before 227]. I had a modified class for a few years and my work was doubled, too, like yours. Yet I was discriminated against in my own country because I didn't speak the language [Spanish]. And even though those kids are doing well now in fourth and fifth grade, I didn't get the accolades like, "You're doing such a good job." It's a very bitter pill. And I get really irked when during an assembly I see teachers talking to each other during the Pledge of Allegiance. We are teaching the kids to respect this country because this country is giving them a free education. And then you have these teachers who don't care, they got their free education and some of them refused to become citizens and they are living off this country. Go back to your own country, then, live off their money! A lot of people who came here from Europe were not literate and they still managed to fall into the fold of the country. The problem is, the influx of Mexicans.

And, interestingly, several people summarized the post-227 politics in terms almost identical to some of their "Latino/bilingual" counterparts: "They got what they wanted." This teacher sounded like others when she charged, "All in all, the bilinguals, they can't complain anymore. We have all been forced to go all English, none of us have a choice, and they're still favored *so they still get what they want.*"

Another "African American/EO" Perspective: Proposition 227 Seen as Resolving the Conflict

Also like some "Latino/bilingual" school community members, a rare few "African American/EO" school community members provided a different version of campus dynamics at this time. These people portrayed the warring factions of the mid-1990s as having reached a truce. However, there were fewer of these views than amongst "Latinos/bilinguals"—only three people on the "African Americans/EO" "side" ever told me that they thought the "war" had subsided. Of these people, two were White and one was African American. And among these three, two argued at *other* points in time that the "war" actually still raged. The one teacher who argued that the situation and the solution were simple was White. He explained,

> I think the school going English can't help but bring us together. We're all getting English materials, even just that. We have a common goal of getting all kids to read. We had that as a common goal before, but just not having a language barrier, like, "I'm EO, you're Spanish," it softens the line between the groups.

The other two teachers constructed the situation in more complex terms: Elizabeth shared that there was definitely still discord. But,

> I think that 227 really stopped some of the divisiveness because now we are all together. [And] it's made my job easier. Before it was the African American kids here [gestures to the left] and the Hispanic kids here [gestures to the right], but now with so much redesignation they're all mixed together by the time they get to the upper grades and it's just everybody. As someone who has worked on redesignation for years, I have seen a big improvement in the writing that the kids [who are redesignating] come with. And their oral skills are so much better. I have even had teachers come to me and show me a second grader's writing and they say, "Do you think they are ready?" And I say "Oh my goodness yes." Now we see that the focus should be on redesignating kids in the primary grades. They are ready to go.

And in the same interview where Michael argued that things were "still the same," that is, that the "war" still raged on, he also reflected that,

> Racial politics here have quieted down because we are so busy with all these changes that we're too busy to fight! If I had known the chaos 227 would cause at this school, I would not have voted for it.

He also pointed out to me that with so many new teachers (turnover was high at California Elementary), there were fewer and fewer people around who even remembered the debates of 1996.

Perhaps the fact that two of these three people who portrayed the conflict as "over" were White, may follow something that potentially was emerging among "Latino/bilingual" school community members—Whiteness allowed a kind of passive refusal to recognize enduring contention over Black-Latino inequity beneath the perceived surface harmony, and an excused absence from a responsibility to address the patterns.

Given these varying experiences and constructions of the post-227 political terrain came varying opinions about how we could better serve all of our children and realize full cultural citizenship for all the adults on campus.

One "African American/EO" Policy Agenda: The Continued Call for English Only

Just as in 1996, and just like many on the "Latino/bilingual" "side," in the post-227 years many "African American/EO" school community members presented fractured policy agendas for the future. Some continued to argue for universal monolingual English instruction, substantiating their position with discourses common in media debates. They talked about creating a level playing field, and fairness and equity as the mission of public education. They placed this agenda within the national context of an America where English is the valued linguistic capital.

Yet this argument was now more complex than the EO argument in the pre-227 days. As much as people continued to argue that English was the linguistic capital that schools should be imparting to children in America, this stance seemed to soften. Now they granted that fairness and equity could be upheld if there was limited bilingual instruction, as long as it was not placed in *competition* with EO—as long as Spanish/Latinos/bilinguals didn't take away from the resources and value of English/African Americans. For example, one staff member explained that bilingual education wouldn't be so bad if it did not rob Black children dollar-for-dollar of a good education. She explained her pro-227 vote this way:

> I know the bilingual program was successful. For that reason I voted for 227, because I don't think it was fair that a successful program was being used on Latinos but no program was being used on African Americans. If African Americans are going to get a crappy education, everyone is going to get a crappy education.

Put another way, a staff member explained to me,

> I'm not against bilingual education so long as it doesn't take away from EOs. The Spanish people, they don't really do anything to support our people

and yet they ask us to support them. I think we're in America and we should speak English. People should teach in English.

From this perspective EO was the preferred way to go. However it was grudgingly acknowledged that this preferred agenda could also share space—equally—with agendas championing a more diverse linguistic landscape.

Another "African American/EO" Policy Agenda: The Continued Call for a Dual Immersion Bilingual Program

The internally contradictory policy agenda—arguing simultaneously for EO and for universal bilingual education—endured at California Elementary in the post-227 era. Arguments for dual immersion bilingual education for all students were articulated to national media discourses about fairness, equity and a level playing field, as were arguments for teaching only English. But arguments for dual immersion were placed within the context of a multilingual, diverse, and global Los Angeles. When I asked one TA a question about the current state of the 1996 "war," he responded,

> It's not going on as much as before, but it's still here. There are still times that people are fixin' to go to blows. I don't see why the Black kids can't learn Spanish. Every time you go for a job in this area, in this city, the first thing they ask you after your name is, "Are you bilingual? Do you speak Spanish?" So the Black kids who don't learn Spanish lose out. Why can't we just teach everybody both? We still want it. The kids have to learn Spanish to go places and do things.

Eleanor confirmed this, saying,

> Let's face it. Hispanics are here, they're going to be here. Their language is going to be a part, so why not? Why not make it a requirement for everyone that when you go to the sixth, seventh grade, everyone learn Spanish?

And a parent connected universal bilingualism to communal respect, caring and opportunity when he stated,

> I think it's wonderful, really, to learn it at a younger age. There is no hatred among babies. You have to remember the Golden Rule: Treat others how you would want to be treated. Yes, bilingual and English, it is a learning tool on both aspects of the pendulum. It is great to be bilingual and to understand what is being said. [Then] we won't feel inferior or insecure. I agree that Spanish should be shared among non-Spanish-speaking students and

that if it's spoken in the house the parents should try to speak English. It's a two-fold situation.

These perspectives bring to mind again, as they did in the earlier phase of my research, Gilroy's (1987) and Hall's (1988) point that social collectivities (interpretive communities) in struggle often negotiate the contingencies of multiple social and material contexts, and as such have multiple—even contradictory—policy agendas: They have both the interest of advancing and improving their position within a certain context—that is, of forwarding the agenda that everyone should learn English, and only English, in America. They also have the interest of not losing their place within another context—that is, of forwarding the agenda that everyone at California Elementary should learn Spanish and English because bilingualism is an increasingly valued local competence.

Further Articulations to National Media Discourses

At this point I also saw an interesting shift in the relationship between micro and macro, local and national discourses. In the mid-1990s,"African American/EO" school community members who argued for dual language bilingual education directly challenged the dominant national media construction of a monolingual English America. When they argued for bilingual education for *African Americans* they reluctantly embraced the increasingly multilingual local ethnoscape of Los Angeles. They drew legitimacy for their pro-bilingual positions from a local context that was in direct contrast to the prevailing popular ideal of a monolingual nation.

By 1998-2000, "African American/EO" school community members could still draw on the deep reservoir of anti-bilingual education media discourses that painted the United States as a traditionally monolingual English, melting pot nation. This lent legitimacy to their continuing EO agenda, and invested in the cultural capital identified with the African American students—English. However, this construction of the sociolinguistic parameters of the American community now sat in competition with the increasingly ubiquitous media reports and popular debates about "Amexica," the "American nation with an identity crisis"—shifting demographics, changing linguistic norms, and multiculturalism ("Welcome to Amexica," 2001). America sat increasingly at the nexus of an interconnected, multilingual world, and effects of this were felt in communities everywhere. The increasingly valued competencies in *this* America were cultural and linguistic fluidity. As such, even continuing EO advocates now ceded a wary acceptance of the importance of bilingualism, and hence of bilingual education alongside EO—as long as it did not slice into the piece of the pie that was the rightful resources of "African Americans/EOs." Moreover, continuing proponents of universal bilingual education could now connect directly to widely-circulated constructions of the American nation as a global nation.

Woolard and Schiefflelin (1994) ask the following question about the co-constructed nature of political discourses in local and national contexts: How does the "constant acting in view of the system" done at local sites "alter the system itself" (p. 16), and to what effects? I believe that my research highlights a dynamic interchange between the local and national sociopolitical contexts, with national discourses reflecting dynamics at local sites as well as local discourses actively drawing on the national: It seemed that the national consciousness and media discourses had, in a way, caught up with the politics at California Elementary: By 1998, a call for universal bilingual education to address issues of changing demographics and changing requirements in the job market, was no longer an odd-ball local case or a bellwether of coming demographic trends. The trends had arrived. The "face of America was changing," and this was reported on and talked about in more and more communities nationwide. So when actors at the state and national level proposed policy agendas such as Ron Unz did in attempting to dismantle bilingual education in California, or such as the Republican Party did when they began to actively court Latino voters, this could be understood as reacting to dynamics both local and national: These popular policy agendas could be seen as both a reaction to the ever-more numerous local shifts in demographics and dynamics, and as forces that shaped dynamics in the local settings.

So far the dynamics I have discussed in this post-227 policy environment have revolved around the ways most people still described the ongoing conflict to me—that is, the "Latino/bilingual" and "African American/EO" "sides." But just like in 1996, I had to look further than these dichotomous descriptions—however true they were in certain senses, and however useful they indeed were for understanding what was going on—in order to get to another layer of complexity. As I asked in the earlier phase of the research, I now continued to ask, Where do White people, and where does Whiteness, fit into this "Black-Brown conflict?"

WHITE PEOPLE, WHITENESS, ME

Although in 1998–2000 White people comprised 21% of the adults on campus (including myself and the principal, vice principal, and new bilingual coordinator), we were still strangely unacknowledged as a group in most descriptions of the conflict.

When I asked Latino and African American school community members how White people fit into the politics on campus, they usually responded in ways very similar to 1996—with either one extreme of *they don't fit in, they're withdrawn*; or the other extreme of *they see both sides; they try to help everybody*. For example, one TA told me, "You [looking at me] can see both sides. You don't choose anybody over anybody. I mean even within Latinos, some of us can't even get along with some of us. That's depressing."

When I asked White people themselves where White people fit into the stories they told me, most said quite flatly something like, "I don't know," or they engaged the same kind of avoidance discourses they did in 1996—those of neutrality, color blindness, and claims to removed rationality and naiveté. For example, just after Elizabeth described to me how she and other EO teachers were "on fire" about racial inequity at the school, she explained to me when I asked what it was like being White in this conflict, that actually she was not part of it at all: "I don't really know, I try to stay out of things. I don't really know this underlying thing you are referring to." After telling me how active she was in statewide campaigns against Propositions 187, 209 and 227, Amy responded to my question about what it was like to be White within these dynamics by claiming remove: "227 and bilingualism don't really affect me. Being White is actually an advantage, the politics here don't affect me at all." Another teacher, an EO teacher, characterized himself as calm and rational, as opposed to African Americans. He then implicitly acknowledged historical racial oppression, but excused himself from complicity:

> I think that when I first got here in 1996 there was tension. Fighting. I mean I never felt it, I always had the materials that I needed, plus I'm just flexible, I go with the flow. I'm not one to say, "I need this!" I don't like to cause conflict. I would hear the TAs talking, saying bad things about the administration, and I would say, "I'm sick of this." I don't know, but if you're a minority in the school, check the numbers, the majority usually takes priority. I tend to get along with everyone. I don't oppress anyone or appear to be oppressive, you know what I mean.

Claiming to be above racial divisions, another White teacher told me that while there was still some lingering tension on campus,

> I tend to cross over where there are probably barriers and just ignore them. I think it's hilarious that they chose me, the one White bilingual teacher from New Jersey, to teach Latino children to sing Negro spirituals in the Black History play.

When Linda and I discussed the disastrous parent institutes that led many Black parents to refuse to return to campus, she shrugged her shoulders and stated:

> African Americans know how ditzy White people are when it comes to race relations, they are used to it, so what we should do is go to them and just admit we do not know how this stuff happened but that we want to work to improve it, and ask them what we could do to improve it.

And the principal said to me at one point (crossing the linguistic and the racial axes of difference in one sentence), "This is all really hard to solve because we're caught between people for whom bilingualism is a religion and people who live by Black Power."

Across campus, when people of whatever background mentioned White individuals in stories that I heard, we were almost never referred to as "white people." Just as in 1996, we were still casually described either as "bilingual" or "EO," depending on the program with which we were associated. Either way, we were still not called to the table as invested, complicit participants in school politics, or as benefactors of a system of racially differentiated access to full cultural citizenship in America. Generally portrayed as outside, unaware of and/or "above" the racial aspects of the conflict, we again got excused from the responsibility of addressing complex, enduring issues of race and inequity, and from the responsibility to contribute to struggles against such inequity.

Of course, I must acknowledge here that as a White person myself I was likely not privy to all of the varied ways in which people on campus talked about White people. However I can say that the general exclusion (as far as I was able to ascertain) of White/ness from the "Black-Brown" conflict was not total. In Latino and African Americans' discursive constructions of post-227 school politics, while the Whiteness of *individuals* may have hardly ever surfaced as salient, *national dynamics of White privilege* did. Whiteness seemed to continue to operate "in and between" subject positions (MacCannell, 1992, p. 131). It was alternately performed, constructed, inhabited, assigned and employed "by actors in a range of subject positions" (Ellsworth, 1997, p. 267). On two occasions, African American school community members equated the positionality of Latinos with that of Whites in national structures of power and privilege. One parent explained his frustration with the school this way: Latinos have assumed a position of power that historically Whiteness has conferred—the power to control access to resources, value in the community, and even existence. He said,

> Somewhere along the line, the federal government must have told these people they are White or something. It's a problem. One of the clerks

downstairs, she's Spanish, or Spanish or Mexican or whatever, uh she thought she was the *Chingadera*—I'm trying to use a nice word instead of a profane word, it means *all that*, you know what I mean? But she wanted to be so important. A Latino could walk into the office, my God, there'd be three or four people over there helping that person. I walk in the office and I have to take a number. We are no longer a minority. We are extinct.

And yet, he followed this stinging critique of local dynamics by drawing upon the national White/of color, dominant/nondominant dichotomy. He continued, "But if we united we could take over. Our fight isn't with each other as individuals or cultures. It's with the government, Uncle Sam, the big machine. America? I'm not part of America. America what?"

In a similar vein, one day during a lengthy interview after school, Michael reflected on the fact that "Latino/bilingual" school community members might not hold the keys to cultural citizenship on the national scene as some people thought:

I think this all goes back to Proposition 187. I mean basically 187 said, "We don't give a fuck about you Mexicans. Don't go to our doctors, don't go to our schools, don't do this, don't do that." But American people voted for it and so it was implemented. Now we're going to pass a law that says you can only be taught in English. Now personally I really feel that they should only be taught in English, because that's the language here. That's what you have to have to survive here. Because I know too many kids that graduated from high school and they can't speak English. So now they're going to a job interview, but oh, they can't speak English so they just get fucked. I used to have prejudice, I'm not going to lie now. I voted for 227. But at the time I voted for it I was thinking of it as a positive aspect, like this is the official language of this country so we're going to teach English and this is how we are going to do it, step one, step two, step three. You know, in a way that would have benefited everybody. What really pisses me off is you [looking at me], your ancestors come over and take over the country looking for religious freedom. Then you start slavery, you take away other people's freedom. And then now you tell other people, the Mexicans, "You can't come over here and find the same freedom that I can."

He then made a connection between the relationships that Latinos and African Americans have with 227, continuing with:

I thought that 227 was a plot against Latinos but now I think it was a divide and conquer kind of thing. It keeps Black and Brown fighting amongst themselves. It hasn't run anybody out of the country and the people that voted for it don't even go to public school and could probably care less about what's going on in an individual classroom. Just because everybody's so gung-ho about red, White, and blue and we want English and we want American everything, you know. It's like, it's like a breakdown of the races.

It's like a breakdown of the languages. We can't even be Americans. We're Africa American, Mexican American. It's so divided. I think 227 was from the get-go a weapon. It's hurting everybody except the people who voted for it. How many people who voted yes for 227 have their children in an all-White school? It was like that when it was only White people in the government but it's not only White people in the government now. It's all races in the government and the same shit is still happening.

Here we see Michael at once recalling his identification with the anti-bilingual education/anti-immigrant English for the Children discourses and his vote for 227, while also manifesting an uneasy relationship with the measure; he disassociates himself from his vote and those discourses due to their connection to the privileged, oppressing subject position of White people within the national racial hierarchy.

The reflections of this parent, and Michael, recall the work of Gilroy (1987) on the makeup and function of "interpretive communities" in struggles for material and social advantage: Members share similar points of location within and against forces of ideological and material opportunity/oppression. Membership in interpretive communities is fluid, constantly (re)articulated in relation to different systems of power. Or as Bourdieu (1991) proposed, groups of people form and reform as they see themselves occupying similar positions in the social space, and hence as possessing similar kinds and quantities of capital, life chances, dispositions, and so forth. And Hall (1988) also reminds us that social collectivities in struggles often have more than one set of agendas: They have both the interest of improving their position within a certain arena, and of not losing their place within another. As such, actors often assume a number of specific subject positions in relation to the issues at hand. On the one hand, African Americans were constructed as an interpretive community aligned around symbolic discourses about English as quintessentially "American," which portrayed "Mexicans" as outsiders in conflict with "America." On the other hand, African Americans and Latinos were portrayed as a single interpretive community, allied within and against an "America" constructed as a bastion of White privilege.

Michael then goes further, pointing out that while privilege and the ability to oppress have historically and traditionally been the purview of White people, today's more diverse governing bodies still enact, support, and maintain policies that disenfranchise people of color—sustaining the "White only" barriers to full cultural citizenship. We see Michael pointing out an example of Gilroy's (1987) important point that hegemonic ideology "is not the exclusive property" of that perceived as "the hegemonic." Its "underlying assumptions," perspectives and motivations are often "duplicate[d] in precise detail" by those in non-dominant or subject positions (pp. 64, 40). Here, then, we can see Whiteness perceived as sets of practices, forms of property, performances, or shifting locations of privilege (Ellsworth, 1997, p. 264), manifesting *through* multiple positionalities, White, Brown, or Black.

Michael's interview was also notable because the White person explicitly mentioned in his reflection was me. I hoped that this indicated a level of comfort that he and I had built over the years. I thought that if it did, it might signal that all of us on campus could talk constructively about our roles in the conflict and our responsibilities in improving our school—if we could build a more pervasive atmosphere of trust and community.

As for my own subject position and agenda within these dynamics, I held a stereotypically White perspective in that I "could see both sides": On the one hand I perceived English for the Children in ways similar to how other "Latino/bilingual" school community members did. It felt to me like an assault on what I knew about language acquisition and good pedagogy for ELLs. It felt like an assault on Latinos, immigrants, nondominant linguistic communities, and on proponents of diversity and equity more broadly. And I knew we had a long way to go to make bilingual instruction as strong as it was meant to be. Finding out that many bilingual teachers rarely actually taught ESL (a key component of *bi*lingual instruction) prior to 227, and that some considered bilingual instruction to be a remedial program compared to immersion Models A and B, was shocking. I came to believe that as much as I detested Ron Unz, his initiative, his motives, and his tactics, the act of *raising questions* about the quality of implementation of bilingual education programs in the late 1990s had been necessary. But I also believed that attempting to gut the program (instead of attempting to address its implementation issues) in favor of a poorly designed, untried, haphazardly-implemented immersion program was horribly wrong. Further, as Ramirez (2000) found in a study of 227 implementation across the state, the blanket focus on English led to a decrease in practices of multiculturalism, instructional differentiation, and constructivist approaches in general. I believe that as a nation we have far to go to provide ELLs—and all students—with a truly world-class education.

On the other hand, I also agreed with "African American/EO" school community members who argued that Proposition 227 did not fulfill many hopes that people had for it as a policy: that it might have offered a cultural and institutional resource for leveraging voice and power for African American children and adults at California Elementary. Proposition 227 could be seen to have failed to elevate EO education to a higher value or standard in our community; to have denied harbor to the goal of common dual language instruction; and to have denied a foothold for professional recognition and cultural citizenship for African American staff members. I support the goals of strengthening the EO program at our school and of establishing a dual language bilingual program available to all our students.

This "seeing both sides" did allow me to identify connections between the experiences and policy goals of the (supposedly) "opposing camps." It allowed me to see connections that would be valuable to any efforts to build collaborative efforts towards improvement. However, being White (and my role as a researcher) also led me to not take a passionate public stance on the issues. Though in private settings I freely expressed my opinions to colleagues, in public settings such as debates in staff meetings I espoused a neutrality which can be critiqued as classic White withdrawal. Taking a critical look at my positionality in the school community after my first phase of research and going into this second phase, I had thought about ways I might actively engage this seemingly neutral, uninvolved positionality of White people in this conflict. I discuss in chapter 8 an attempt I made to engage publicly with colleagues from across the school community about who we were, where we had been, and where we could go together (the Professional Discussion Group project). I believe that only when we do this—together—will we be able to reach our common goal of engaging all of us as full cultural citizens on our campuses and in our communities.

WAR OR COMMON CAUSE?
LOOKING ACROSS WHITE, BLACK, LATINO, EO, BILINGUAL

As I have tried to convey in this chapter about post-227 dynamics at California Elementary, just like in 1996 there was much diversity within the simple dichotomy of "African American/EO versus Latino/bilingual." There were of course the school community members who defied the simple definitions of who was "on" each "side." And I found even more complex border crossing dynamics now. Reflecting on life with Proposition 227, a few people actually changed their minds completely about what kind of educational agenda they supported. There was Linda, as mentioned earlier, who had long been a vocal bilingual education advocate but who was so pleased with how much English students were learning in her immersion class that she became completely pro-227. And there was the bilingual teacher-turned Title I coordinator who said, "We hated 227 but I think slowly we have come to see that teaching in English to these children really, it's kind of a good thing. It really is what's best." (I return to this quotation in the next chapter.)

Further cross-pollination of perspectives also occurred post-227: There were moments when people drew connections between the educational trajectories and cultural citizenship struggles of African Americans, EOs, Latinos, and bilinguals. Two examples were noted in the previous section—the parent referring to Latinos' and African Americans' common struggle against "Uncle Sam," and Michael's discussion of 227 policy as a "divide and conquer" mechanism of the White power structure. And the bilingual coordinator in 1999 made this connection:

> I was shocked that there were kids who weren't being served effectively by the bilingual program. I did work at the cluster [the midway administrative level within the district at the time], in the Instructional Cabinet there. It opened my eyes to learn that there were eighth graders dropping out because they couldn't access the curriculum in English, and these kids had been in our system since kindergarten! Yes, over 50% of the kids in the bilingual program, by eighth grade, were dropping out because they didn't have the English skills to access the curriculum. It was always the first thing on our agenda at the cluster meetings: "LEP issues." I think it was there for compliance, so we could show that we were addressing it. But no one was ever like, "Oh my God let's do something." It's just like with the EO kids. We have to do something about it but since I've been here we still haven't. We are failing kids from *both* groups.

I believe that by 2000 people began to talk more about these connections in part due to the simple fact that more staff members began to work across programs. The number of classrooms that mixed EO with Model A, Model B and/or bilingual (yes, sometimes all in one classroom) went from 9 in 1999–2000 to 19 in 2000–2001. Further, the fact that we were *all* affected by the first chaotic years of 227, with multiple classroom reorganizations, materials redistributions, and so forth, may have led people to see some commonality across lines of division.

This cross-pollination of perspectives may have contributed to another major finding of this phase of research: As I have tried to show, while tensions and around the same issues from earlier years remained, they now generated what felt more like low-grade skirmishes than a war. I believe that this was at least in part because there was a kind of resignation after the 1998 ballot measure. It had passed, and it had not gone to court and been dismissed like Proposition 187. There did not seem to be anything we could do about it except work within it. Recall the sentiments of people on both "sides" who argued that the *other* "side" "got what they wanted" with Proposition 227, that things were *still* not where they should be, but that there was not much room for change agendas because the policy was "here to stay." A certain sense of resignation had settled in. There no longer seemed to be the cultural, political, or policy space within which to launch an offensive for any of the future policy agendas that school community members advocated. And so, although English for the Children had brought the possibility of dissolving the conflict at California Elementary and of ushering in an era of more harmonious campus dynamics (it ostensibly outlawed the supposed issue at hand, after all, bilingual instruction), what it actually could be seen to do in the daily lives of many school community members was extinguish further their sense of choice and voice in the struggle to bring full participation in campus life to all adults, and to bring equitable and excellent education to all our students

Perhaps a shared sense of loss of agency and possibility (though clearly *not* a good thing) might allow some space to see a common present—and perhaps, a shared future. Looking at the achievement data for California Elementary, it would be hard not to see this: In 1998–1999 and 1999–2000, our school scored at the bottom of the state's API scale—a 1 on a scale of 1 to 10. One side having an advantage over the other becomes hard to argue for too long, when both sides are so far behind where they should be. Where and how might common ground, a coalitional approach to shared cultural citizenship, be found? A vocal advocate for language minority education, Kenji Hakuta, advised the United States Commission on Civil Rights in 2001, that decision makers "need to think more broadly" about programs and instruction. "What is critical," he argued, "is finding and communicating a set of program components that work for the children in a given community of interest, within the context of the goals, demographics, and resources of the community" (Hakuta, 2001, p. 10).

This has encouraged me as a researcher and practitioner to continually reach for a place where I can see that sometimes, "*La frontera es lo único que compartimos.*" ("The border is the only thing we share" [my translation]) (Gómez Peña, 1987, p. 47). It has motivated me to always look for boundaries as not only lines of demarcation but also as where *things begin their presencing* (Bhabha, 1994, p. 1), as windows into common cause and possibility. It is with this sentiment in mind that I discuss in the next chapter an insight about language policy processes that I gleaned from looking across the first two phases my research.

CHAPTER 6

REFLECTIONS ON POLICY PROCESSES AND CULTURAL CITIZENSHIP

In the previous chapter I presented the basic outline of school community members' experiences and constructions of the language policy shift we underwent from 1998 through 2000. The way I described how people on the two "sides" saw things is indeed the way a majority of folks described things to me, and how in a most basic sense I read the landscape as a school community member myself. However, even considering the varying impressions and agendas that I laid out within each of the opposing "sides," a still richer understanding can be explored.

POLICY PROCESSES WITHIN
NEGOTIATIONS OF CULTURAL CITIZENSHIP

An important insight about *policy as process* became clear to me in 2000. During after-school interviews, three "Latino/bilingual" school community members expressed a sentiment about the English immersion policy that mirrored a sentiment some "African American/EO" school community members had expressed about bilingual education policy in 1996: They did not bristle against 227 as a policy itself, but against their

War or Common Cause? A Critical Ethnography of
Language Education Policy, Race, and Cultural Citizenship , pp. 131–138
Copyright © 2008 by Information Age Publishing
All rights of reproduction in any form reserved.

perceived lack of choice or voice in the policy planning and implementation process. The bilingual teacher-turned Title I coordinator explained to me that,

> With the vote for 227 approaching, there was disbelief on the part of bilingual teachers that the measure would pass. We just didn't think it could go. And so when the votes came in I guess also we thought that it would be dismissed, that we would fight it in court like Prop 187. But because we knew it was on the ballot, because we knew what was going on, I think that there came a time when we realized that in fact we were doing a poor job of developing the children's English language. We focused so much on the Spanish—our kids were beautifully literate. They could write a three-page paper in the third grade. But we did not have the resources or the staff development or the energy at the end of the day to teach English language development. So there was a moment when we recognized our fault and said, "Hey, the reason this is on the ballot is because we—this, this has been lacking. So we are going to do a better job of it now." *We hated 227 but I think slowly we have come to see that teaching in English to these children really, it's kind of a good thing. It really is what's best. What we resented was the form and the haphazard manner in which it was all just given to us. How can someone who's never been in the classroom write some stupid law and tell us what to do in our classroom?*

Another teacher put it this way:

> It was disgusting. 227 wasn't implemented, it was just *told*. Some people I knew decided, "What are they going to do, come in my room and count the minutes I teach in English vs. Spanish?" It's kind of like, when the door closes, it's my room. *They resented people trying to tell them what to teach.*

Similarly, as "African American/EO" school community members negotiated community dynamics post-227, regardless of whether they felt that 227 was a positive or negative policy step, whether they argued for EO or dual language bilingual instruction or both, many echoed this teacher when she broke it down like this:

> It's a very bitter pill. We ask for things, we don't get them. Nobody listens. We do the same job, we don't get paid the same. Our students struggle, nobody cares. *See, Kim, I'm not against bilingual education, I'm against the way the system is handling it, and us, and them.*

When I heard these reflections, I was immediately struck. I had heard this sentiment before. It sounded just like some "African American/EO" school community members in 1996 who, like Janice, explained to me the inner complexities of their policy stance this way:

I know there's a need for bilingual education. People don't know this but I have studied bilingual education, I know the theory. I see it work at this school and I agree with it in principle. But I don't support it here because of how it was *pushed on us*. When they started the bilingual program *we got no input* and suddenly EOs became disrespected, *second class citizens* in our own school. Bilingual ed has to go!

Here we see what I believe to be a crux of the conflict at California Elementary: Choice and voice in the policy process as a key component of people's sense of cultural citizenship. Defining cultural citizenship as *both the process and the outcomes* of how a community defines itself, its interests and purpose, its binding solidarities, its boundaries, its valued membership and its voice (Flores & Benmayor, 1997), enables us to examine how policies function as (and in and through) ongoing processes of daily life, becoming lenses through which people see and tools they use to forge the dynamics of cultural citizenship. For these school community members, it was not so much the technical *policy* of English immersion or bilingual education itself that they objected to. They resented that they felt it was *forced upon them (the process)* and that it *robbed them of their value, voice and agency (the outcome)*.

In other words, the policy as mandate was less an issue than the policy as *contested cultural resource* (Levinson & Sutton, 2001) in daily social, professional, material, and academic life. As Urciuoli (1996) might say, it was the pragmatics of the language policies, the usage of these resources, that gave them their meaning. Questions about language education policies seemed to crystallize for people as less a single topic of contention and more a complex constellation of sites across which groups with distinct and overlapping political, economic, and cultural visions attempted to define what the socially legitimate means and ends of the community were to be (Apple, 1993; McCarthy & Critchlow, 1993). When I realized this I came to understand the study of education policy processes as also a study of how people negotiate cultural citizenship.

KEY POINTS TO THE STUDY OF POLICY PROCESSES AND CULTURAL CITIZENSHIP

When we take the study of education policy processes as also a study of cultural citizenship, a few key points arise. I believe educators, school community members, researchers, and policymakers should consider these kinds of things as we seek to understand the complexities of creating, implementing, advocating for or challenging, and assessing the effectiveness of language instruction policies. I frame these points in terms of the ethnographic details at California Elementary, but I believe they are general points applicable, ultimately, to perhaps any kind of policy.

Point 1: People Negotiate Multiple Social, Material, and Political Contexts

First, consider the dual arenas that the conflict played out in: Both interpretive communities, "Latino/bilingual" and "African American/EO," could be seen striving for legitimacy and advantage in both the local and national (even global) contexts. Within the local context of our school and Los Angeles, school community members tended to interpret the bilingual education or English immersion policy and the attendant professional, fiscal, and intergroup dynamics in one way; and they tended to assert one particular agenda for future policy. In efforts to justify the position and agenda they drew on a specific set of popular media imaginings of American culture, race relations, English and Spanish, immigration, and equal opportunity. Simultaneously, within the national (and even global) context of politics and job markets, school community members tended to interpret the situation in a different way, and tended to assert a different (even contradictory) agenda for future policy. In efforts to substantiate this position and agenda they drew upon a different set of popular media constructions. Both interpretations of the situation and both agendas could be seen as legitimate and appropriate and powerful, according to the differing contexts. Changes to perspectives and agendas was necessitated by shifting sets of relationships, pressures and opportunities within the different contexts.

As I have quoted earlier, Hall (1988) reminds us that social collectivities in struggle often have multiple agendas: They "have both the interest of advancing and improving their position" within one arena, "and of not losing their place" within another (p. 45). As such, people can take on multiple agendas in relation to the issues at hand (p. 49); and these agendas can even be contradictory. Rosaldo (1994) and Flores and Benmayor (1997), too, urge us that to understand how people construct their struggles for cultural citizenship we must study how powerful "cultural artifacts" look and feel from varied subject positions in the community, to examine the "multiplicity of socio-material concerns" that people negotiate, and the differential political and material outcomes that they experience (Rosaldo, 1994, pp. 244–245). Taking this analytical perspective on language education policies, following Levinson and Sutton (2001) I believe that through the fine-grained approach of multi-sited ethnography, anthropologists can study policies as ongoing processes of cultural production. We can study them as moments of appropriation, creation, and contestation, constituted by diverse actors across diverse social and institutional contexts (p. 1). This will enable us to better understand why and how policies are created and play out in the ways that they do, and empower us to craft future policies that better serve the myriad needs of today's school communities.

Point 2: People Negotiate Intertwined Dynamics of Agency and Structure

A second key point to consider is the concurrent dynamics of action and constriction that people negotiated: In 1996 the flames of "war" at California Elementary seemed to be fanned by a sense of possibility. Given all of the changes and uncertainties that the school community was experiencing, there seemed to be a sense of possibility. By 2000, however, while the conflict continued the intensity had subsided a bit. It seemed to me that this was because there was to some extent a loss of the sense of possibility: Proposition 227 had passed, it had not been overturned in the courts as had earlier controversial state ballot measures, and we had to work within it. Recall the sentiments of people on both "sides" who argued that the *other* "side" "got what they wanted" with 227, that things were *still* not where they should be, but that there was no real room for innovative agendas because the policy was "here to stay."

As we seek to understand such dynamics, Levinson and Holland (1996) remind us that "cultural production" is a continual process of creating and appropriating and contesting meaning within social and material contexts (p. 13). Schools are not sites of seamless cultural transmission, such as in much social reproduction and cultural transmission theory (e.g., Bourdieu & Passeron, 1977; Bowles & Gintis, 1976). And yet neither are they sites of unimpeded agency or the pure invention of social relations. As public institutions schools straddle the line between the local, the state, and the national, and school community members navigate between forces of structure and agency that ebb and flow. Researchers, policymakers, and practitioners must leave the surface level (a policy "works" here or it does not, we "like it" or we do not. We must dig into the depths of how policies and their outcomes are shaped over time by differential and shifting resources for, and constraints upon, social interaction (Levinson & Holland, 1996, pp. 1, 3; also Fordham, 1996; Willis, 1977). Understanding the interplay of these forces can put us in a position to leverage the strengths and meet the challenges of daily practice in schools that are implementing increasing numbers of high-stakes policy and program "solutions."

Point 3: There is Diversity Within Dichotomy

A third key point to the study of education policy processes and cultural citizenship is to interrogate the diversity within the dichotomy: The conflict at California Elementary was described as "African American/EO vs. Latino/bilingual." These competing "sides" were constructed as homogeneous within, and as clearly oppositional. Yet as I explored school community dynamics I found that "African American/EO vs. Latino/bilingual" just did not capture all that was going on. Many borders were crossed in this supposedly clear-cut dichotomy. People crossed the divide racially and linguistically—for example there were African American teachers in the bilingual program, bilingual teachers who espoused an English Only agenda, and White people on both "sides." And, though I did find a general consensus within each "side" about experiences of school politics and agendas for the future, there were also large and important variations in how people saw themselves, their relationships, and the politics at hand. Further, aspects of both "sides' " agendas actually coalesced around the shared concepts of valuing all as equal members of the school community, equipping all children with necessary linguistic competencies, providing all children with the best instruction and life opportunities, and involving all adults in decision making. As demographic shifts make American communities ever-more diverse, and as globalization makes questions about professional qualifications and linguistic and cultural competencies more complex, I believe that policy studies must require an exploration of diversity within the dichotomies that people all-too-easily assign to the questions they ask and the answers they give.

As Gilroy (1987) argues, instead of perpetuating understandings of social conflicts as only simple oppositions, a more fruitful approach for researchers and practitioners is to *also* recognize dynamics in school communities as inherently complex (see also Gutiérrez, 2002). In Gilroy's terms, at California Elementary people could be seen as members of "interpretive communities," loosely united around overlapping sets of experiences, discourses, and future goals. Membership in the "African American/EO" and the "Latino/bilingual" interpretive communities was at times clear and stable, and at times contingent and shifting, depending on the issue and context at hand. A way into understanding struggles between and diversity within interpretive communities, then, is to examine their shared, "multi-accented symbolic repertoires" (p. 235). We can ask, What are the common discourses and symbols deployed, what are their stable and enduring elements? What are their contradictory and shifting logics? How do these discourses and symbols manifest in particular argumentative structures, and how do they change with context? Asking these kinds of questions can provide us with richer understandings of all that "goes on" in school communities and in education politics. This can empower us to create and act upon language education policies in ways that intentionally address the both the straightforward, dichotomous nature of politics in American schools as well as the inherent complexities.

Point 4: Politics of Race, Language, and Nation Have Enduring Power

A fourth key point to keep in mind is the need to account for the enduring forces of race, language, and national identity politics. These dynamics shape social interactions sometimes implicitly, sometimes explicitly. They act independently of each other sometimes, and are thoroughly co-constitutive at other times. These forces are woven throughout the fabric of daily life in today's increasingly diverse schools. At California Elementary, for example, we must explore how and why people organized the conflict in racial terms ("this Black/Brown war"). These racial parameters grew out of people's experiences of the world and out of the very powerful ways in which racial hierarchies and race relations function in our society. They gave shape and momentum to each set of perspectives, discourses and agendas. But they also left hidden a significant amount of heterogeneity of perspectives within the dichotomy. Further, we must examine why, how and to what effect these racial categories *mapped so easily* to language ("Latino/bilingual," "African American/EO") and then played so well into dynamics of privilege/marginalization in the local and national arenas. Untangling the categories of language, race, and nation is a key, I believe, to seeing how these structures of domination are maintained, and how our own discourses and actions contribute to this. Leaving them unexamined can neutralize the potential for people to coalesce around shared aspects of their subject positions in the name of shared goals. For example, California Elementary school community members shared the goal of educating students to become bilingual and hence able to meet the increasing requirements of linguistic and cultural fluidity in the local and global economy.

I do not mean to make this last point too simply. Just "seeing common goals" would not have magically dissolved lines of difference and conflict on campus. However, I believe that questioning our common sensibilities about who is "us" and who is "them" is crucial to a politics that was sorely needed by the mid-1990s at California Elementary (and that still is, in the United States more generally). As Smitherman (1992, 2002), Darder (1997), Perry and Delpit (1998), and Attinasi (1997) have pointed out, the English Only movement that gained steam in the mid-1990s has implications not only for supporters of bilingual education for Latino students.

These efforts to narrow and police the language considered "correct" and officially "American," and to legislate it as solely proper for use in schools, has implications for African Americans and for all linguistic minorities—and indeed for advocates of pluralism and diversity generally. The English Only movement and other similar "backlash pedagogies" (Gutiérrez, Asato, Santos, & Gotanda, 2002) continue to threaten school communities across the United States that struggle to find innovative ways to educate all of their students to high standards—students increasingly varied by language, race/ethnicity, culture, socioeconomic level, legal status, and academic preparation. Language education policies will be placed on better footing to be vehicles for success in diverse school communities if they are created, implemented, and researched in ways that account for the power of enduring experiences and politics of race, language and national identity—both in local and national contexts.

LOOKING FORWARD

I left California Elementary (again) in 2000, and from 2001 through 2004 I worked for a local nonprofit organization that engaged in equity-focused policy advocacy statewide and that provided school improvement consulting services to districts in the Los Angeles area. I served the organization in two capacities. I conducted research and evaluation projects for the organization, and I worked directly with local schools as a coach. In this second capacity I came to see that many schools in the area were struggling with the same kinds of conflicts and questions that we were at California Elementary. Then, in the next "chapter" of my life (2005 through 2007) I had the opportunity to extend my research to the southeastern United States. I came to see that people in this new place and years later *also* struggled with similar conflicts and questions. In the next chapter of this book I take a look at media discourses, legislative politics and the education policy context nationally and in the "New South," and at some emerging research on the region's increasingly diverse schools. I examine these in light of my findings from this California research and then in the final chapter, outline some thoughts on the implications of similarities found across space and time.

CHAPTER 7

IMMIGRATION DEBATES, LEGISLATIVE POLITICS, AND EDUCATION POLICY CONTEXT, 2005–2007

From the National Stage to the "New South"

In the summer of 2005 I moved to Atlanta, Georgia to take a position with a regional research and policy center.[1] As soon as I arrived in Atlanta and picked up the newspaper, turned on the TV, and listened to the radio, I realized that people were talking constantly about immigration. Within this ubiquitous discourse, the fear was often expressed that the influx of immigrants to the state would mean that Georgians would soon be living in *Georgiafornia* (Campos, 2006a). People worried that the population shift and attendant controversies over economics, politics, culture and education that erupted in California were now imminent in the Peach State.

The anthropologist in me got to work. I was compelled to "follow the conflict" (Marcus, 1998), which was so obviously now playing out in the Southeast (the Southeast here meaning roughly North Carolina, South Carolina, Georgia, Alabama, and Mississippi). In June of 2005 I began

War or Common Cause? A Critical Ethnography of
Language Education Policy, Race, and Cultural Citizenship , pp. 139–158
Copyright © 2008 by Information Age Publishing
All rights of reproduction in any form reserved.

tracking media debates about immigration, language, race and education. I scanned the *Atlanta Journal-Constitution (AJC)* daily. The *AJC* is the major paper in Atlanta, arguably *the* major metropolitan area not only in Georgia but in the Southeast (Atlanta is the largest city in the region, with the one major regional airport, and it is where some departments of the federal government have their regional office, such as the U.S. Department of Education). In addition to scanning the *AJC* daily, I also regularly tracked some national newspapers such as the *Washington Post*, the *New York Times*, *USA Today*, and *Education Week*. I also continued to track, at least weekly, television and radio coverage on national channels such as CNN and National Public Radio.

This new period of research adds not only a longer look at the dynamics explored in California but a wider scope as well, adding the geographic and social contrasts of a place where, at least compared to mature immigrant destinations like California, immigration—and Latino immigration in particular—is new. It also adds to the limited existing research on Latinos, immigrants, and multiracial/multilingual school communities in the Southeast (Beck & Allexsaht-Snider, 2002).

In this chapter I first provide an overview of trends, politics, and discourses on the national scene in order to contextualize the subsequent discussion of the issues in the Southeast (and particularly in Georgia). The chapter concludes with reflections on the questions that began brewing for me the moment I arrived in Atlanta: How do the social terrain and the media discourses about immigration, race, language and education compare to those in California? What are the implications of this for struggles for educational equity and cultural citizenship, particularly as pertains to language policymaking?

NATIONAL MEDIA DEBATES ABOUT IMMIGRATION

In 2005–2007, the flow of immigration to the United States that was so controversial in the 1990s was continuing. One national 2005 report stated that the annual influx of foreign-born people was about 1.2 million, with more illegal immigrants entering than legal immigrants (Moscoso, 2005). The most obvious impact of these trends is that immigrants are more visible than ever across the entire nation, in communities large and small, urban and rural; in communities long associated with large immigrant populations as well as those considered "new immigrant destinations" (Hernández-León & Zúñiga, 2005). One *USA Today* article reported that "almost a third of the nation's 361 metropolitan areas have registered declines in their White populations this decade as minorities bring ethnic and racial diversity to vast sections of the USA" (El Nasser,

2006). In 2003, Latinos became the largest minority group in the land, comprising 14% of the population while African Americans were now 12%, Asians 4%, and Whites 68%.

During this time period, public discourse continued to engage around the same dominant topics as in the earlier years explored in this book: questions of what was to become of the "American" identity; culture clashes and the issue of assimilation versus separatism; and the economic pros and cons of diversity. Articles on immigration and diversity appeared regularly in national papers and magazines; television news outlets such as CNN also had extensive coverage—the nightly Lou Dobbs CNN segment called "Broken Borders" is a good example.

The discourse of cultural and linguistic assimilation versus separatism remained a dominant refrain. Those charging that Latinos remained separate and unwilling to assimilate continued to press their case. To the contrary, assimilationist arguments were made, such as that in *Newsweek* of May 30, 2005. The article, called "A Latin Power Surge," highlighted the assimilationist perspective with the subtitle, "Why we're the new Irish: Mexican-Americans, too Began Apart—and are now a Thread in the Tapestry." Whatever position one took on the topic of assimilation versus separatism, however, what was not debatable was the continued growth of the political power of Latinos. The media highlighted "Latino Power," evidenced by, for example, the increasing visibility of Latino politicians such as Bill Richardson, who competed for the Democratic Party nomination for president in 2008, and Los Angeles's mayor Antonio Villaraigosa, a new star on the national Democratic party scene. As well, there was much coverage of Latinos' increasing importance as a voting bloc for both political parties (Campo-Flores & Fineman, 2005).

Indeed, just how immigrants, and Latino immigrants in particular, "fit into" idealized visions of "America" remained a very contentious topic. For example, one could still read frequently about employers who aggressively recruited immigrant workers, but whose workplace policies indicated a discomfort with the culture(s) the workers brought. There were reported lawsuits by Latinos against their employers because the employers required that they utilize their commercially valuable linguistic skills to speak Spanish to customers, but mandated that they "communicate in a common language—English" to each other, even in such private settings as the lunchroom (Jordan, 2005). There was the case of the pizza parlor owner in a Midwestern town who began accepting pesos as payment to take advantage of the Mexican currency that immigrant workers often brought back from visits home; this set off a tide of public complaints. And in April 2006 when a Spanish-language version of the U.S. national anthem was released, an energetic debate ensued, with President Bush even weighing in (Associated Press, 2006b).

The culture backlash persisted. Chapters of the anti-immigration group The Minuteman Project sprouted up in several states, to fight what they called the "uncontrolled demographic and cultural transformation of the country," which "threatened the values" of America (Tumulty, 2006). The group lobbied lawmakers to enact anti-immigration legislation, stalked day labor work sites to observe and photograph laborers, patrolled stretches of the border with Mexico (in April 2006 the group claimed to have nearly 7,000 members on guard), and even launched ambitious publicity campaigns (Dart, 2006; Pasco & Weikel, 2005).

Interestingly, while protests about immigration raged, there was continued national recognition—though less prominently reported in the media—of the need for Americans to increase their cultural and linguistic repertoires. Experts stressed that America's continued economic strength and national security depended on a commitment to producing students with knowledge of world languages and cultures (Committee on Economic Development, 2006). Resolutions in both houses of Congress established 2005 as the "Year of Languages," and in January 2006 President Bush announced the National Security Language Initiative, pledging investment in language education programs across the country.

How did this recognition of the need for linguistic and cultural interaction in the global economy compare to debates about the economic effects of immigration at home? Just what were the costs to cities, states, and the nation? Answers varied greatly. In 2006, members of the U.S. House of Representatives held field hearings on the topic of immigration. Often in these debates emotions seemed to trump facts. One representative at a hearing in Tennessee was quoted as saying there was a total "disconnect" between facts and reality. For example, figures that state Medicaid program directors cited didn't match the accusations from citizens about the burdens put on their local health care system by illegal immigrants (Baxter, 2006b). Another issue was whether immigrants take jobs from American workers and depress wages (McNaughton, 2007). Debates about this now focused not only on the lower-paying industries of agriculture, meat processing, carpet manufacturing, and construction (the types of industries focused on in debates of earlier years), but also on high-tech computer industry jobs. Influential companies such as Microsoft lobbied Congress to increase the number of H-1B visas for high-tech workers, while others opposed this, arguing that these foreign workers—though highly paid—were paid much less than their American colleagues, depressing wages industry-wide (McNaughton, 2007). And, it became increasingly noted that immigrants were often the key to a community's future: Demographers found that "an area's ability to attract and hire immigrants increasingly can make or break it economically" (El Nasser, 2006).

In the years following the tragedy of September 11, 2001, debates about immigration came to be dominated by national security concerns, spurred by the fear that terrorists could enter the country through its porous borders (with attention blatantly focusing more on the southern border with Mexico than the northern border with Canada— indeed in popular discourse the very term "the border" simply came to denote the border with Mexico). Immigration provisions became key points in congressional intelligence legislation debates, and books with such provocative titles as *The 50% American: Immigration and National Identity in an Age of Terror* gained attention (Jacoby, 2005). By 2007 newspapers were reporting that immigration had "supplanted Iraq as the leading issue on TV and radio talk shows" (Babington, 2007).

Efforts by the government to enforce existing immigration laws made the headlines. In 2004 U.S. customs, border control, and immigration agencies began increasingly utilizing the tactic of raids in cities both near and far from the border. Immigration and Customs Enforcement began to coordinate with other government agencies such as the Social Security Administration to fine violators and to deport illegal immigrant prison inmates (Editorial Board, 2006). The government also began to utilize the Racketeer Influenced and Corrupt Organizations (RICO) laws. Formerly used against the mob and big tobacco, RICO was now used to go after companies known to employ large numbers of undocumented immigrants (Poole & Joyner, 2007). President Bush increased the number of border patrol agents on the Mexico-U.S. border. In March of 2006 it was reported that the number of agents was approximately 10,000, up from 7,000 before September 11, 2001 (Johnson, 2006; Leinwand, 2006a).

Regarding the movement for immigrant rights as it relates to historical movements in the United States for civil rights, some in the media at this time pointed out how far apart people saw the campaign for immigrant rights and African Americans' long struggle for equity. Opined one nationally-known Black social activist (Hutchinson, 2006): The "great irony" of the huge immigration marches in 2006 was that "the old civil rights groups have been virtually mute on immigration and the demonstrations," and the Congressional Black Caucus "has issued mostly perfunctory, tepid and cautious statements opposing the draconian provisions" of some of the proposed immigration statutes. This relative silence departed from the past when, for example, the Congressional Black Caucus actively opposed tough immigration proposals in the 1980s. Currently, he argued, Black leaders "see immigrant rights as a reactive, narrow, single issue movement whose leaders have not reached out" to African Americans. And they must respond to many who "blame illegal immigrants" for taking jobs from African Americans, fueling "an odd alliance" between Black anti-immigrant activists, GOP conservatives, and thinly disguised, racially tinged "America first" groups.

On the other hand, some media coverage painted a picture of a common Black and Latino struggle for civil rights. A few editorials argued that anti-immigrant groups such as the Minutemen were simply throwbacks to the days of the Ku Klux Klan, and should be actively opposed by both African Americans and Latinos. One noted that the fight against offering a path to citizenship for those undocumented workers already in the country was simply a ploy to keep that population subject to unregulated, low-wage labor, similar to fights to maintain the free and cheap labor of African Americans in the past (Hernandez, 2006).

In all the discourses about immigration at this time, I noticed a clear emergence in linguistic markers: "illegal" became a noun. "Illegal" became a term to refer to illegal *immigrants*—or carelessly, to all immigrants (Harris-Bosselmann, 2006). Along with this linguistic turn, the criminalization of immigrants in general became even more common than in earlier years: Article after article talked about an underground "epidemic" industry in fake driver's licenses and passports, and about "highly sophisticated crime networks" providing services to those coming to the United States (Malone, 2006).

Here we see continuing evidence of what Balibar (1991) calls "an immigration complex": a myriad of social concerns condensed into one overwhelming malady, and posited as caused by the singular fact of the presence of "illegals" (p. 220). In this linguistic move, the loaded signifier, "illegal," becomes "a gloss for a national Other" (p. 222), a gloss for things undesirable and dangerous. As I have pointed out in earlier chapters, Bourdieu (1991) calls such moves performative utterances (p. 128): attempts "to produce and impose representations of the social world" in order to influence the actions people can "undertake to transform the social world in accordance with their interests" (p. 128). With the moniker of "illegals" and the image of immigrant communities as riddled with crime, those who considered themselves law-abiding citizens were encouraged to assume that the only right thing to do was to treat immigrants indiscriminately like criminals. Reactionary arguments to "deport them all" or "run them out of town" were bolstered.

NATIONAL LEGISLATIVE POLITICS

Federal immigration legislation overhaul became *the* hot political topic of this time. Regardless of where people stood on the issue, what most could agree on was that the current immigration system was "broken." Many harkened back to the 1986 overhaul of immigration legislation, that had been expected to control the influx of illegal immigrants by making it a crime to hire undocumented workers and offering amnesty to those who had already been in the United States for at least 5 years. What instead happened was that the number of illegal immigrants went from the estimated 3 million in 1986 to an estimated 12 million or more by 2007. As Senator John McCain said, creating new immigration legislation would be "a defining moment in the history of the United States of America" (Tumulty, 2006).

The immigration issue was particularly complex for Republicans. On the one hand, many remarked on the necessity of increasing the Latino vote for Republicans. They noted that President Bush had furthered the GOP nationally by recruiting socially conservative Latinos during his first election campaign (Campo-Flores, 2004). Many cautioned that the GOP risks being on the wrong side of electoral politics if it failed to embrace immigrant issues. And the business arm of the party pressured against extremist legislation, acknowledging the need for cheap immigrant labor in many industries. On the other hand, the cultural conservatives favored tough provisions to close the border and deport "illegals."

Throughout 2005, 2006, and 2007 the ideas of a "path to citizenship" (or, "amnesty") and of securing the border became the organizing (hegemonic) concepts of immigration legislation debates. Other ideas that came and went were making illegal immigration a federal crime (not a civil violation as it has been); mandating English as the official language of the United States (enacting such legislation has been an ongoing effort of social conservatives for many years) (Reynolds, 2006); penalties for those who smuggle and those who hire illegal immigrants; and a national identification system to verify the legal status of job applicants, prisoners, and people at border checkpoints. Various versions of a "path to citizenship" were considered (with varying proposals of timelines, paperwork and fees required, etc.). Arguments for and against these proposals often talked about illegal immigrants either "stealing the American dream" (e.g., King, 2006a) or helping to fulfill it (e.g., Alonso-Zaldivar, 2004). While media debates were heated, actual productive work on the issues was hampered by the fact that many legislators were "leery of anything approaching amnesty in an election year" (Abrams, 2006). One news report quoted a lawmaker saying that there was "virtually no agreement on anything" in the various bills in committee (Shepard, 2006).

Public participation in these debates spread to a mass level unseen in many years. There were demonstrations in cities across the country. One day in April of 2006 was said to have nearly 2 million people marching, including at least 40,000 in Atlanta and upwards of half a million in Los Angeles (Riechmann, 2006). It was the "biggest coordinated demonstration on immigration this country has ever seen" (Borden & Rockwell,

2006). Television and radio outlets emerged as particularly powerful forums—it was reported that lawmakers (particularly Republicans) felt the need to "placate" popular talk show hosts, "even to the point of accepting their ideas for amendments" (Babington, 2007). And just before the final vote, the number of telephone calls placed by constituents to their senators was so great that the Senate's phone system crashed.

The death blow for comprehensive federal immigration reform was struck on June 27, 2007, when the Senate voted to end consideration of the proposed bill. No compromise could be found, and no further attempts were anticipated until after the 2008 presidential elections.

NATIONAL EDUCATION POLICY CONTEXT: NO CHILD LEFT BEHIND

The year 2001 saw the sweeping reauthorization of the Elementary and Secondary Education Act, as the No Child Left Behind Act, or NCLB (U.S. Department of Education, 2001). I do not attempt here to provide either a comprehensive description of NCLB or an exhaustive summary of debates about it. I instead highlight a few key points of relevance for the topics addressed in this book.

The key concept of NCLB is "accountability." While schools, districts, and states had long been working to improve student achievement via various types of "accountability" efforts (I mentioned some of the steps California began to take in chapter 5), with NCLB the accountability for improvement was now enforced by the U.S. Department of Education (USED), to a level as yet unseen in American public education. There were mandated outcomes that USED began to monitor, applying sanctions where they were not met. Data on school and student progress now had to be made available to the public. It was a policy "sea change."

A key starting point provision of the legislation had to do with creating and operationalizing standards. It required states to create student learning standards (what students need to know and be able to do) in the content areas. The law further required states to administer assessments in reading and mathematics in Grades 3 through 8, and at least once in high school (science was added as a required assessment area for 2008). Specifically for English Language Learners (ELLs), Title III of NCLB required states to develop English language development standards and to implement English language proficiency assessments aligned to those standards.

Utilizing these standards and assessing students against them lead to another key provision of NCLB: the disaggregation of student achievement data. Schools and districts are now held accountable not only for raising the achievement scores of all the students at a school as a whole group, but also for raising the achievement scores of each and every student subgroup the school serves.[2] NCLB defined subgroups as racial/ethnic groups (White, African American, Latino, Asian, Native American), socioeconomic groups (free/reduced lunch, i.e., low socioeconomic level, and not free/reduced lunch), language groups (ELLs), and those served by special programs (students with disabilities). Achievement of students in every subgroup is required for schools to make Adequate Yearly Progress (AYP), towards the ultimate goal of proficiency for 100% in 2014.

As such, even for schools that have high achievement scores on average, if one subgroup of students is not making AYP, the whole school is considered "in need of improvement." And this "needs improvement" label comes with very high stakes: Consequences of not meeting AYP range from having to implement school improvement plans to full scale state takeover and reconstitution. Debates about the nature and impact of this accountability system have been spirited (e.g., Skrla & Scheurich, 2004; Valenzuela, 2005).

For the subgroup of ELLs, school systems that receive federal Title III funding have additional accountability measures. Title III funds are disbursed to states that then allocate funds to school districts to pay for targeted teacher professional learning and instructional materials. Title III accountability is operationalized through the requirement that states create (and have USED-approved) Annual Measurable Achievement Objectives (AMAOs). AMAOs track the achievement of ELLs in three ways: first, progress made towards full English proficiency; second, rates of "crossing the finish line" into full English proficiency; and third, making AYP as normally calculated.

A major point of contention as NCLB approaches its next season for reauthorization is how accountability, and consequences, are conceptualized and operationalized. Regarding ELLs, many object to students being assessed in a language they have not yet mastered (i.e., English). Others point out that because new ELLs enter U.S. schools each year, this subgroup is being continually infused with students in the lowest proficiency levels and hence with the lowest scores on assessments in English, making it unrealistic that schools be held accountable for continually improving scores of this population. There are other points of contention as well. A major advocacy group, the National Association for Bilingual Education (NABE), had the following policy statement on their Web site in 2004 (NABE, 2004):

> Among [our] concerns are: over-emphasizing standardized testing, narrowing curriculum and instruction to focus on test preparation rather than richer academic learning; over-identifying schools in need of improvement; using sanctions that do not help improve schools; inappropriately excluding

low-scoring children in order to boost test results; and inadequate funding. Overall, the law's emphasis needs to shift from applying sanctions for failing to raise test scores to holding states and localities accountable for making the systemic changes that improve student achievement.

In particular, NABE advocated holding schools accountable for "a comprehensive picture of students' and schools' performance by moving from an overwhelming reliance on standardized tests to using multiple indicators of student achievement in addition to these tests."

When it first passed, NCLB effectively repealed the Bilingual Education Act (Title VII of the Elementary and Secondary Education Act), which had previously funded the basic costs of educational programs for ELLs as competitive grants awarded to school districts. NCLB renamed the Bilingual Education Act the English Language Acquisition, Language Enhancement, and Academic Achievement Act (Title III), and changed its basic program funding approach to providing funds to schools attached to students—a flat amount per student, regardless of the program implemented to serve the students at their school. Although some policymakers argue that NCLB neither prohibits nor encourages bilingual instruction, others argue that because it does not foreground bilingualism, it in effect removes a focus on linguistic diversity (NABE, 2006). Though NCLB does allow for some limited testing of students in their first/native language, most states have opted for state standardized content area assessments all in English (Virginia and New Jersey are two states that have made headlines for bucking this trend [Zehr, 2007a, 2007b]). Because most states have opted for assessments solely in English, many states that previously championed the use of native language instruction have "gone with the flow," moving to implement English Only instruction (Zehr, 2007d). Further, bilingual education advocates note, because it can take several years for students in bilingual programs to reap the benefits of bilingual instruction to perform at or above grade level in *both* languages, this multiyear achievement horizon does not fit the demand of meeting annual AYP requirements (Zehr, 2007d).

This "policy effect" of migration to English-focused instruction and assessment has continued to spread even though research has also continued to emerge that counters such a trend (reports were published heralding the benefits of bilingual education, and finding little or no difference between outcomes in bilingual settings and monolingual English settings). Of particular interest to my research was that in 2000 the California Department of Education commissioned a multiyear evaluation of the effects of the English immersion approach mandated by Proposition 227. The overall finding of the evaluation (American Institutes for Research and WestEd, 2006) was:

Our overall conclusion, based on the data currently available, is that there is no clear evidence to support an argument of the superiority of one EL [English Learner] instructional approach over another.... Little to no evidence of differences in EL performance by model of instruction was found. (p. ix)

In 2000 USED appointed the National Literacy Panel, a nonpartisan group of university researchers, to do an extensive study of the existing research on bilingual education. While officials from USED publicly tout that NCLB "puts a strong emphasis on using education practices and programs based on sound, scientifically-based research," when the panel's findings "cast doubt on the efficacy of teaching immigrant children through English-only lessons," and highlighted moderate benefits of utilizing the first/native language in the classroom, the administration decided not to publish the report (Toppo, 2005; Zehr, 2007c). It was eventually published privately (August & Shanahan, 2006).

In this policy environment of high-stakes accountability for improving the academic achievement of all student subgroups, and of English Only instruction and assessment, communities across the nation are struggling to serve increasingly linguistically diverse student bodies. This struggle is heightened in places such as the Southeast where schools are serving ELLs for the first time.

IMMIGRATION DEBATES IN GEORGIA AND THE SOUTHEAST

As noted earlier, in recent years the Southeast has become a hypergrowth region for immigration, with many states showing exponential gains in their immigrant populations (Campo-Flores, 2004). In particular, Latinos (many immigrant, some from elsewhere in the United States) began settling in the Southeast. Georgia and North Carolina are states often recognized in national population studies as among the top, if not *the* top, destinations for immigrants (Tomás Rivera Policy Institute, 2004; Mikow-Porto et al., 2004). From 2000 to 2005, Georgia's estimated population of illegal immigrants alone jumped 470,000, an increase of 114%, putting it behind only California, Texas, Florida, New York, Illinois, and Arizona in total estimated raw numbers (Campos, 2006a, 2006b). By 2006, an oft-cited statistic was that there were up to 800,000 illegal immigrants in the Peach State (Tharpe, 2006a).

Scholars have begun to call the influx of Latinos to the region the "New Latino Diaspora" (Hamann, Wortham, & Murillo, 2002). Because of this, some have revived the moniker of the "New South" (Hamann, 2003). The "New South" is a term originally coined to refer to the Southern states after the Civil War. It signaled change, and the hope that the Confederacy would become a region of rebirth; of industrialization, economic regeneration, political renovation, and racial harmony. In later decades it referred to the social changes spurred by the Civil Rights Movement. Many note that the Dixie states are today catching up to (and beginning to lead) the national demographic trends, undergoing transformative change due to immigration. People are asking again today—how will the South define itself, how will we *be*, in this "new" era?

Immigrants began moving to the Southeast for the plethora of jobs in the construction, agriculture, poultry processing, and carpet manufacturing industries. All of these are major Georgia industries that literally keep the state economy going (Borden, 2005; Kemper, 2007). By 2005, Gwinnett County, a particularly popular immigrant destination in suburban Atlanta, came to be referred to locally as "GwiMexico" or, acknowledging another of its new, large populations, "Korean Uptown" (Feagans, 2006d).

As Georgia's neighborhood demographics have changed, other social institutions once homogeneous have become diverse. For example, businesses began putting up signs in multiple languages. Emergency 911 call centers began contracting translation services (Feagans, 2006b). And, historically Black churches began to actively court Spanish language parishioners (Varela, 2007).

These changes in Georgia are similar to the changes experienced earlier in more mature immigrant destination areas around the country, and in some ways these changes are even more drastic. The South missed much of the "Great Immigration" of the late 1800s and early 1900s that completely changed the makeup of other regions (Beck & Allexsaht-Snider, 2002). Until relatively recently, Georgia was largely comprised of European-origin Whites and African Americans, both groups English speaking. Reported one newspaper in 1999, "Georgia is experiencing a wave of immigration unlike anything since the colonial era…. [This is] the most significant social and cultural upheaval in Georgia since the early days of racial desegregation" (*Athens Daily News*, cited in Beck & Allexsaht-Snider, 2002, p. 42).

That this quotation invokes Southerners' experiences of desegregation speaks to the fact that recent demographic shifts move within and against a race consciousness in the South which, compared to mature immigrant destinations such as California, has remained much longer deeply dichotomous along a Black-White line (Hansen, 2005). For example, in 2006 as debates raged nationally about immigration, in Georgia (with Atlanta often considered a geographic center of the Civil Rights Movement) there was also much media coverage of politics surrounding what is sometimes called "the crown jewel" of the Civil Rights Movement (Coker, 2006): Sections of the 1965 Voting Rights Act were scheduled in Congress for a 25-

year extension. A Georgia-led coalition of lawmakers pressured members of Congress to indefinitely delay a planned vote, challenging certain provisions of the statute. The issue was contentious but in July, 2006, the law was fully renewed. There was also much media attention to the fact that in 2007 the state legislatures of Alabama, Virginia, and North Carolina issued public apologies for the states' roles in the regime of racial slavery (Rawls, 2007). An effort to issue a similar apology in Georgia failed in 2006 and in 2007.

Aside from these regional particularities, media coverage of debates about immigration in the "New South" reflected the themes of the national discourses (hence I will only touch on them again here): A clash of cultures was a continuing theme. The argument that immigrants—and particularly Latino immigrants—are "just different than Americans" was often voiced (e.g., Weed, 2005). Latino immigrants were accused of destroying an otherwise homogeneous or "happily melted pot" of American culture (Rogers, 2005).

Language became a key issue in this argument, and some charged that Latinos' "failure to assimilate linguistically" (Hymo, 2006; Ross, 2006) was causing English to "become an optional language in Georgia" (King, 2006a). The opposing cultural perspective painted immigrants as, "as American as apple pie and chile rellenos" (Chávez, 2005), with "American" values like family, religion, and work (Cowen & Rothschild, 2006). Others pointed out that Latino immigrants learned to speak English just as fast as immigrants of the previous century, and argued that language is not an essential component of American identity, anyway—the "ties that bind" are "common values and truths held self-evident, such as liberty and justice for all" (Pitts, 2006). Further, advocates maintained that even the illegal workers of today are just one group in a long historical flow of new Americans (Downes, 2006), and they produced the obligatory stories of immigrants in Georgia who fulfilled the American Dream to prove it (Ramos, 2006).

Economic arguments like those in the national media also saturated local debates during this time period. A typical anti-immigration argument was that illegal immigrants drive down wages (Hermann, 2006; King, 2005). Another complaint was the "burden" that illegal immigrants place on social services—it is "simply unfair to poor, legal Georgia residents who depend on the government program[s]" (King, 2006b). Many blamed businesses for "cheating" by hiring undocumented workers (Smith, 2005). A Georgia State Senator quipped in March, 2006, "America wants to export a higher standard of living to other people, not import a lower standard of living to ours…. Our heart has no limit, but our pocketbook does" (Tharpe & Campos, 2006).

To the contrary, the argument was presented that immigrant workers both legal and illegal are the lifeblood of many local Georgia industries (Tharpe, Campos, & Pickel, 2006). Even Georgia's U.S. Senator Saxby Chambliss, otherwise hawkish on the idea of securing the border, at one point argued that as an agricultural state Georgia needed a way to make foreign laborers legal (Baxter & Galloway, 2007; Kemper, 2007). And business advocates complained that "the current process for *legally* hiring immigrant farmworkers is so cumbersome and expensive that it encourages farmers to risk hiring illegal workers" (Kemper, 2006b; King, 2007a).

Another theme running through the immigration debate in Georgia also reflected national discourses: the attribution of criminality to all things immigrant. Articles ran in the newspaper that described an "underworld" of nefarious activity. There were false document sellers providing fake social security numbers and drivers licenses (Borden, 2006). There were people running services transporting illegal immigrants from the U.S.-Mexico border to Georgia (Rodríguez, 2006). Warning against these dangerous forces, billboards around Atlanta began to pop up, saying things like "The INVASION: Secure Our Borders" (Kemper, 2006a). Clearly, the national immigration discourses were speaking loudly and clearly to some people in this deep southern state which does not even border a foreign country.

LEGISLATIVE POLITICS IN GEORGIA: SENATE BILL 529

State and municipal governments became very active at this time in passing illegal immigration laws. Towns in Pennsylvania, New Jersey, Missouri and other states passed measures to fine landlords for renting to illegal immigrants, to deny business permits to companies hiring illegal immigrants, and to make English the municipality's official language (Koch, 2006). The National Conference on State Legislatures reported in April, 2006 that legislators in 42 states had recently introduced more than 360 bills related to immigration (Tharpe, 2006b). In 2005, Republicans in the Georgia General Assembly announced that they would make illegal immigration "a top priority" of the upcoming legislative session (Moscoso, 2005). This reflected what was happening in other Southeastern states as well, the issue being particularly controversial in North Carolina and Alabama (Baxter, 2005, 2006a).

Georgia Senate Bill 529 was the major piece of immigration legislation passed by the Georgia General Assembly in 2006. It became effective in July, 2007. Senate Bill 529 was similar in intent to California's Proposition 187 in that it limited a wide range of services to immigrants: The bill required that employers verify the legality of all new employees and participate in the federal work authorization program to do so. It outlawed trafficking in people for labor or sexual servitude. It established that the state of Georgia and the United States Departments of Justice and Homeland Security would collaborate to allow law enforcement entities in Georgia to enforce federal immigration and customs laws. It limited the "immigration assistance services" that could be provided to immigrants by private individuals. It stipulated limits on how much per employee per year could be claimed by employers as a deductible business expense for state income tax purposes. It stated that all persons 18 or older who apply for federal public benefits will be required to verify their lawful presence in the United States (exempting as per federal law health emergency services, disaster relief, assistance such as soup kitchens, short-term shelters, and notably, K–12 public education).

A related bill also passed: Senate Bill 23 provided that during criminal sentencing and probation procedures local courts should consider a person's legal status in the United States as a factor. A proposed law to prevent official state documents from being translated into any language other than English, and a proposed resolution to amend the state constitution to make English the official language of the state, did not pass. (There is, however, an existing law, Official Code of Georgia section 50-3-100, which has established English as the official language of the state.)

Senate Bill 529 and the related bills, along with the dominant arguments against immigration in the major media outlets, imparted an unwelcoming social and legal atmosphere to newcomers to the Peach State during this time period. Some even charged that Senate Bill 529 threatened to chill the environment for basic human and civil rights (Sager, 2005). It is within these political, demographic, cultural and economic changes that I have described, that Georgia educators struggle to serve a growing population of immigrants and ELLs. To this struggle I now turn.

EDUCATION POLICY CONTEXT IN THE "NEW SOUTH"

With so many immigrants moving to Georgia it is no surprise that between 1994 and 2004 the state's public schools experienced a 378% increase in the kindergarten through 12th grade ELL population (Georgia Department of Education, 2006a).[3] By 2006, 5% of the total K–12 population was ELLs, and of the 75,000 ELLs enrolled across the state in 2006, 70% were Spanish speakers, with the remaining 30% representing over 100 different languages (Georgia Department of Education, 2006a). By 2005 some districts were enrolling very small numbers of ELLs for the first time ever. Other districts, most of which are clustered in the Atlanta metro and northern regions of the state, were serving large and somewhat more established populations. Though these demographic statistics may seem small (5% of the total state K–12 population of approximately 1.5 million in 2006) compared to states like California (which in the same year served approximately 1.5 million ELLs K–12 alone), Georgians have experienced these changes as rapid and drastic. For example, the Clayton County school district in metro Atlanta experienced a 60% growth in its Latino student population between 2000 and 2005. A county school official was quoted in the newspaper in 2006 as saying that the "shift came so quickly that we are actually functioning behind the curve" (Varela, 2006).

Looking at student achievement statewide, statistics on the ELL subgroup are worrisome. ELLs are the demographic subgroup consistently scoring the lowest on state assessments (Georgia Department of Education, 2007b). The Hispanic/Latino subgroup had a graduation rate in 2007 of 60.3% and the ELL subgroup had a rate of 46.6%. These were far lower than the statewide graduation rate of 72.3% and the lowest for all subgroups except for students with disabilities and migrant students (migrant students themselves often being Latino and ELL) (Georgia Department of Education, 2007b). Of note in comparison to my research findings from California, is also the fact that these statistics are not extremely different from statistics for the African American subgroup in Georgia. Black students' assessment scores also often fall below the state average, and their graduation rate in 2007 was 65.5%, also below the statewide rate (Georgia Department of Education, 2007b). Considering that Georgia as a whole often ranks near the bottom of national comparisons of state educational data, these statistics are even more troubling.

Yet with Georgia's largely conservative, Republican social and political atmosphere, widespread changes to "business as usual" monolingual English instruction in public schools have not occurred. Indeed, Beck and Allexsaht (2002) point out that, "The conservative agenda of nativism and English Only has found many receptive ears in this New Latino Diaspora region" (p. 58). They describe how in the mid-1990s, as the population of ELLs first began to get attention at the state level, the state superintendent of schools espoused an actively pro-English Only policy agenda, and very little was done to meet the particular needs of ELLs. The U.S. Department of Education Office of Civil Rights even took issue with the fact that so little attention was being paid to providing targeted educational services to ELLs (it was not uncommon for local school systems to leave ELLs unidentified as such and to simply place them in the regular classroom to "sink or swim").

Current state language education policy is outlined in state board rule 160-4-5-.02, *Language Assistance Services: Program for English Language Learners* (Georgia State Board of Education, 2006). The rule stipulates that all schools serving ELLs are to implement a curriculum with the dual purpose of achieving proficiency in the English language and in the academic content areas, and of developing "American cultural concepts." It stipulates that ELLs are to be served either by the state ESOL (English for Speakers of Other Languages) program or an alternative program approved in advance by the Department (see the following paragraph). The state ESOL program provides that ELLs be placed in the mainstream English-speaking classroom, with additional support from an ESOL specialist teacher (the ESOL teacher can pull the students out of the mainstream class for one period of daily ESL lessons, or "push in," providing these lessons within the context of the mainstream classroom). Alternately, additional support can be provided through transporting students to a special language resource/newcomer center, and in the secondary grades students can take an ESOL class as one of their regular class periods.

Schools are technically allowed, however, to use students' first language for instruction: The Georgia Department of Education's main Web site for the ESOL program states (Georgia Department of Education, 2007a),

> The program's overarching standard is that students will use English to communicate and demonstrate academic, social, and cultural understanding. To reach this standard, it is critical that instructional approaches both in ESOL and general education classes accommodate the needs of Georgia's linguistically and culturally diverse student and parent populations. To the extent practicable, it is appropriate to use the home language as a means of facilitating instruction for English language learners and communication with their parents.

Schools that wish to implement an approach that utilizes languages other than English for instruction must have their plan approved by the State Department of Education (Georgia State Board of Education, 2006).[4]

So we find that the twin issues of immigration and the rapidly increasing population of ELLs in Georgia schools have not produced the drastic language education policy movements that happened in California (e.g., mass implementation of bilingual programs and then a seesaw back to English immersion). As a relatively new immigrant destination area with a still-relatively low amount of linguistic diversity compared to states like California, and being overwhelmingly socially conservative, there has been little in the way of a public push to innovate at the statewide policy level. While immigration is a hot political topic in Georgia, public K–12 education is not an arena in which advocates for linguistic diversity have yet gained a foothold.

However, conflicts are occurring in school communities that press the issue of diversity and its implications for policy and practice. Struggles over cultural citizenship are on the rise. As such, the California case examined in earlier chapters has some important lessons for practitioners, policymakers, and researchers in Georgia.

STRUGGLES FOR CULTURAL CITIZENSHIP IN THE "NEW SOUTH"

The major finding of this phase of my research is that what happened in California with Proposition 227 (draconian and reactionary language education policy as cultural backlash), and what happened at California Elementary School (a "war" between factions of a school community divided by language and race), could happen in the Southeast. Immigration is projected to continue to rise in coming years. Even more schools in more states in the region will therefore soon experience the kind of population shift that South Elementary experienced. And as the immigrant (and particularly Latino immigrant) population matures, one would expect their political clout to grow, as has happened in California. If we fail to take into account the kinds of dynamics that I document in the California chapters, we are inviting the same kinds of conflicts to happen in schools in the "New South" states as happened in the Golden State.

Indeed, these kinds of controversies are already happening, according to existing research in the region. In his study of Latino immigration and education politics in a small community in north Georgia, Hamann (2003) noted that conflict ensued when longtime residents and newcomers alike became suddenly unsure of who was part of the community or what the community's shared mores and values were (p. 6). Hamann, Wortham, and Murillo (2002) have pointed out that in Southern communities with growing populations of immigrants, a sense of "panic" is growing amongst longtime residents, with "home" seen as undergoing a "metamorphosis" into a "world dominated by sinister aliens" (p. 6, cited in Suárez-Orozco, 1998). Hernández-León and Zúñiga (2005) have also identified clear patterns of interracial "antagonisms" akin to those I saw at California Elementary, that "indicate the redrawing and invention of new boundaries" in Georgia (p. 271). And in 2004 the Tomás Rivera Policy Institute published a research study on educational practices and perceptions in several "emerging Latino immigrant communities" in Southeastern states. Included in the sample were two counties in Georgia. The study identified a troubling issue gaining traction in these communities: tension between African American and Latino stakeholders. The study cited the fact that (p. 36),

> Some African American administrators believe that Latino students have received preferential treatment compared to African Americans.... There is

a very established African American community here and they fought hard to be part of the city schools. They see immigrants coming in and getting what they think are special classes.

Alternately, the report cited people who shared that, "recent changes in the school district leadership have resulted in resources being diverted from immigrant education issues toward African Americans" (p. 19). These quotations could have easily come from my data at South Elementary.

Clearly, more studies of inter-racial/ethnic relations in emerging immigrant communities in the Southeast is needed (Tomás Rivera Policy Institute 2004, p. 2). Study authors remind us that, "most of the day-to-day tension between immigrants and other populations is due to lack of understanding" (p. 9).

This research is sorely needed to support communities and decision-makers as they seek to address these and other issues brought about by the changing demographics in the region. Indeed, the Georgia Partnership for Excellence in Education (2008), a leading education policy organization, has called this the "number one" educational issue in the state for 2008:

> Our public schools are educating a new, diverse body of students, and with no past blueprint of policies to reference on this issue, Georgia's response to the population transformation will be truly historic.... A lack of proactive initiatives by policy makers and educators could have detrimental consequences for our state.... Adequate resources must be allocated to ensure that minority and low income students have access to an excellent education that prepares them to grow into engaged, gainfully employed Georgia citizens. (pp. 2, 3)

They then remind us that Georgia's collective response to this challenge "will be all-important in determining Georgia's future quality of life, economic prosperity, and cultural legacy. *How will Georgia embrace its growing diversity?*" (p. 3 [italics added]). I address this in the final chapter, by way of a discussion of the implications of commonalities I found between the conflict studied in California and emerging dynamics in the Southeast.

NOTES

1. Though the 2005–2007 Georgia phase of this research project corresponds to me moving to Atlanta to take this position at the regional research and policy center, my professional work for the center is separate from this independent research project. All the inquiries I made were done separately from my work for the center, and all the sources that I cite are

publicly available (e.g., information from the Georgia Department of Education's Web site).

2. That is, student subgroups of sufficient size—states set their minimum thresholds for this.

3. One should be careful not to simply equate immigrants with ELLs, or ELLs with immigrants. Many immigrants, by virtue of coming from other countries, do not speak English and their children enter U.S. schools as English Language Learners. However this is not true in all cases, such as immigrants from countries where English is a widely spoken language. Alternately, some children born and raised in the U.S. live in households where another language is spoken, and so enter school as ELLs.

4. For example, see Hamann et al. (2002, 2003) for discussion of a controversial project to launch a bilingual program in one community in the Northern region of the state.

CHAPTER 8

WAR OR COMMON CAUSE?

Conclusions and Implications for Research, Policy, and Practice

At the beginning of this book I framed my research questions as, How can language education policies be understood not only in their traditionally acknowledged, instrumental role (policy as imposed directive to be implemented) but also as themselves cultural resources that are constantly created, appropriated, and challenged in daily interaction; as *processes* through which people understand and construct ways of living, relationships, and political agendas (Levinson & Sutton, 2001)? After Levinson and Sutton (2001) and Stein (2004) I aimed to account more thoroughly for the "cultural, contextual, and political dimensions of educational policy" in practice (Levinson & Sutton, 2001, p. 2). Further, I asked how such a conceptualization of policy processes can impart a sophisticated understanding of the ways in which people negotiate their roles to define "the distribution and allocation of rights, privileges, and institutional access" (Rocco, 1997, p. 98). In other words, I explored struggles for cultural citizenship that cultural citizenship that underly relationships to and outcomes of policy mandates. After Flores and Benmayor (1997), Rosaldo (1994, 1997), and Ong (1996), I distinguished cultural citizenship from the traditional concept of legal citizenship, seeing it in the sense of a

War or Common Cause? A Critical Ethnography of
Language Education Policy, Race, and Cultural Citizenship , pp. 159–171
Copyright © 2008 by Information Age Publishing
All rights of reproduction in any form reserved.

"citizen as political subject" (Flores & Benmayor, 1997, p. 11). Cultural citizenship can be considered the state in which a person or a group has voice, belonging, and the power to participate fully in a community.

First, I conducted ethnographic research on a conflict over language education policy in my own school in South Los Angeles, where I was a teacher before and during most of the research. In the 1980s and 90s the community surrounding California Elementary was undergoing a rapid demographic shift due to immigration. I investigated how the school community negotiated dramatic policy changes in the late 1980s through 2000, from establishing a bilingual program for incoming Latino English Language Learners (ELLs) in this school that had until then been predominantly African American and monolingual, to then careening in the other direction to implement English immersion as per the state's Proposition 227 mandate. I asked, how did Latino, African American, and White school community members struggle to define the community and their relationships to it through debates about the roles of language/s in teaching and learning, community relations, and life in America? I also analyzed national media coverage of debates about immigration, race, language, and education policy, and looked at how school community members strategically drew upon these discourses to make sense of their experiences and to legitimate their agendas. Finally, I asked, how did these local and national politics shape the academic and professional environments on campus, and with what effects?

Second, in 2005 through 2007 I continued my inquiry in another locale, asking, how does the social terrain and public discourse about immigration, race, language and education policy in the Southeast, particularly Georgia, compare to what I explored in California? What could common dynamics in these two contexts—one a mature immigrant destination (California) and one a relatively new immigrant destination (the "New South")—tell us about issues that more and more communities nationwide are experiencing? How can this help us understand the critical factors at play in shaping the social contexts of schooling, and relationships to and outcomes of language education policies? And, how can this support the work of better formulating, implementing, and researching policies for increasingly diverse communities—so as to ultimately improve student achievement? I analyzed media coverage, legislative politics, and the education policy context both nationally and locally.

As described in chapters 3 and 5, at California Elementary I found that as people negotiated the changing language instruction policies on campus, talk about language was also talk about race. Racial categories were mapped on to linguistic and pedagogical ones as people made sense of and imagined their relationships to each other, to the community, and to the policies. People tended to construct dynamics on campus as dichotomous, with those described as "Latino" and "bilingual" on one "side" and those described as "African American" and "English Only" (EO) on the other. As the "Latino/bilingual" "versus" "African American/EO" opposition highlights, I found that it was the racial oppositions *as connected to* the linguistic and pedagogical ones that became "metacommunicative" (Urciuoli, 1996, p. 8): These compound categories served as rhetorical "place markers" for a whole set of assumptions about beliefs, group membership, and policy agendas (McCarthy & Crichlow, 1993, p. viii).

In debating the value and future of the EO, bilingual, and English immersion programs, people on both "sides" maintained that the academic program serving "their" students suffered unfairly, citing several sets of analogous concerns. There were accusations on both "sides" of exclusion from positions of administrative power (e.g., "We don't have enough Latino representation on decision-making committees."). There were charges of racism and discrimination against staff, parents, and students (e.g., "African American boys are disproportionately and more harshly disciplined."). People were accused of ignoring sound instructional practice because of greed (e.g., "Teachers are 'cheating,' purposefully not redesignating their students as fluent in English because they want to keep their bilingual stipend."). Things were the way they were, people charged, because the other group's "culture" was inferior and less "American" (e.g., "African American families don't care about education, they just want to draw on welfare, and that is why EO students are failing."). And, to prepare students to be academically and professionally successful "Americans," each "side" maintained that only "their" teachers had the appropriate sets of expertise and experience (e.g., "Experience counts more than language ability in making someone a good teacher. Being bilingual isn't enough."). Throughout these arguments, school community members alternately drew upon and challenged national media discourses in strategic ways to substantiate their opinions and agendas.

Yet, as discussed in chapter 6, when I dug deeper, listened more closely to my colleagues, and reflected more critically on my own experiences as a teacher at the school, I found that these concerns were manifestations of a still more fundamental issue in the community: People across both "sides" of the conflict did not feel they had a choice or a voice in the policy changes they were experiencing. When California Elementary implemented bilingual education, and then years later when it implemented English immersion, at each point of policy change one "side" or the other felt that it was just "pushed on them," they "got no input," and "suddenly" they were "second-class citizens in our own school." They resented their sense of powerlessness in the process and the perceived negative, unfair results of the change for students, parents, and staff members on "their side." Ultimately, the policy as mandate was less an issue than the policy as *cultural resource in the processes of* daily social, professional, material, and academic life (Levinson & Sutton, 2001).

In other words, people felt a lack of cultural citizenship. Looking at these issues as moments in a struggle for cultural citizenship illuminated the competing social, historical, political, and professional contexts within which people functioned, and the overlapping forces of agency and constriction that they navigated. This in turn allowed examination of how the policies became tools that people used to forge identities, relationships, and strategic agendas (Levinson & Sutton, 2001). It brought to light how the conflict over language policies contributed to a lack of morale and collaboration among the staff, to strained relationships with parents, and to a weakened academic environment on campus.

I think that these findings are crucial for educators, practitioners, researchers and policymakers. Today's communities are ever more diverse, and schools are in many ways woefully unprepared to serve effectively students with varying backgrounds, strengths, and needs. One has only to examine educational outcome data on student achievement, high school and postsecondary graduation, and income and other social statistics, to see wide gaps. And these gaps are evident not only between disaggregated groups (e.g., at California Elementary, between Latino and Black students) but also between where students are as a whole and where they should be (e.g., at California Elementary the school as a whole was ranked at the lowest level of the California Academic Performance Index). What is more, American students overall compare poorly to their peers in most other industrialized nations.

Today policy has become an increasingly powerful technical governing tool in attempts to address the systemic challenges faced in civil society (Shore & Wright, 1997). The No Child Left Behind Act (NCLB), discussed in chapter 7, is a classic example of a federal law promulgating sweeping public education policy mandates. This policy proscribes expectations and carries increasingly high stakes for just about every aspect of schooling such as funding, organizational structure, service delivery, administration, instruction, assessment, and evaluation. Institutions and actors throughout the system are impacted, from state education agencies, to local school districts, to schools, to teachers, to parents, to students.

The Ecology of Policy Processes

To gain more sophisticated understandings of how policies take shape in school communities, and to what effects they articulate to struggles for cultural citizenship, it is important to consider what I call the *ecology* within which policy processes are situated.[1] I discussed in chapter 6 the importance of accounting for *four key points as relate to the ecology of policies.* The *first point* is to keep in mind the multiple contexts within which people function, and the sometimes competing interests they juggle. What are the experiences—from all stakeholders' vantage points—of the dynamics that a policy sets out to "fix" and the dynamics the policy creates? And how do these experiences shift with context? That is, what are the contingencies, relationships, and agendas important to people in their local school and neighborhood context, and how do these compare to contingencies, relationships, and agendas at play when people consider larger contexts such as national politics? The *second key point* is to account for the historical and enduring structures of domination/subordination and action/constriction that people navigate in the local community and in larger contexts. How might experiences of and attitudes about a policy change according to whether people feel a sense of (or a lack of) possibility for garnering advantages within their local context versus within a national or even global context? The *fourth key point* is that within all relevant contexts we must ask why, how, and to what effects policy issues articulate to historical forces of privilege and marginalization organized around categories of race, language and imaginations of an idealized "America." (I return to the *third key point* in the next few paragraphs.)

In the California Elementary case, for example, I saw how people changed their understandings of policy dynamics and their language policy goals depending on the context (local or national) within which they considered the issues: Those on the "African American/EO" "side" saw large amounts of material and human resources at the school targeted only at incoming "Latino/bilingual" students (and benefiting "Latino/bilingual" staff members), just as Latinos on a state and national scale were gaining political clout and becoming more numerous than African Americans. In this national context they argued that "bilingual ed has to go," drawing on discourses in the media that it was un-American, unfair, and ineffective in providing students with the dominant "American" cultural capital of English. However they also saw that bilingual program students at the school were higher achieving than EO students and that bilingual adults had more job opportunities in the local economy. So in this local context they (simultaneously) argued a contrary position—for expanding the program into a dual immersion program to equip Latino *and* African American students with locally valued bilingualism, drawing on the discourses of fairness and equal opportunity. Those on the "Latino/bilingual" "side" also tended to stake out a context-specific agenda: Looking locally they argued that Latinos were still struggling for full acceptance and inclusion at the school and that the bilingual program was still new and needed continued growth and resources. As such they pushed for strengthening the program, drawing upon popular media constructions of it as a way to bring ELLs "up" to a level (English-speaking) playing field. Looking nationally though they recognized bilingualism as a valuable advantage in the international economy, and so (simultaneously) they argued against expanding the program to African American students by characterizing it as a needed strategic advantage for Latinos (drawing on popular characterizations of bilingual education as a "Latino issue"). I also found that people's sense of their ability to affect change or not—their sense of agency (or lack thereof)—played an important role in shaping the intensity of the conflict: When there seemed to be numerous ways in which school community members could make changes to and garner advantages from the way things were done on campus (pre-227), the conflict erupted into an all-out "war." People vied for advantageous positions vis-à-vis personnel, fiscal, social, and program changes they championed. When there seemed to be no way for anyone to make advantageous changes to how things were done (in the post-227 policy context), the conflict persisted but calmed to a series of disagreements less public and less extreme.

Leaving such complex, context-specific dynamics unexamined can impede understandings of how and why policy processes play out as they do. This can quash the potential for people to coalesce around shared aspects of their multifaceted subject positions in the name of shared aspirations. For example, I found that at California Elementary, though people tended to paint the conflict as a "war" between opposing "sides," aspects of both "sides'" agendas actually coalesced around shared goals of including all as equal members of the school community, equipping all children with valued linguistic competencies, providing all children with the best of academic and life opportunities, and involving all adults in decision making.

These findings become even more important as we consider the findings of my third phase of research, in Georgia from 2005 through 2007. As discussed in chapter 7, years after the struggles exploded in California, they are now bubbling up in earnest in the "New South." The region is receiving national attention for becoming a hypergrowth destination area for immigrants, particularly Latino immigrants. Debates in the media about immigration in 2005 through 2007 strongly resembled those analyzed in the earlier California years, indicating continued struggles to define who a legitimate "American" is, what "Americans" look like and talk like, and what "American" culture is. However, given Georgia's strongly conservative, sociopolitical environment and the still *relatively* low percentage of immigrants in the state (that is, low compared to states like California), there has not been a movement to replicate, for example, something like California's once-widespread, mandated implementation of bilingual education. Language education policy at the state level in Georgia favors a basically English immersion/EO platform. But as demographics change and schools pursue innovative ways to meet the needs of diverse student bodies, research studies are already beginning to identify the negative effects of intergroup misunderstandings, culture clashes, and contestation over moral, fiscal, programmatic, and human resources—all of these hauntingly reminiscent of those at California Elementary.[2]

This should serve to remind us of the *third key point that I make about the ecology of education policies* (in chapter 6): We must continually account for the complexities within the dichotomies of policy debates. The politics of race can be both very dichotomous and simultaneously, much more complex than a dichotomy. As Pollock (2004) states, regarding race relations people's "lives are often far more disputed than educational research on race suggests" (p. 27). We must therefore embrace a dual perspective: One, we must continue to interrogate what one might call the "simple" or straightforward constructions of race (e.g. the American tendency to construct race relations as Black/White or White/of color) and dynamics of race (e.g., the undeniable, enduring ways in which racial hierarchies get reproduced through such things as unequal distribution of high-quality facilities, effective teachers, and other essential resources). Two, we must *also* interrogate the situational, context-specific, multifaceted ways in which racial identities, differences, and inequalities take shape (p. 27); how they move within and between other sociopolitical dynamics, and how they play out with varying effects for different groups of people. A deeper look at race politics at California Elementary showed that while constructing the issues at hand as a dichotomy ("Black vs. Brown") shaped and gave needed momentum to peoples' experiences, discourses, and agendas, it also could be seen to cover up a significant amount of heterogeneity both within and across the line of division—heterogeneity that revealed common causes across the policy agendas of both "sides."

Further, the politics of language can be both very dichotomous and simultaneously, much more complex than a dichotomy such as "EO versus bilingual." Bourdieu and Passeron (1977) remind us that one cannot talk about a language without also talking about relationships to that language. Looking at the "political economy of language" (Urciuoli, 1996) at California Elementary, it became clear that bilingual education was much more than just "a Latino issue," as it is usually characterized in the media and politics. As Smitherman (1992, 2002), Darder (1997), Perry and Delpit (1998) and Attinasi (1997) have pointed out, the anti-bilingual education EO movement has implications not only for Latino immigrants and supporters of bilingual education. These efforts to narrow the mode of communication considered "correct" and officially "American," and to legislate it as solely proper for use in public schools, have implications for all linguistic minorities and indeed for all advocates of linguistic and cultural diversity.[3]

What is more, like at California Elementary where in the words of the principal, "Here, language *is* race" (reflected in the "African American/ EO" and "Latino/bilingual" characterizations of the two "sides" of the conflict), politics of language in diverse communities are often co-constitutive with politics of race (Attinasi, 1997; Delpit & Kilgour Dowdy, 2002). So, in order to better understand and address dynamics of conflict we must critically analyze how race and language politics shape and are shaped by each other and how they are informed by other political symbols such as "immigrant" and "American." We must then interrogate how these dynamics play into policy processes and outcomes. Had such complexity across lines of division been openly explored at California Elementary, I believe it might have spurred coalitional actions toward shared goals.

The Role of Research

Here is where I believe critical ethnography can play a role in improving language education policy processes "on the ground" in schools, districts and communities. The very essence of ethnography is to examine the complexities of everyday life. Fine-grained ethnographic analyses can account for the "cultural, contextual, and political dimensions of educational policy" that tend to be overlooked in conventional policy analysis (Levinson & Sutton, 2001, p. 2; see also Pollock, 2004; Stein, 2004). This helps to illuminate the multiple meanings and effects of policies and "the place and role of values, beliefs, and identities" when people engage in decision making (p. 3). Levinson and Sutton argue that such a perspective can not only contribute to better understandings of policy processes, but also enliven efforts to democratize policy processes (p. 15), by equipping stakeholders with information and perspectives that make them more savvy implementers and creators of policy in their daily lives.

School community members and education decision makers are, after all (in the words of Corson [1999]), "applied language planners": How language policy initiatives are created and implemented in schools can be seen as de facto policymaking. And as I have earlier quoted Hakuta (2001, p. 10), what is critical in applied language planning "is finding and communicating a set of program components that work for children in a given community of interest, within the context of the goals, demographics, and resources of the community," and according to the nonnegotiable criteria of creating high achievement for *all* students.

Working together, researchers and practitioners can produce ethnographic data to explore and critique their knowledge, interpretive categories, communication, and norms of practice. When these connections are understood dynamically, people are poised to improve their realities. Along with Hargreaves (1996), I believe that collaborative action and study is an essential step that the education community as a whole needs to take, on a wider scale than we have so far. Ethnographic research publications only sit on a shelf unless they are *used* in real settings of practice and policymaking. And they are most *useful* if they are used in "real time"—supporting practitioners, stakeholders, and leaders in advancing their understandings of the issues at hand at any given moment.

In this current moment there is a movement among scholars to create a synergy between research, policy, and practice. For example, Valenzuela, Prieto, & Hamilton (2007) urge more anthropologists of education to study the implementation and impacts of perhaps the most important piece of education policy legislation in recent times, the NCLB Act (see also Sloan, 2007). They also urge researchers to engage in collaborations with people in school communities who are not normally given voice in policymaking processes, in order to support their involvement with the policy questions that impact their lives. And the American Anthropological Association Council on Anthropology and Education has launched an organizational effort to encourage scholars to become more active in public education policy issues (Ladson-Billings et al., 2007).

I believe that we as anthropologists can and should continue to do this "in our own right," providing fine-grained, sophisticated, critical examinations of policy processes. I also believe that there is great potential for researcher collaboration: Scholars utilizing varying methodologies can produce perspectives on the issues that are broader and richer than any one methodology alone. For example, a major line typically drawn between different methodological approaches is that between qualitative and quantitative methodologies. There is currently a growing movement in education (given great momentum by NCLB) to increase (and even favor) quantitative studies of instructional interventions (e.g., quasi-experimental and experimental random controlled trials). This movement champions the value of testing "what works" for kids as gauged by statistical analyses of quantitative measures such as assessment scores (What Works Clearinghouse, 2006; Whitehurst, 2004). (Debates about this have been vigorous [e.g., Viadero, 2008].) I do believe that undertaking experimental evaluations of instructional interventions is one productive step for the field, but such inquiries provide a *very* limited look at what goes on in educational settings, and certainly they cannot be relied upon as defining the universe of important questions or the definitive set of useful findings. Findings from such inquiries could become much more robust and informative if they were enriched by explorations of *how* interventions and policy initiatives function in the lived experiences of students, schools, and communities.

Another approach to creating a symbiotic relationship between research and action, that has informed *this* ethnographic project, is participatory action research (PAR). Atweh, Kemmis, and Wilkinson's (1998) idea of PAR is similar to Freire's idea of conscientização (1973), and draws on Fals-Borda & Rahman (1991). Participatory action researchers do research "on themselves" (Atweh, Kemmis, & Wilkinson, 1998, p. 23), investigating reality in order to change it and changing reality in order to investigate it (p. 21). Participants strive to understand the ways in which their assumptions are shaped by social structures, discourses and power in and across the dimensions of personal/local and collective/national/global (pp. 23, 25). And they then act on this new learning to create positive change.

PAR is akin to some current work in the area of teacher professional development[4] that pushes educators to become more involved in research on their own practice, and in the area of multicultural education.[5] In a way, it is also reflective of the current national movement to make education an "evidence based" field: Today decisions about everything from what instructional strategies to implement, to what curriculum programs to buy, to how school improvement plans should be crafted, are expected to be "evidence based" (or "research based" or "data based"). And this "evidence" encompasses more than just student achievement statistics and results published in peer-reviewed journals. It is also expected that decision making account for various other types of data about schools that can impact the success of any strategy, program, or plan. These other types of data are things like campus demographics, teacher behaviors and attitudes, school norms and routines, and challenges facing the community (see for example Georgia Leadership Institute for School Improvement, 2007; Johnson, 2002; Killion & Bellamy, 2000).[6] Given this imperative, educators must become adept at identifying, collecting, analyzing, and acting upon a variety of data sets as part of their daily practice.

My own personal attempt to create synergy between research, policy and practice in this project was instructive: During the second phase of my study at California Elementary I set out to participate in a PAR-inspired project (as an added component to the ethnographic work and teaching that I describe in chapter 5). When I returned to the school in 1998 I hoped to establish a kind of forum where we teachers could engage in collegial, critical discussions about the conflict that was raging on campus and our efforts to improve our practice. It was my hope that these discussions might become a springboard for projects to improve our practice and to counter forces of division and inequity on our campus and beyond. Establishing what came to be called the Professional Discussion Group (PDG) took more time than I expected and met with many challenges. It took me a whole year (of that 2-year research period) to get settled into my teaching position and research activities, and to then organize, with colleagues, the PDG meetings. Even with support from the administration and initial enthusiasm from some teachers, participation was low and it fizzled out after a few semesters. One reason was surely the hectic pace of activity on campus. With all we had going on at that time (including the chaotic implementation of 227), the principal opined: "We wanted to do it, I thought it was a great idea. We need to do it. But we're just burned out." Another reason the PDG did not flourish may have been the divisions of the campus conflict itself. The few teachers who did participate were White and Latino. The "Latino/bilingual" and "African American/EO" "sides" had been constructed as "against" each other for so long, perhaps many people assumed that a discussion group organized by a bilingual—and White—teacher (me) would not truly address *all of our* concerns. As I wrapped up my research in 2000 I wondered about all kinds of scenarios that might have made this PAR endeavor more attractive to and worthwhile for more people in my school community.

It is difficult to know what "the most effective" kind of collaborative inquiry and activism is for any school community until one is deeply engaged there—and even then it is no small task to make it thrive, as I found out. Atweh, Kemmis, and Wilkinson (1998) stress that the most important criterion of successful PAR is not whether one or another plan for the PAR is followed faithfully, but whether the participants "have a strong and authentic sense of development and evolution in their practices" (p. 21). So together, we must continue to search for the kinds of joint research and problem solving that works for our school communities.

The stakes are high for this work. The achievement, opportunities, and futures of all of our students hang in the balance. At California Elementary, the academic environment on campus during the "war" left much to be desired. Conflict was high. Morale was low. Divisions ruled the day, and student achievement suffered for it. In Georgia, student achievement is a major issue. The state posts student outcome statistics at some of the lowest levels in the nation (and this is particularly true of schools in the typically high poverty communities where immigrants are settling). In the "New South," where diversity beyond a Black/White dichotomy is experienced as a relatively new phenomenon, addressing head-on the interconnected issues of immigration, language, race, cultural citizenship, and teaching and learning is paramount if policies are to be put in place that give voice to all stakeholder groups and that provide benefit to all students.

Meaningfully involving researchers together with practitioners and policymakers in collaborative study and action is a challenging task. But as mentioned, there is already growing awareness of the need to do this among anthropologists of education. And if the current trends in school improvement and teacher professional development continue, educators and policymakers will become ever-more comfortable with critical self reflection, and more expert at the utilization of data and research in their decision making. It is going to take people in school communities seeking out researchers more often, and researchers connecting to communities more intentionally. I believe that the more we embrace a truly coalitional approach to investigating, understanding and engaging in policy processes, the more all students and all stakeholder groups in school communities will benefit. If we strive for this *together*, issues that arise will have a better chance of becoming a common cause for constructive action, than of becoming either a policy "backlash" or a "war" that tears apart a school.

NOTES

1. Similarly, Mora [2002] has talked about the intertwined nature of multiple policy mandates and varying relationships to these mandates, as a "policy web."

2. Beck and Allexsaht-Snider (2002), Hamann, Stanton, and Murillo (2002), Zúñiga et al. (2002), Tomás Rivera Policy Institute (2004), Hansen (2005), Godziak and Martin (2005), Hernández-León and Zúñiga (2005).

3. Recognizing this, Smitherman (2002) forwards the following three-pronged language education policy agenda, that could be seen to address many of the concerns at California Elementary, and perhaps also the concerns of many in Georgia's increasingly multilingual communities: First, reinforce the teaching of the language of wider communication (e.g., Standard English) to all students; second, reinforce and reaffirm the legitimacy of nonmainstream languages and dialects in communities and schools (e.g., nonstandard forms of English); third, promote the acquisition of foreign languages by all students, particularly Spanish because of its widespread use in this hemisphere. This, Darder (1997) agrees, would encourage multidialectal understanding," enabling a coalitional politics of "cross-linguistic and cross-cultural dialogue" to create a joint voice against the monolingual norm (p. 336).

4. For example, Hitchcock and Hughes (1995), Hale Hankins (1997), Ulichny and Schoener (1996), McLean (1995), Livingston and Castle (1989), Bullough and Gitlin (1995), Duncan-Andrade (2005), Jolly (2005), Hord (1997).

5. For example, Banks (1988), Lee (1996), Cazden and Dickinson (1981), Hidalgo (1993), Kagan and Kagan (1998), Trueba (1987), Pumfrey (1989), Gilmore (1991), Sleeter and Grant (1994), Delgado-Gaitan and Trueba (1991), hooks (1994), Delpit (1993, 1995), Delpit and Kilgour Dowdy

(2002), Apple (1996), Fine, Weis, Addelston, & Marusza (1997), Darder, Torres, and Gutiérrez (1997), Ladson-Billings (1994, 1998).

6. As another example, in Georgia, the state Department of Education anchors its statewide school improvement efforts around the Georgia "School Keys," a set of standards and resources to guide reform (Georgia Department of Education, 2007d). States one standard (p. 55 [italics added]),

> Teachers and administrators collaboratively analyze disaggregated student learning, *demographic, perception, and process data* to identify student and adult learning needs and goals. They continuously ... collect and analyze relevant student and teacher data (e.g., *action research,* analyzing student work, classroom observations, Awareness Walk, and surveys) to monitor and revise school and classroom improvement strategies.

REFERENCES

Abrams, J. (2006, March 16). More time sought to craft immigration bill. *Atlanta Journal-Constitution*, p. A14.

Abu-Lughod, L. (1991). Writing against culture. In R. G. Fox (Ed.), *Recapturing anthropology: Working in the present* (pp. 137–162). Santa Fe, NM: School of American Research Press.

Agar, M. H. (1996). *The professional stranger: An informal introduction to ethnography.* San Diego, CA: Academic Press.

Almaguer, T. (1994). Racial fault lines: The historical origins of White supremacy in California. Berkeley, CA: University of California Press.

Alonso-Zaldivar, R. (2004, December 6). What's in a racial identity? American Latinos all over the map, study finds. *Los Angeles Times*, p. A17.

Alvarez-Cáccamo, C. (1996). Building alliances in political discourse: Language, institutional authority and resistance. *Folia Linguistica, 30*, 3–4.

Amador, L. (2000, July 22). Manifestación fronteriza. *La Opinión*, pp. 1B, 2B.

American Institutes for Research and WestEd. (2006). *Effects of the Implementation of Proposition 227 on the Education of English Learners, K-12: Findings of a Five-Year Evaluation. Submitted to the California Department of Education* (Final Report for AB56 AB1116). Retrieved August 1, 2007 from http://www.air.org/news/documents/227Report.pdf

Anderson, B. (1983). *Imagined communities.* London: Verso.

Anderson, N., & Sahagun, L. (1998, October 22). Bilingual classes still thriving in wake of prop 227. *Los Angeles Times*, pp. A1, A32.

Antrop-González, R. (2002). Watch what you read: Not all policies or newspaper articles are research-based. *NABE News, 25*(5), 14–19.

Appadurai, A.(1991). Global ethnoscapes: Notes and queries for a transnational anthropology. In R. G. Fox (Ed.), Recapturing anthropology (pp. 191–210). Santa Fe, NM: School of American Research Press.

Apple, M. (1993). Constructing the "other:" Rightist reconstructions of common sense. In C. McCarthy & W. Crichlow (Eds.), *Race, identity and representation in education* (pp. 24–39). New York: Routledge.

Apple, M. (1996). *Cultural politics and education.* New York: Teachers College Press.

Applewhite, S. R. (1979). The legal dialect of bilingual education. In R. Padilla (Ed.), *Ethnoperspectives in bilingual education research: Bilingual education and public policy in the United States* (pp. 3–17). Ypsilanti, MI: Eastern Michigan University.

Applied Research Center. (1999, February 24). Advertisement. *New York Times*, p. A19.

Associated Press. (2006b, April 28). Bush says anthem should be in English. *NYTimes.com.* Retrieved April 28, 2006, from http://www.nytimes.com/SP-Bush-National-Anthem.html?ei"

Astroff, R. J. (1988, Winter). Spanish gold: Stereotypes, ideology, and the construction of a US Latino market. *Howard Journal of Communications*, 155-173.

Attinasi, J. (1997). Racism, language variety, and urban minorities: Issues in bilingualism and bidialectalism. In A. Darder, R. Torres, & H. Gutiérrez (Eds.), *Latinos and education: A critical reader* (pp. 279–301). New York: Routledge.

Attinasi, J. (1999). English Only for California children and the aftermath of Proposition 227. *Education, 119*(2), 263–283.

Atweh, B., Kemmis, S., & Wilkinson, M. (1998). Participatory action research and the study of practice. In S. Kemmis, B. Atweh, & P. Weeks (Eds.), *Action research in practice: Partnerships for social justice in education* (pp. 21–36). London: Routledge.

Aubrey, E. (2000, January 21-27). Held back: The miserable state of Black education. *L.A. Weekly*, 26–32.

August, D., & Hakuta, K. (Eds.). (1997). *Improving schools for language-minority children: A research agenda*. Washington, DC: National Academy Press.

August, D., & Shanahan, T. (Eds.). (2006). *Developing literacy in second-language learners: Report of the national literacy panel on language-minority children and youth*. Mahwah, NJ: Erlbaum.

Babington, C. (2007, June 24). On-air hosts drive immigration. *Atlanta Journal-Constitution*, p. A3.

Balibar, E. (1991). Is there a "neo-racism?" In E. Balibar & E. Wallerstein (Eds.), *Race, nation, class: Ambiguous identities* (pp. 17–28, 217–227). London: Verso.

Ballesteros-Coronel, M. (2000, May 17). Persiste segregación escolar [There will be more Latinos in the legislature]. *La Opinión*, pp. 3A, 4A.

Balotta, A. (2000, February 9). Esperan a mas latinos en la Legislatura. *La Opinión*, pp. 1A, 10A.

Barrera, M. (1997). A theory of racial inequality. In A. Darder, R. Torres, & H. Gutiérrez (Eds.), *Latinos and education: A critical reader* (pp. 3–44). New York: Routledge.

Barrera, V. (2002). Two states turn to California for support on election day 2002. *CABE Multilingual News, 26*(4), 1.

Baugh, J. (1984). *Language in use: Readings in sociolinguistics*. Englewood Cliffs, NJ: Prentice Hall.

Baxter, T. (2005, November 11). Pressure mounts to solve illegal immigration mess. *Atlanta Journal-Constitution*, pp. C1, C6.

Baxter, T. (2006a, February 20). Illegal immigrant bills slow legislatures, cloud issues. *Atlanta Journal-Constitution*, pp. A1, A5.

Baxter, T. (2006b, August 11). Facts not easy to verify in a hearing on immigration. *Atlanta Journal-Constitution*, p. A3.

Baxter, T., & Galloway, J. (2007, May 20). Chambliss takes on immigration critics. *Atlanta Journal-Constitution*, p. A4.

Beck, S. A. L., & Allexsaht-Snider, M. (2002). Recent language minority education policy in Georgia: Appropriation, assimilation, and Americanization. In S. W. Enrique, G. Murillo, Jr., & E. T. Hamman (Eds.), *Education in the New Latino Diaspora* (pp. 37–66). Westport, CT: Ablex.

Behar, R. (1993). Translated woman: *Crossing the border with Esperanza's story*. Boston: Beacon Press.

Behar, R. (1996). *The vulnerable observer: Anthropology that breaks your heart*. Boston: Beacon Press.

Bell, D. A. (1997a). Thank you, doctors Murray and Herrnstein (or, who's afraid of critical race theory?). In R. Delgado & J. Stefancic (Eds.), *Critical white studies: Looking behind the mirror* (pp. 534–537). Philadelphia: Temple University Press.

Bell, D. A. (1997b). White superiority in America: It's legal legacy, its economic costs. In R. Delgado & J. Stefancic (Eds.), *Critical white studies: Looking behind the mirror* (pp. 596–600). Philadelphia: Temple University Press.

Bhabha, H. (1994). *Locations of culture*. New York: Routledge.

Bianco, J. L. (2003, May/June). Globalisation and language: An explosion of policy for second language learners. *NABE News*, pp 13-14.

Blankstein, A., & Luo, M. (1999, February 3). Principal badly beaten in alleged hate crime. *Los Angeles Times*, pp. B1, B8.

Blume, H. (2002, May 3–9). Dueling for an education: Some parents win, others lose English-Spanish program. *L.A. Weekly*, pp. 18-20.

Blume, H., & Ehrenreich, B. (1998, May 29–June 4). Squeeze play (English, Español. The failure of bilingual education and the proposition that would make things worse). *L.A. Weekly*, pp. 18–25.

Borden, T. (2005, August 21). Van services a conduit for illegal immigrants. *Atlanta Journal-Constitution*, pp. A1, A17.

Borden, T. (2006, May 7). Social Security cards $40 each in Atlanta area. *Atlanta Journal-Constitution*, p. A14.

Borden, T., & Rockwell, L. (2006, April 11). Immigration rallies fill nation's streets. *Atlanta Journal-Constitution*, pp. A1, A6.

Bourdieu, P. (1991). *Language and symbolic power*. Cambridge, MA: Harvard University Press.

Bourdieu, P., & Passeron, J-C. (1977). *Reproduction in education, society and culture*. London: SAGE.

Bourgois, P. (1995). *In search of respect*. Cambridge, England: Cambridge University Press.

Bowles, S., & Gintis, H. (1976). *Schooling in capitalist America: Educational reform and the contradictions of economic life*. New York: Basic Books.

Breslau, K. (2000, March). Hable Ingles, por favor. *Newsweek*, pp. 12, 64.

Bullough, R. V., Jr., & Gitlin, A. (1995). *Becoming a student of teaching: methodologies for exploring self and school context*on. (2000). *1999 Academic Performance Index (API) school report: Summary for grades 2-8*. Retrieved December 12, 2007, from www.LAUSD.k12.ca.us

California Department of Education. (1999a). *Ed-Data, School Report, Student Information*. Retrieved September 14, 2008, from http://www .ed-data.k12.ca.us/Navigation/fsTwoPanel.asp?bot- tom=%2Fprofile.asp%3Flevel%3D07%26reportNumber%3D16

California Department of Education. (1999b). *STAR Stanford 9 report. "California Elementary."* Retrieved September 14, 2008, from http://star.cde.ca.gov/star99/ indexes/19/64733/0000000.html

California Secretary of State. (1998). *Voter Guide. Proposition 227—Full text of the proposed law.* Retrieved December 12, 2007, from http://primary98.sos.ca.gov/ VoterGuide/ Propositions/ 227text.htm

Campo-Flores, A. (2004, January). *Se habla* electoral votes. *Newsweek, 19,* 32.

Campo-Flores, A., & Fineman, H. (2005). A Latin power surge. *Newsweek, 30,* 24–35.

Campos, C. (2006a, March 27). Warrior against illegals lives, breathes the issue. *Atlanta Journal-Constitution,* pp. B1, B4.

Campos, C. (2006b, April 18). Illegal immigration protest draws crowd. *Atlanta Journal-Constitution,* p. B5.

Carspecken, P. F., & Apple, M. (1992). Critical qualitative research: Theory, methodology, and practice. In M. de LeCompte, W. L. Millroy, & J. Preissle (Eds.), *The handbook of qualitative research in education* (pp. 507–553). New York: Academic Press.

Cazden, C. B., & Dickinson, D. K. (1981). Language in education: Standardization vs. cultural pluralism. In C. A. Ferguson & S. B. Heath (Eds.), *Language in the USA* (pp. 446–468). Cambridge, MA: Cambridge University Press.

Chávez, L. (2005, December 22). Cut the promises, solve immigration. *Atlanta Journal-Constitution,* p. A17.

Clough, M. (1997, July 27). Birth of nations. *Los Angeles Times,* pp. M1–M6.

Coker, M. (2006). Georgia bloc wins delay in rights vote. *Atlanta Journal-Constitution,* p. A3.

Collard, W. (1999, August 7). Cut immigration now. *New York Times,* p. A18.

Colvin, R. L. (1996, April 8). Battle heats up over bilingual education. *Los Angeles Times,* p. A1.

Committee on Economic Development. (2006). *Education for global leadership: The importance of international studies and foreign language education for U.S. economic and national security.* Washington, DC: Committee for Economic Development.

Cooper, M. (1994, October 4). The war against illegal immigrants heats up. *Village Voice,* p. 28.

Cooper, R. T. (1999, September 16). Inquiry into English-only tests ordered. *Los Angeles Times,* pp. A3, A20.

Corson, D. (1999). *Language policy in schools: A resource for teachers and administrators.* Mahwah, New Jersey: Earlbaum.

Cowen, T., & Rothschild, D. M. (2006, June 14). Immigration: Latinos do blend into US life. *Atlanta Journal-Constitution,* p. A17.

Cox, K. (2005). *Georgia department of education motto.* Retrieved January 1, 2008, from http://public.doe.k12.ga.us/index.aspx

Crawford, J. (1992a). *Hold your tongue: Bilingualism and the politics of English only.* Upper Saddle River, NJ: Addison-Wesley.

Crawford, J. (1992b). *Language loyalties: A sourcebook on the official English controversy.* Chicago: University of Chicago Press.

Crawford, J. (1995). *Bilingual education: History, politics, theory and practice* (3rd ed). Los Angeles, CA: Bilingual Educational Services.

Crawford, J. (1997). *Issues in U.S. language policy.* Retrieved September 19, 2000, from http://ourworld.compuserv.com/homepages/JCRAWFORD/

Crawford, J. (1998, June 26). *The bilingual education story: Why can't the news media get it right?* Presentation to the National Association of Hispanic Journalists, Miami. Retrieved September 19, 2000, from http://ourworld.compuserv.com/homepages/JCRAWFORD/

Crenshaw, K., Gotanda, N., Peller, G., & Thomas, K. (Eds.). (1995). *Critical race theory: The key writings that formed the movement.* New York: The New Press.

Crowley, T. (1989). *Standard English and the politics of language.* Chicago: University of Illinois Press.

Darder, A. (1997). Creating the conditions for cultural democracy in the classroom. In A. Darder, R. Torres, & H. Gutiérrez (Eds.). *Latinos and education: A critical reader* (pp. 331-350). New York: Routledge.

Darder, A., Torres, R., & Gutiérrez, H. (Eds.). (1997). *Latinos and education: A critical reader.* New York: Routledge.

Dart, B. (2006, April 5). Minutemen shadow town's day labor site. *Atlanta Journal-Constitution*, p. A6.

de la Cruz, E. (2000, April 3). Tras el fin de la educación bilingüe [As bilingual education ends]. *La Opinión*, pp. 1A, 12A.

de la Torre-Jimenez, L., & Botello, A. E. (1999, November 14). Nueva 187 antiinmigrante [New 187 is anti-immigrant]. *La Opinión*, pp. 1A, 8A.

Delgado, R., & Stefancic, J. (Eds.). (1997). *Critical White studies: Looking behind the mirror.* Philadelphia: Temple University Press.

Delgado-Gaitan, C., & Trueba, H. (1991). *Crossing cultural borders: Education for immigrant families in America.* New York: The Falmer Press.

Delpit, L. (1993). The politics of teaching literate discourse. In J. Fraser & T. Perry (Eds.), *Freedom's plow* (pp. 285-296). New York: Routledge.

Delpit, L. (1995). *Other people's children: Cultural conflict in the classroom.* New York: The New Press.

Delpit, L., & Dowdy, J. K. (Eds.). (2002). *The skin that we speak: Thoughts on language and culture in the classroom.* New York: The New Press.

Domínguez, V. (1997). *White by definition: Social classification in Creole Louisiana.* New Brunswick, NJ: Rutgers University Press.

Downes, L. (2006, March 9). Immigration counts. *Atlanta Journal-Constitution*, p. A13.

Du Bois, W. E. B. (1940). *Dusk of dawn: An essay toward an autobiography of a race concept.* New Brunswick, NJ: Transaction.

Duncan-Andrade, J. M. R. (2005, March). Developing social justice educators. *Educational Leadership*, 70–73.

Duranti, A. (1994). *From grammar to politics: Linguistic anthropology in a western Samoan village.* Berkeley, CA: University of California Press.

Editorial Board. (2006, February 21). Our opinion: Better, but still short. *Atlanta Journal-Constitution*, p. A10.

El Nasser, H. (2006, March 7). Sun Belt, suburbs get more diverse: Minorities propel fastest-growing areas. *USA Today*, pp. 1A, 5A.

Ellsworth, E. (1997). Double binds of whiteness. In M. Fine, L. Weis, L. C. Powell, & L. M. Wong (Eds.), *Off white: Readings on race, power, and society* (pp. 259–269). New York: Routledge.

Estrada, L. J. (1979). A chronicle of the political, legislative and judicial advance for bilingual education and the American southwest. In R. Padilla (Ed.), *Ethnoperspectives in bilingual education research: Bilingual education and public policy in the United States* (pp. 97–108). Ypsilanti, MI: Eastern Michigan University Press.

Fals-Borda, O. (1979, March). Investigating reality in order to transform it: The Colombian experience. *Dialectical Anthropology, 4*, 33–55.

Fals-Borda, O., & Rahman, M. A. (Eds.). (1991). *Action and knowledge: Breaking the monopoly with participatory action-research*. New York: The Apex Press.

Fanon, F. (1967). *Black skin White masks*. New York: Grove Press.

Feagans, B. (2006b, May 15). 911 faces a crisis of its own: Callers who don't speak English. *Atlanta Journal-Constitution*, pp. B1, B3.

Feagans, B. (2006d, August 15). Immigrants transform Gwinnett. *Atlanta Journal-Constitution*, pp. A1, A4.

Fears, D., & Olivo, A. (1999, April 15). Results suggest race card's power in elections is fading. *Los Angeles Times*, pp. A1, A31.

Fillmore, L. W. (1992). Against our best interest: The attempt to sabotage bilingual education. In J. Crawford (Ed.), *Language loyalties: A sourcebook on the official English controversy* (pp. 367–375). Chicago: University of Chicago Press.

Fine, M. (1997). Witnessing Whiteness. In M. Fine, L. Weis, L. C. Powell, & L. M. Wong (Eds), *Off White: Readings on race, power, and society* (pp. 57–65). New York: Routledge.

Fine, M., Weis, L., Addelston, J., & Marusza, J. (1997). White loss. In M. Seller & L. Weis (Eds.), *Beyond Black and White: New faces and voices in U.S. schools* (pp. 283–302). Albany, NY: State University of New York Press.

Fishman, J. A. (1976). The sociology of language: An interdisciplinary social science approach to language in society. In J. A. Fishman (Ed.), *Advances in the sociology of language: Basic concepts, theories and problems: Alternative approaches* (Vol. I, pp, 217–404). The Hague: Mouton.

Fishman, J., & Keller, G. (Eds.). (1982). *Bilingual education for Hispanic students in the United States*. New York: Teachers College Press.

Flagg, B. J. (1997a). The transparency phenomenon, race-neutral decisionmaking, and discriminatory intent. In R. Delgado & J. Stefancic (Eds.), *Critical White studies: Looking behind the mirror* (pp. 220–226). Philadelphia: Temple University Press.

Flagg, B. J. (1997b). "Was blind, but now I see:" White race consciousness and the requirement of discriminatory intent. In R. Delgado & J. Stefancic (Eds.), *Critical White studies: Looking behind the mirror* (pp. 629–631). Philadelphia: Temple University Press.

Flores, W. V., & Benmayor, R. (1997). Constructing cultural citizenship. In *Latino Cultural Citizenship* (pp. 1–26). Boston: Beacon Press.

Foley, D. (1990). *Learning capitalist culture deep in the heart of Tejas*. Philadelphia: University of Pennsylvania Press.

Foley, D. (1995). *The heartland chronicles*. Philadelphia: University of Pennsylvania Press.

Foley, D. (1999). The fox project: A reappraisal. *Current Anthropology, 40*(2), 171–191.

Fordham, S. (1996). *Blacked out: Dilemmas of race, identity, and success at capital high.* Chicago: University of Chicago Press.

Foucault, M. (1972). *The history of sexuality.* New York: Vintage Press.

Frankenberg, R. (1993). *White women, race matters: The social construction of whiteness.* Minneapolis, MN: University of Minnesota Press.

Gal, S. (1987). Codeswitching and consciousness in the European periphery. *American Ethnologist, 14,* 637–653.

Gal, S. (1989). Language and political economy. *Annual Review of Anthropology, 18*(3), 45–67.

Gal, S. (1994). Gender in the post-socialist transition: The abortion debate in Hungary. *East European Politics and Societies, 8*(2), 256–287.

Gallegos, B. (Ed.). (1994). *English: Our official language?* New York: The H. W. Wilson.

García-Irigoyen, L. (1999, October 2). Demandan a arrendatario por discriminación racial [Demand racial discrimination]. *La Opinión,* pp. 1B, 2B.

Georgia Department of Education. (2006a, March 22). *Title III and ESOL education subcommittee report to the strategic multiples committee of the governor's education financial task force.* Retrieved July 21, 2007, from http://public.doe.k12.ga.us/ci_iap_esol.aspx

Georgia Department of Education. (2006a). *Annual yearly progress (AYP) statewide report: summary.* Retrieved July 21, 2007, from http://www.gadoe.org/ayp2007/summary.asp?SchoolID=000-0000-b-1-2-3-4-5-0-0-8-0-10

Georgia Department of Education. (2007b). *State report card.* Retrieved January 4, 2008 from, http://public.doe.k12.ga.us/ReportingFW.aspx?PageReq=102&StateId=ALL&T=1

Georgia Department of Education. (2007c). *School Keys: Unlocking Excellence through the Georgia School Standards.* Retrieved January 13, 2008 at http://public.doe.k12.ga.us/tss_school.aspx

Georgia General Assembly. (2006). Senate Bill 529. Retrieved January 20, 2007 at http://www.legis.state.ga.us/legis/2005_06/sum/sb529.htm

Georgia Leadership Institute for School Improvement. (2007). *Analyzing Data: Performance Data Scan Elementary School.* Atlanta, Georgia: Board of Regents of the University System of Georgia. Retrieved February 1, 2008 from http://www.galeaders.org/site/aboutus/BaseCamp_Summit_Resources%20docs/AD%20-%20Performance%20Data%20Scan%20-%20ES%20Sample.pdf.

Georgia Partnership for Excellence in Education. (2008). *Top 10 Issues to watch in 2008.* Atlanta: Author.

Georgia State Board of Education. (2006). *Language Assistance Services: Program for English Language Learners* (State board rule 160-4-5-.02). Retrieved January 4, 2008, from http://public.doe.k12.ga.us/_documents/doe/legalservices/160-4-5-.02.pdf

Gerstenzang, J. (2000, February 6). Candidates keeping schools at forefront of campaign issues. *Los Angeles Times,* p. A3.

Gilmore, P. (1991). Gimme room: School resistance, attitude, and access to literacy. In C. Mitchell & K. Weiler (Eds.), *Rewriting literacy: Culture and the discourse of the other* (pp. 57–76). New York: Bergin and Garvey.

Gilroy, P. (1987). *There ain't no Black in the union Jack: The cultural politics of race and nation.* Chicago: University of Chicago Press.

Ginsburg, F. (1989). *Contested lives: The abortion debate in an American community.* Los Angeles: University of California Press.

Ginsburg, F. (1993). The case of mistaken identity: Problems in representing women on the right. In C. B. Brettell (Ed.), *When they read what we write: The politics of ethnography* (pp. 163–176). Westport, CT: Bergin and Garvey.

Girion, L. (2000, September 20). 13 Phone operators win record $709,284 in English-only suit. *Los Angeles Times*, pp. C1, C4.

Giroux, H. A. (1992). *Border crossings: Cultural workers and the politics of education.* New York: Routledge.

Giroux, H. A. (1993). Living dangerously: Identity politics and the new cultural racism, towards a critical pedagogy of representation. *Cultural Studies, 7,* 1.

Gittelsohn, J., & Chey, E. (1999, May 19). Glitch on prop 227 road? *The Orange County Register*, pp. 1, 10.

Gladstone, M. (1999, February 24). Davis' education bills head for full vote. *Los Angeles Times*, pp. A3, A18.

Glaser, B. G., & and Strauss, A. L. (1967). *The discovery of grounded theory: Strategies for qualitative research.* New York: Aldine de Gruyter.

Godziak, E. M., & Martin, S. F. (2005). Challenges for the future. In *Beyond the gateway: Immigrants in a changing America* (pp. 277–284), Lanham, MD: Lexington Books.

Golab, J. (1999, November, 28). The color of hate. *Los Angeles Magazine.*

Goldberg, D. T. (1996). In/visibility and super/vision on race, veils, and discourses of resistance. In L. R. Gordon, T. D. Sharpley-Whiting, & R. T. White (Eds.), *Fanon: A critical reader* (pp. 179–202). Oxford, England: Blackwell.

Gómez-Peña, G. (1987). Documented/undocumented. In R. Simonson & S. Walker (Eds.), *Multicultural literacy: Opening the American mind* (pp. 37–44). Saint Paul, MN: Greywolf Press.

Gordon, E. T. (1998). *Disparate diasporas: Identity and politics in an African-Nicaraguan community.* Austin, TX: University of Texas Press.

Greenhouse, S. (2000, May 16). Coalition urges easing of immigration laws. *New York Times*, p. A16.

Gregory, S., & Sanjek, R. (1994). *Race.* New Brunswick, NJ: Rutgers University Press.

Grober, F., Jr. (2000, February 28). Debate over immigration. *Los Angeles Times*, p. B4.

Groves, M. (2000a, February 16). Flaws found in rankings of schools. *Los Angeles Times*, pp. A3, A21.

Groves, M. (2000b, May 30). Breather urged for school reforms. *Los Angeles Times*, pp. A3, A21.

Gumperz, J. J. (1982). *Discourse strategies.* Cambridge, England: Cambridge University Press.

Gumperz, J. J., & Hymes, D. (1972). Preface. In *Directions in sociolinguistics: The ethnography of communication* (pp. v–viii). New York: Holt, Rinehart and Winston Inc.

Gupta, A., & Ferguson, J. (1998). Discipline and practice: The field as site, method, and location in anthropology. In *Anthropological locations: Boundaries and grounds of a field science* (pp. 1–46). Berkeley, CA: University of California Press.

Gupta, A., & Ferguson, J. (Eds.). (1998). *Anthropological locations: Boundaries and grounds of a field science*. Berkeley, CA: University of California Press.

Gurza, A. (1999, May 18). A language is a terrible thing to lose. *Los Angeles Times*, p. B1.

Gutiérrez, K. D. (2002). Studying cultural practices in urban learning communities. *Human Development, 45*, 312–321.

Gutiérrez, K. D, Baquedano-Lopez, P., & Asato, J. (2000 Winter-Spring). English for the children: the new literacy of the old world order, language policy and educational reform. *Bilingual Research Journal, 24*(1–2), 87–112.

Gutiérrez, K. D., Asato, J., Santos, M., & Gotanda, N. (2002). Backlash pedagogy: Language and culture and the politics of reform. *The Review of Education, Pedagogy, and Cultural Studies, 24*, 335–351.

Haguchi, D. (1999). *Into the education age: A message from the president* (1998–1999 Annual Report). Los Angeles: United Teachers.

Hakuta, K. (2001, April 13). Education of language minority students: Testimony to the United States commission on civil rights. *CABE Multilingual News, 24*(6), 1–11.

Hale, H., K. (1997). Cacophony to symphony: Memoirs in teacher research. *Harvard Educational Review, 68*(1), 80–95.

Hall, S. (1988). The toad in the garden: Thatcherism among the theorists. In C. Nelson & L. Grossberg (Eds.), Marxism and the interpretation of culture (pp. 35–37). Chicago: University of Illinois Press.

Hall, S. (1996). New ethnicities. In D. Morely & C. Kuan-Hsing (Eds.), *Stuart Hall: Critical dialogues in cultural studies* (pp. 441–449). New York: Routledge.

Hamann, E. T. (2003). *The educational welcome of Latinos in the new south*. Westport, CT: Praeger.

Hamann, E. T., Wortham, S., & Murillo, E. G., Jr. (2002). Education and policy in the New Latino Diaspora. In S. W. Enrique, G. Murillo, Jr., & E. T. Hamman (Eds.), *Education in the New Latino Diaspora* (pp. 1–16). Westport, CT: Ablex.

Handler, R. (1988). *Nationalism and the politics of culture in Quebec*. Madison: University of Wisconsin Press.

Hansen, A. (2005). Black and White and Other: International immigration and change in metropolitan Atlanta. In E. Godziak & S. F. Martin (Eds.), *Beyond the gateway: Immigrants in a changing America* (pp. 87–110). Lanham, Maryland: Lexington Books.

Haraway, D. (1988). Situated knowledge: The science question in feminism and the privilege of partial perspective. *Feminist Studies, 14*, 3.

Hargreaves, A. (1996). Transforming Knowledge: Blurring the Boundaries between Research, Policy, and Practice. *Educational Evaluation and Policy Analysis, 18* (2), 105–122.

Harris, C. L. (1995). Whiteness as property. In K. Crenshaw, N. Gotanda, G. Peller, & K. Thomas (Eds.), *Critical race theory: The key writings that formed the movement* (pp. 276–291). New York: The New Press.

Harris-Bosselmann, T. (2006, March 5). Illegal immigration: Paper should avoid racial undertones. *Atlanta Journal-Constitution*, p. B5.

Harrison, F. V. (1998). Introduction: Expanding the discourse on "race." *American Anthropologist, 100*(3), 609–631.

Hartigan, J., Jr. (1997). Establishing the fact of whiteness. *American Anthropologist, 99*(3), 495–505.

Hartigan, J., Jr. (1999). *Racial situations: Class predicaments of whiteness in Detroit.* Princeton, NJ: Princeton University Press.

Hastings, M. (2000a, March 16). Riley solicita más escuelas bilingües [Riley promotes more bilingual schools]. *La Opinión*, p. B6.

Hastings, M. (2000b, June 16). Educación de hispanos preocupa a Clinton [Clinton concerned with Hispanic education]. *La Opinión*, pp 1A, 12A.

Hayden, T. (1999, October 19). We're a city in denial about race. *Los Angeles Times*, p. B9.

Hayes-Bautista, D. E. (2000, February 7). Latinos are the new "American dream makers." *Los Angeles Times*, p. B5.

Heath, S. B. (1983). *Ways with words: Language, life, and work in communities and classrooms.* Cambridge, MA: Cambridge University Press.

Helfand, D. (1998, September 25). School board seeks waiver for 227. *Los Angeles Times*, p. B5.

Helfand, D., & Sahagun, L. (1999, February 5). Principal's account of being attacked exposes tensions. *Los Angeles Times*, pp. A1, A26.

Heller, M. (1995). Language choice, social institutions, and symbolic domination. *Language in Society, 24*(3), 373–405.

Henry, J. (1963). *Culture against man.* New York: Vintage Books.

Hermann, J. (2006, March 2). Illegals make for unfair competition. *Atlanta Journal-Constitution*, p. A15.

Hernandez, E. (2006, July 16). Illegal immigration: Senator simply for cheap labor. *Atlanta Journal-Constitution*, p. C5.

Hernández-León, R. & Zúñiga, V. (2005). Appalachia Meets Aztlán: Mexican Immigration and Intergroup Relations in Dalton, Georgia. In V. Zúñiga & R. Hernández-León, (Eds.). *New destinations: Mexican immigration in the United States* (pp. 244–274). New York: Russell Sage Foundation.

Hidalgo, N. (1993). Multicultural teacher interest action. In J. Frasier & T. Perry (Eds.), *Freedom's plow* (pp. 99–108). New York: Routledge.

Higham, J. (1994). *Strangers in the land: Patterns of American nativism, 1860-1925.* New Brunswick, NJ: Rutgers University Press.

Hill, J. H., & Irvine, J. T. (1992). Introduction. In *Responsibility and evidence in oral discourse* (pp. 1–23). Cambridge, MA: Cambridge University Press.

Hitchcock, G., & Hughes, D. (1995). *Research and the teacher: A Qualitative introduction to school-based Research.* New York: Routledge.

hooks, b. (1989). *Talking back: thinking feminist, thinking black.* Boston,: South End Press.

hooks, b. (1994). *Teaching to transgress: Education as the practice of freedom.* New York: Routledge.

hooks, b. (2000). *Where we stand: Class matters.* London: Routledge.

Hord, S. M. (1997). *Professional learning communities: Communities of continuous inquiry and improvement*. Austin, TX: Southwest Educational Development Laboratory.

Horton, J. (1995). The politics of diversity: Immigration, resistance, and change in Monterey Park, California. Philadelphia: Temple University Press.

Hutchinson, E. O. (2006, April 5). Blacks wrongly blame their woes on foreigners. *Atlanta Journal-Constitution*, p. A13.

Hymes, D. (1972). Toward ethnographies of communication: The analysis of communicative events. In P. Giglioli (Ed.), *Language and social context* (pp. 21–44). New York: Penguin Books.

Hymo, L. (2006, May 21). Immigration: Europe faces a similar problem. *Atlanta Journal-Constitution*, p. C5.

Irvine, J. T. (1989). When talk isn't cheap: Language and political economy. *American Ethnologist, 16*(2), 248–267.

Jacoby, T. (2005, December 1). Borderline public policy [Review of the book]. *Washington Post*, p. C4.

Johnson, R. (2002). *Using data to close the achievement gap: How to measure equity in our schools*. Thousand Oaks, CA: Corwin Press.

Jolly, A. (2005). *A Facilitator's Guide to Professional Learning Teams*. Greensboro: SERVE Center, University of North Carolina at Greensboro.

Jordan, M. (2005, November 8). Testing "English only" rules. *Wall Street Journal*, pp. B1, B13

Kagan, S., & Kagan, M. (1998). *Multiple intelligences: The complete MI Book*. San Clemente, CA: Kagan Cooperative Learning.

Keeler, C. (1999, November 19). 'Of 187' initiative. *Los Angeles Times [Editorial]*, p. B8.

Keller, F. D., & Van Hooft, K. S. (1982). A chronology of bilingualism and bilingual education in the United States. In J. A. Fishman & G. Keller (Eds.), *Bilingual education for Hispanic students in the United States* (pp. 3–19). New York: Teachers College Press.

Kemper, B. (2006a, March 2). Solutions elusive, divisive for illegal immigration. *Atlanta Journal-Constitution*, pp. A1, A5.

Kemper, B. (2006b, March 27). Chambliss: Farms need immigrants. *Atlanta Journal-Constitution*, pp. A1, A5.

Kemper, B. (2007, June 21). Ga. business leaders push immigration bill. *Atlanta Journal-Constitution*, p. A3.

Killion, J., & Bellamy, T. (2000). On the Job: Data Analysts Focus School Improvement Efforts. *Journal of Staff Development, 21*, 1. Retrieved January 13, 2008, from http://www.nsdc.org/library/publications/jsd/killion211.cfm

King, D. A. (2005, December 11). No way to compete with "guest workers." *Atlanta Journal-Constitution*, p. C5.

King, D. A. (2006a, May 21). Immigration: Americans' views are loud and clear. *Atlanta Journal-Constitution*, p. C5.

King, M. (2006b, June 1). Illegal immigrants strained health system. *Atlanta Journal-Constitution*, p. A15.

King, M. (2007a, May 29). MYTH: Illegal immigrants depress wages of Americans. *Atlanta Journal-Constitution*, p. A8.

Kirby, S. (2000, January 21). Illegal aliens and identity theft. *Los Angeles Times*, p. B6.

Koch, W. (2006, October 9). Push for "official" English heats up: Legislation reacts to immigration. *USA Today*, pp. 1A, 3A.

Kondo, D. K. (1990). *Crafting selves*. Chicago: University of Chicago Press.

Labov, W. (1972). *Language in the inner city: Studies in Black English vernacular*. Philadelphia: University of Pennsylvania Press.

LaClau, E., & Mouffe, C. (1984). *Hegemony and socialist strategy: Towards a radical democratic politics*. New York: Verso.

Ladson-Billings, G. (1994). *The dream keepers: Successful teachers of African American children*. San Francisco: Jossey-Bass.

Ladson-Billings, G. (1998). Just what is critical race theory and what's it doing in a nice field like education? *International Journal of Qualitative Studies in Education, 11*(1), 7–24.

Ladson-Billings, G., McCarty, T., Brayboy, B., Cammarota, J., Erickson, F., & Gutiérrez, K.. (2007, November). *Council on anthropology and education ad hoc task force on advancing anthropology and education perspectives in public policy*. Presentation at the annual meeting of the American Anthropological Association, Washington, DC.

La Opinión News Services. (2000a, March 12). Legislatura de Nebraska propone ley de ayuda para los inmigrantes [Nebraska legislature proposes law to help immigrants]. *La Opinión*, p. 7A.

La Opinión News Services. (2000b, May 20). Aumenta demanda de personal bilingüe [Demand for bilingual personnel grows]. *La Opinión*, p. 6B.

Lau v. Nichols. (1974). 414 US 563. Retrieved December 1, 2007, from http://caselaw.lp.findlaw.com/scripts/getcase.pl?court=US&navby=case&vol=414&invol=563.

Lee, E. (1996, March). *Anti-racist education: Pulling together to close the gaps*. Addressed to annual METCO conference, Boston.

Leinwand, D. (2006a, March 8). Loose border saps county coffers. *USA Today*, p. 3A.

Leovy, J. (1999, October 20). Immigrants protest reduction of classes. *Los Angeles Times*, p. B1, B3.

Lesher, D. (1999, March 25). Davis weighs dropping defense of prop. 187. *Los Angeles Times*, pp. A3, A28.

Levinson, B. A. U., & Sutton, M. (Eds.). (2001). *Policy as practice: Toward a comparative sociocultural analysis of educational policy*. Westport: Ablex.

Levinson, B., & Holland, D. (1996). The cultural production of the educated person: An introduction. In B. A. Levinson, D. E. Foley, & D. C. Holland, (Eds.). *The Cultural Production of the Educated Person: Critical ethnographies of schooling and local practice* (pp. 1-56). Albany, NY: State University of New York Press.

Lewin, T. (1998, November 29). Public schools confronting issue of racial preferences. *New York Times*, pp. A1, A34.

Lewis, A. (1999, September 21). Is this America? *New York Times*, p. A31.

Lewis, O. (1966). *Anthropological essays*. New York: Random House.

Lewis, O. (1964). *The children of Sanchez: Autogiography of a Mexican family*. London: Penguin Books.

Linares, J. J. (2000, March 2). Candidatos a favor de más inmigración [Candidates Are in Favor of More Immigration]. *La Opinión*, pp. 1A, 8A.

Linquanti, R. (2001). The redesignation dilemma—A policy analysis. *Multilingual News, California Association of Bilingual Educators, 25*(1, 2), 11–13.

Lipman, P. (1998). *Race, class and power in school restructuring*. Albany, NY: State University of New York Press.

Livingston, C., & Castle, S. (Eds.). (1989). *Teachers and research in action*. Washington, DC: National Education Association.

Loar, R. (1995, February 26). In person: Speaking in favor of bilingual education. *Los Angeles Times*, p. B3.

López, I. F. H. (1995). The social construction of race. In R. Delgado (Ed.), *Critical race theory: The cutting edge* (pp. 191–203). Philadelphia: Temple University Press.

Lopez, R. J., & Connell, R. (2000, June 7). The class of '89: Journeys into the new Los Angeles. *Los Angeles Times*, pp. A1, S1-S6.

Los Angeles Unified School District. (1996a). *School racial/ethnic history information statistics, Jefferson cluster*. Los Angeles: School Information Systems Branch.

Los Angeles Unified School District. (1996b). *Language development program for African-American students: Literacy and language, blueprint for learning*. Los Angeles: Division of Instruction, Language Acquisition and Bilingual Development Branch.

Los Angeles Unified School District. (1996c). *The master plan for English learners* (draft). Los Angeles: Language Acquisition and Bilingual Development Branch.

Los Angeles Unified School District. (1998a). *Proposition 227 and English language* [Staff Development Packet]. Los Angeles: Los Angeles Unified School District.

Los Angeles Unified School District. (1998b). *Proposition 227 and the educational options for parents of limited-English-proficient students* [Branch packet for parents and schools]. Los Angeles: Author.

Los Angeles Unified School District. (1998c, September 8). *Spotlight newsletter for LAUSD employees—No. 5*. Los Angeles: Author.

Los Angeles Unified School District. (1998e). *Finger tip facts*. Los Angeles: Los Author.

Luykx, A. (1999). *The citizen factory: Schooling and cultural production in Bolivia*. New York: State University of New York Press.

Lyons, J. J. (1998). Message from the executive director: Impact of proposition 227 on California classrooms. *NABE News, 22*(1), 1–3.

MacCannell, D. (1992). *Empty meeting grounds: The tourist papers*. New York: Routledge.

MacLeod, J. (1987). *Ain't no makin' it: Aspirations and attainment in a low-income neighborhood*. Boulder, CO: Westview Press.

MacSwan, J. (2001). Implications of the New York City schools research report for program-restrictionist legislation in the United States. *NABE News, 24*(4), 4–16.

Maharidge, D. (1999, March 29). In California, the numbers tell the story. *New York Times*, p. A25.

Malone, J. (2006, April 6). Feds take aim at illegals' fake IDs: Atlanta among 10 cities cited in crackdown. *Atlanta Journal-Constitution*, pp. A1, A6.

Marcus, G. E. (1998). *Ethnography through thick and thin*. Princeton, NJ: Princeton University Press.

Marrero, P. (1999, October 24). Proposición 187, parte II: la escuela [Proposition 187, Part 2: The School]. *La Opinión*, p. 3A.

Martinez, Y. (1998, March). Bilingual education under siege. *Hispanic Magazine*, 26–29.

Mauss, M. (1954, 1925). *The gift*. London: Cohen and West.

McCarthy, C., & Crichlow, W. (Eds.). (1993). Theories of identity, theories of representation, theories of race. In *Race, identity and representation in education* (pp. xiii–xxix). New York: Routledge.

McDonnell, P. (1996, March 20). Campaign '96/issues: California election puts focus on multiculturalism concerns. *Los Angeles Times*, p. A5.

McIntosh, P. (1989, July/August). White privilege: Unpacking the invisible knapsack. In *Peace and Freedom*, 10–12.

McLean, J. E. (1995). *Improving education through action research: A guide for administrators and teachers*. Thousand Oaks, CA: Corwin Press.

McNaughton, D. (for the Editorial Board). (2007, April 22). Our opinion: How America can win job race. *Atlanta Journal-Constitution*, p. C6.

McQuillan, J., & Tse, L. (1996, Winter). Does research matter?: An analysis of media opinion on bilingual education, 1984–1994. *The Bilingual Research Journal*, 2(1), 1–27.

Medina, E. (2000, May 21). AFL-CIO: por una nueva amnestia general [AFL-CIO: For a New General Amnesty]. *La Opinión*, p. B1.

Menchaca, M. (1993). Chicano Indianism: A historical account of racial repression in the United States. *American Ethnologist, 20*(3), 583–603.

Menchaca, M. (1995). *The Mexican outsiders: A community history of marginalization and discrimination in California*. Austin, TX: University of Texas Press.

Merriam, S. B. (1998). *Qualitative research and case study applications in education*. San Francisco: Jossey-Bass.

Mikow-Porto, V., Humphries, S., Egelson, P., O'Connell, D., Teague, J., & Rhim, L.. (2004). *English language learners in the Southeast: Research, policy, and practice*. Greensboro, NC: SERVE, The Regional Educational Laboratory of the Southeast.

Mora, J. K. (2002). Caught in a policy web: The impact of education reform on Latino education. *Journal of Latinos and Education, 1*(1), 22–44.

Mora, J. K. (1999, December 17-23). Unz Scathed. *LA weekly*, p. 6.

Morganthau, T. (1997, January 27). America 2000, demographics: The face of the future. *Newsweek*, 58–60.

Morrison, T. (1992). *Playing in the dark: Whiteness and the literary imagination*. New York: Vintage Books.

Morse, J. (2000, March 6). Sticking to the script. *Time*, 60–61.

Moscoso, E. (2005, September 20). Most immigrants enter U.S. illegally. *Atlanta Journal-Constitution*, pp. A1, A5.

National Association for Bilingual Education. (2006, February 28). *Advocacy Update*. Retrieved February 28, 2006, from http://www.nabe.org.advocacy/nclb.html

National Association for Bilingual Education. (1999). *NABE News, 23*(1), 27.

National Association for Bilingual Education. (2004, October 21). *NABE Joins Alliance for Fair and Effective Accountability, Endorses Broad Critique of No Child Left Behind*. Retrieved June 15, 2007, from http://www.nabe.org/press/press4.html

National Education Association. (2003, March/April). The NEA'S voice on teacher preparedness for English language learners. *NABE News*, pp. 15-29.

Navarro, M. (2000, July 13). Bricks, mortar and coalition building: How race is lived in America. *New York Times*, pp. A1, A16.

Niebuhr, G. (1999, September 23). Across America, immigration is changing the face of religion. *New York Times*, p. A16.

Oakes, J. (1985). *Keeping track: How schools structure inequality*. New Haven, CT: Yale University Press.

O'Connor, A. M. (1999, August 25). Learning to look past race. *Los Angeles Times*, pp. A1, A9.

Ong, A. (1996). Cultural citizenship as subject-making: Immigrants negotiate racial and cultural boundaries in the United States. *Current Anthropology, 37*(5), 737–762.

Omi, M., & Winant, H. (1994). *Racial formation in the United States from the 1960's to the 1990's*. New York: Routledge.

Pape, E. (1999, April). The reckoning: The 10th district city council race code marks the end of an era. *Los Angeles Magazine*, p. 26.

Pasco, J. O., & Weikel, D. (2005, December 5). Illegals' foe rocks Calif. race. *Atlanta Journal-Constitution*, p. A7.

Peirce, C. S. (1956). Logic as semiotic: The theory of signs. In J. Buchler (Ed.), *The philosophy of Peirce: Selected writings* (pp. 98–119). London: Routledge and Kegan Paul.

Peller, G. (1995). Race consciousness. In K. Crenshaw, Gotanda, N., Peller, G., & Thomas, K. (Eds.), *Critical race theory: The key writings that formed the movement* (pp. 127–158). New York: The New Press.

Perry, T., & Delpit, L. (Eds.). (1998). *The real Ebonics debate: Power, language, and the education of African-American children*. Boston: Beacon Press.

Phinney, D., & Reza, H. G. (1996, August 2). OC's congressmen support language bill unanimously. *Los Angeles Times* (Orange County Edition), p. A16.

Piatt, B. (1997). *Black and brown in America: The case for cooperation*. New York: New York University Press.

Pinar, W. (1993). Notes on understanding curriculum as a racial text. In C. McCarthy & W. Crichlow (Eds.), *Race, identity and representation in education* (pp. 60–70). New York: Routledge.

Pitts, L. (2006, May 24). English can survive on its own. *Atlanta Journal-Constitution*, p. A17.

Pollock, M. (2004, November). Race wrestling: Struggling strategically with race in educational practice and research. *American Journal of Education, 111*, 25–67.

Porter, R. P. (1990). *Forked tongue: The politics of bilingual education*. New York: Basic Books.

Pumfrey, J. (1989). Multicultural education revisited: Towards a policy for social justice. In P. D. Pumfrey & G. K. Verma (Eds.), *Race relations and urban education: Contexts and promising practices* (pp. 143–162). New York: The Falmer Press.

Purdum, T. S. (2000, July 4). Shift in the mix alters the face of California. *New York Times*, pp. A1, A12.

Pyle, A. (1996, January 13). Bilingual classrooms boost performance, study finds. *Los Angeles Times*, p. A1.

Ramirez, D. (2000, March 21). *Proposition 227: Who wins? Who loses?* Paper presented at the California Association for Bilingual Education, San Francisco.

Ramirez, M. (1999, October 30). Hope grows as church struggles to let go of past, embrace future. *Los Angeles Times*, pp. A1, A22.

Ramos, P. A. (2006, March 12). Immigration: Parents' arrival benefits children. *Atlanta Journal-Constitution*, p. C5.

Rawls, P. (2007, April 22). Ala. governor would sign slavery apology. *Atlanta Journal-Constitution*, p. A10.

Regalia, M. A. (1999, April 8). Immigrants wanted. *New York Times*, p. A26.

Reed-Danahay, D. E. (Ed.). (1997). *Auto/ethnography: Rewriting the self and the social*. Oxford, England: Berg.

Reid, H. (2000, October 6). Inmigración y ciudadania. *La Opinión*, p. 9A.

Reynolds, M. (2006, May 22). Immigration debate turns to culture. *Atlanta Journal-Constitution*, pp. A1, A6.

Ricento, T. (2000). Proposition 227 and the future of antibilingual education legislation in the U.S. *The Multilingual Educator, 1*(1), 30–33.

Riechmann, D. (2006, March 26). Illegal immigration fight spills into streets. *Atlanta Journal-Constitution*, p. A3.

Rocco, R. (1997). Citizenship, culture, and community: Restructuring in southeast Los Angeles. In W. V. Flores & R. Benmayor (Eds.), *Latino cultural citizenship* (pp. 97–123). Boston: Beacon Press.

Rodríguez, G. (1998, October 30). Going native: California's anti-immigration movement vanished when facts finally caught up with its apocalyptic prophecies. *Los Angeles Magazine*, p. 30.

Rodríguez, O. R. (2006, May 8). Illegals' kids face danger in smugglers' grip. *Atlanta Journal-Constitution*, p. A8.

Rodríguez, R. (2000, July 9). The salsa zone. *Los Angeles Times*, pp. M1, M6.

Roediger, D. (1991). *The wages of whiteness: Race and the making of the American working class*. New York: Verso.

Rogers, S. (2005, October 22). Immigration: Too many see U.S. as a gold mine. *Atlanta Journal-Constitution*, p. A11.

Rosaldo, R. (1994). Social justice and the crisis of national communities. In P. F. Baker, P. Hulme, & M. Iverson (Eds.), *Colonial discourse/postcolonial theory* (pp. 293–252). Manchester, England: Manchester University Press.

Rosaldo, R. (1997). Cultural citizenship, inequality and multiculturalism. In W. V. Flores & R. Benmayor (Eds.), *Latino cultural citizenship* (pp. 27–38). Boston: Beacon Press.

Ross, W. (2006, May 21). Immigration: Want to stay? Learn language. *Atlanta Journal-Constitution*, p. C5.

Ryan, W. (2002). The Unz initiatives and the abolition of bilingual education. *Boston College Law Review, 43*, 487–519.

Sachs, S. (2000, January). More screening of immigrants for TB sought. *New York Times*, pp. A1, A22.

Sadek Sanchez, C. (1998, December 27). Dos leyes que aseguran el fracaso [Two laws that guarantee failure]. *La Opinión*, pp. B1, B4.

Sager, B. (2005, November 5). Kennesaw State forum tackles immigration. *Atlanta Journal-Constitution*, pp. E1, E2.

Sahagun, L. (1999a, February 14). Diversity challenges schools to preserve racial harmony. *Los Angeles Times*, pp. A1, A33.

Sahagun, L. (1999b, April 7). Retreat brings teachers face to face with other races—and themselves. *Los Angeles Times*, p. B2.

Sahagun, L. (1999c, December 13). Bilingual teachers may face cut in extra pay. *Los Angeles Times*, pp. B1, B3.

Sahagun, L. (1999d, January 13). LA students take to English immersion. *Los Angeles Times*, pp. A1, A3.

Sahagun, L., & Anderson, N. (1998, October 23). Hundreds wait for bilingual education. *Los Angeles Times*, pp. B1, B6.

Sahagun, L., & Smith, D. (1999, October 28). School board majority plans to oust Zacarias. *Los Angeles Times*, pp. A1, A20.

Sahagun, L., & Helfand, D. (2000, May 18). ACLU sues state over conditions in poor schools. *Los Angeles Times*, pp. A1, A24.

Schmidt, Sr., R. (2000). *Language policy and identity politics in the United States*. Philadelphia: Temple University Press.

Searle, J. (1972). What is a speech act? In P. Giglioli (Ed.), *Language and social context* (pp. 136–154). New York: Penguin Books.

Seelye, K. Q. (1998, October 14). Budget talks trip over school aide and other issues. *New York Times*, pp. A1–A16.

Segal, D. A. (1993). "Race" and "color" in pre-independence Trinidad and Tabago. In K. A. Yelvington (Ed.), *Trinidad ethnicity* (pp. 81–115). London: Macmillan Press.

Seller, M., & Weis, L. (Eds.). (1997). *Beyond black and white: New faces and voices in U.S. schools*. Albany, NY: State University of New York Press.

Shah, H., & Thornton, M. C. (1991). Racial ideology in US mainstream news magazine coverage of black-Latino interaction, 1980-1992. *Critical Studies in Mass Communication, 11*, 141–161.

Shepard, S. (2006, March 3). Senate panel polishes illegal immigration bill. *Atlanta Journal-Constitution*, p. A3.

Shore, C., & Wright, S. (1997). Policy: A new field of anthropology. In C. Shore & S. Wright (Eds.), *Anthropology of policy: Critical perspectives on governance and power* (pp. 3–35). London: Routledge.

Shore, C., & Wright, S. (Eds.). (1997). *Anthropology of policy: Critical perspectives on governance and power*. London: Routledge.

Silverstein, M. (1976). Shifters, linguistic categories and cultural description. In K. Basso & H. Selby (Eds.), *Meaning in anthropology* (pp. 11-55). Albuquerque, NM: University of New Mexico Press.

Silverstein, S. (1999, December 8). Crossing language barriers. *Los Angeles Times*, pp. A1, A34, A35.

Silverstein, S. (2000, March 9). U.S. dividing into immigrant zones, report contends. *Los Angeles Times*, p. A33.

Skelton, G. (1999, March 29). Prop 187 decision puts governor to no-win test. *Los Angeles Times*, p. A3.

Skrla, L., & Scheurich, J. J. (Eds.). (2004). *Educational equity and accountability: Paradigms, policies and politics*. New York: Routledge-Falmer Press.

Slavkin, M. (2000, June 18). Las preguntas que Romer debe hacerse. *La Opinión*, pp. 1B, 4B.

Sleeter, C. E., & Grant, C. A. (1994). Making choices for multicultural education: Five approaches to race, class, and gender in American education (2nd ed.). Columbus, OH: Merrill.

Sloan, K. (2007). High-stakes accountability, minority youth, and ethnography: Assessing the multiple effects. *Anthropology and Education Quarterly, 38*(1), 24–41.

Smith, C. (2005, August 1). Employers cheat to deserve scorn. *Atlanta Journal-Constitution*, p. A10.

Smith, H. L., & Heckman, P. E. (1995). The Mexican-American war: The next generation. In E. E. García & B. McLaughlin (Eds.), *Meeting the challenge of linguistic and cultural diversity in early childhood education* (pp. 64–83). New York: Teachers College Press.

Smitherman, G. (1992). African-Americans and "English only." *Language Problems and Language Planning, 16*, 235–248.

Smitherman, G. (2002). Toward a national public policy on language. In L. Delpit & J. K. Dowdy (Eds.), *The skin that we speak: Thoughts on language and culture in the classroom* (pp. 163–178). New York: The New Press.

Smitherman, G., & Van Dijk, T. A. (Eds.). (1988). *Discourse and discrimination*. Detroit, MI: Wayne State University Press.

Solá, M., & Bennet, A. T. (1991). The struggle for voice: Narrative, literacy, and consciousness in an east Harlem school. In C. Mitchell & K. Weiler (Eds.), *Rewriting literacy: Culture and the discourse of the other* (pp. 35–56). New York: Bergin & Garvey.

Staples, B. (1999, August 23). California schools, after affirmative action. *New York Times*, p. A18.

Stein, S. J. (2004). *The culture of education policy*. New York: Teachers College Press.

Steinberg, J. (1999, December 3). Academic standards ease as a fear of failure spreads. *New York Times*, pp. A1, A25.

Sterngold, J. (2000, February 1). A citizenship incubator for immigrant Latinos. *New York Times*, p. A12.

Strong, P. T. (1992). Captivity in white and red: Convergent practice and colonial representation on the British-Amerindian frontier, 1606–1736. In D. Segal (Ed.), *Crossing cultures: Essays in the displacement of western Civilization* (pp. 33–104). Tucson, AZ: The University of Arizona Press.

Suárez-Orozco, M. (1998). State Terrors: Immigrants and Refugees in the Post-National Space. In Y. Zou & E. Trueba (Eds.), *Ethnic Identity and Power: Cul-*

tural Context of Political Action in Schools and Society (pp. 283–319). Albany: State University of New York Press.

Takaki, R. (1990). *Iron cages: Race and culture in 19th century America*. New York: Oxford University Press.

Tharpe, J. (2006a, February 10). Bill on illegals set to go. *Atlanta Journal-Constitution*, pp A1, A6.

Tharpe, J. (2006b, February 19). Center stage in illegals debate. *Atlanta Journal-Constitution*, pp. A1, A5.

Tharpe, J. (2006c, March 22). House recasts bill on illegals: worker verification program included. *Atlanta Journal-Constitution*, pp. A1, A7.

Tharpe, J., & Campos, C. (2006, March 9). Senate ratifies limits on illegals. *Atlanta Journal-Constitution*, pp. A1, A12.

Tharpe, J., Campos, C., & Pickel, M. L. (2006, February 20). Senate bill reveals rift on illegals. *Atlanta Journal-Constitution*, pp. A1, A5.

Thompson, J. (1991). Editor's introduction. In P. Bourdieu (Ed.), *Language and symbolic power* (pp. 1–31). Cambridge, MA: Harvard University Press.

Tobar, H. (2000, June 23). Heartland tuning in to Spanish. *Los Angeles Times*, pp. A1, A18.

Tollefson, J. W., & Tsui, A. B. M. (Eds.). (2004). *Medium of instruction policies: Which agenda? Whose agenda?* Mahwah, NJ: Lawrence Erlbaum Associates, Inc.

Tomás Rivera Policy Institute. (2004). *The new Latino south and the challenge to public education: Strategies for educators and policymakers in the emerging immigrant communities*. Los Angeles: University of Southern California.

Toppo, G. (2005, August 25). Is bilingual education report being downplayed? *USA Today* (Education section). Retrieved February 1, 2008, from http://www.usatoday.com/news/education/2005-08-24-bilingual-education_x.htm.

Trueba, H. T. (Ed.). (1987). *Success or failure? Learning and the language minority student*. Cambridge, MA: Newbury House Publishers.

Trujillo, A. (1996). In search of Aztlán: Movimiento ideology and the creation of a Chicano worldview through schooling. In B. Levinson, D. Foley, & D. Holland (Eds.), *The cultural production of the educated person: Critical ethnographies of schooling and local practice* (pp. 119–152). Albany, NY: State University of New York Press.

Tumulty, K. (2006, April 10). Should they stay or should they go? *Time*, pp. 30–41.

Turner, K.(1998, December 8,). In the news: Quick reads on issues teachers care about: Prop 227 lawsuit filed. *United Teacher*, p. 2.

20/20. (1996, July 26). *Television broadcast*. New York: ABC.

Uchitelle, L. (2000, March 9). INS is looking the other way as the legal immigrants fill jobs. *New York Times*, pp. A1, C14.

Ulichny, P., & Schoener, W. (1996). Teacher-researcher collaboration from two perspectives. *Harvard Educational Review, 66*(3), 496–524.

Unz, R. (2001, October 26). Rocks falling upward. National Review Online. Retrieved March 15, 2002, from http://nationalreview.com/common/comment-unz102601.shtml

Urciuoli, B. (1996). *Exposing prejudice: Puerto Rican experiences of language, race and class*. Boulder, CO: Westview Press.

Urciuoli, B. (1997, December). *"Official English" as U.S. cultural defense against a complex world*. Paper presented at the conference on Globalization and Ethnicity. University of Amsterdam, the Netherlands.

U.S. Department of Education. (2001). *No Child Left behind Act*. Retrieved January 1, 2008, from http://www.ed.gov/policy/elsec/leg/esea02/index.html

Valdés, A. (1979). The role of the mass media in the public debate over bilingual education. In R. Padilla (Ed.), *Ethnoperspectives in bilingual education research: Bilingual education and public policy in the United States* (pp. 175–188). Ypsilanti, MI: Eastern Michigan University.

Valdés, G. (1997). Dual-language immersion programs: A cautionary note concerning the education for language minority students. *Harvard Educational Review, 67*(3), 391-429.

Valdez, E. (2001). Winning the battle, losing the war: bilingual teachers and post-Proposition 227. *The Urban Review, 33*(3), 237–253.

Valenzuela, A. (2005). *Leaving children behind: How "Texas style" accountability fails Latino youth*. Albany, NY: State University of New York Press

Valenzuela, A., Prieto, L., & Hamilton, M. P. (2007). Introduction to the special issue: No Child Left behind and Minority Youth: What the qualitative evidence suggests. *Anthropology and Education Quarterly, 38*(1), 1–8.

Varela, A. (2006, November 20). Hispanics swell Clayton's school rolls, roles. *Atlanta Journal-Constitution*, pp. B1, B6.

Varela, A. (2007, February 18). Megachurch courts Latinos. *Atlanta Journal-Constitution*, p. A8.

Velásquez, N. (1995, December 11). Bilingualism enhances our competitiveness [Letter to the editor]. *New York Times*, pp. 14A.

Verhovek, S. H. (1999, June 26). The new language of American labor. *The New York Times*, p. A8.

Viadero, Debra. (2008). U.S. position on research seen in flux. *Education Week, 27*(26), 1, 14.

Visweswaran, K. (1994). *Fiction of feminist ethnography*. Minneapolis, MN: University of Minnesota Press.

Visweswaran, K. (1998). Race and the culture of anthropology. *American Anthropologist, 100*(1), 70–83.

Weed, C. (2005, August 1). Illegal immigrants don't respect others. *Atlanta Journal-Constitution*, p. A10.

Weinstein, B. (1983). *The civic tongue: Political consequences of language choices*. New York: Longman Press.

Weis, L. (1996). Foreword. In B. Levinson, D. Foley, & D. Holland (Eds.), *The cultural production of the educated person: Critical ethnographies of schooling and local practice* (pp. ix–xiv). Albany, NY: State University Press.

Welcome to Amexica: The border is vanishing before our eyes, creating a new world for all of us. (2001, June). *Time Magazine*, Special Issue cover page.

West, C. (1994). *Race matters*. New York: Vintage.

Weston, K. (1998). The virtual anthropologist. In A. Gupta & J. Ferguson (Eds.), *Anthropological locations: Boundaries and grounds of a field science* (pp. 163–184). Berkeley, CA: University of California Press.

What Works Clearinghouse. (2006). *Study design classification. U.S. Department Of Education Institute of Education Sciences.* Retrieved March 3, 2008, from http://ies.ed.gov/ncee/wwc/twp.asp.

Whitehurst, G. (2004). Making Education Evidence-based: Premises, Principles, Pragmatics and Politics. Northwestern University Institute for Policy Research distinguished public policy lecture. Retrieved January 1, 2008 from http://ies.ed.gov/director/pdf/2004_04_26.pdf

Wilcox, K. (1982). Ethnography as a methodology and its application to the study of schooling: A review. In G. Spindler (Ed.), Doing the ethnography of schooling: Educational anthropology in action (pp. 457–488). Prospect Heights, IL: Waveland Press.

Williams, B. F. (1989). A class act: Anthropology and the race to nation across ethnic terrain. *Annual Review of Anthropology, 18*, 401-444.

Williams, B. F. (1991). *Stains on my name, war in my veins: Guyana and the politics of cultural struggle.* Durham, NC: Duke University Press.

Willis, P. (1977). *Learning to labor: How working class kids get working class jobs.* London: Gower.

Winddance Twine, F. (1997). Brown-skinned white girls: Class, culture, and the construction of white identity in suburban communities. In R. Frankenberg (Ed.), *Displacing whiteness: Essays in social and cultural racism* (pp. 214–243). Durham, NC: Duke University Press.

Wrigley, J. (1982). *Class politics and public schools.* New Brunswick, NJ: Rutgers University

Woolard, K. A. (1989). *Double talk: Bilingualism and the politics of ethnicity in Catalonia.* Stanford, CT: Stanford University Press.

Woolard, K. A., & Schiefflelin, B. B. (1994). Language ideology. *Annual Review of Anthropology, 23*, 55–82.

Yon, D. A. (2000). *Elusive culture: Schooling, race and identity in global times.* New York: State University of New York Press.

Zehr, M. A. (2007a, January 10). NJ bucks tide on reading for English-learners. *Education Week, 26*(18), 1, 12.

Zehr, M. A. (2007b, January 31). Tussle over English-language learners: Harrisonburg, Va., officials call it unfair to require stricter reading test for some still working on skills. *Education Week, 26*(21), 1, 18.

Zehr, M. A. (2007c, February 7). Research advancing on "academic English." *Education Week, 26*(22), 13.

Zehr, M. A. (2007d, May 9). NCLB seen as damper on bilingual programs. *Education Week, 26*(36), 5, 12.

Zentella, A. C. (1990). Returned migration, language, and identity: Puerto Rican bilinguals in dos worlds/two mundos. *International Journal of the Sociology of Language, 84*, 81–100.

Zúñiga, V., Hernández-León, R., Shadduck-Hernández, J. L., & Villarreal, M. O. (2002). The new paths of Mexican immigrants in the United States: Challenges for education and the role of Mexican universities. In S. W. Enrique, G. Murillo, Jr., & E. T. Hamman (Eds.), *Education in the New Latino Diaspora* (pp. 99-116). Westport, CT: Ablex.

CPSIA information can be obtained
at www.ICGtesting.com
Printed in the USA
BVHW04s1548180818
524549BV00001B/1/P